Human Being: Insights From Psychology and the Christian Faith

Jocelyn Bryan

No use of Banksy /
Kenny / Harris
Ricoeur in ready
but not indexed

no Kierkegaard.

scm press

© Jocelyn Bryan, 2016

First published in 2016 by SCM Press
Editorial office
3rd Floor, Invicta House,
108–114 Golden Lane,
London EC1Y OTG

SCM Press is an imprint of Hymns Ancient & Modern Ltd
(a registered charity)
13A Hellesdon Park Road, Norwich,
Norfolk, NR6 5DR, UK

www.scmpress.co.uk

British Library Cataloguing in Publication data

A catalogue record for this book is available
from the British Library

978 0 334 04924 1

Typeset by Regent Typesetting
Printed and bound in Great Britain by
CPI Group (UK) Ltd

Contents

Preface

During the past 20 years interdisciplinary academic research has become increasingly prevalent. Most, if not all, disciplines recognize an overlap of interests with other fields and are open to engaging with different perspectives in order to enrich our understanding of the world. Furthermore, there has been a significant shift in attitudes towards intra-disciplinary working. Thirty years ago, those engaged in neuropsychology were rarely in conversation with social psychologists; but today the perspectives of neuropsychology, evolutionary psychology, cognitive and social psychology are frequently brought into dialogue with one another. In parallel with these moves, practical theology has established the importance of cross-disciplinary dialogue between theology and other disciplines so that we might respond to the situations and issues which confront us with both theological integrity and wisdom.

An obvious dialogue partner for theology is psychology. Both disciplines take human experience seriously. Psychology studies human nature and experience to explain human thinking, feeling and action. It is also concerned with what enables human beings to develop and flourish. Theology and the Christian faith assert that God is active in the lives of human beings and indeed in all creation. Thus, identifying the work of God through and in human experience is one of the tasks of theology. In his letter to the Romans, Paul writes that, 'Ever since the creation of the world his eternal power and divine nature, invisible though they are, have been understood and seen through the things he has made' (1.20). Creation, including human nature and experience, is a source of revelation. Furthermore, our knowledge and beliefs concerning God begin and develop through our experience. In both theology and psychology human experience is analysed and a source of knowledge. They are markedly different in their approach; psychology is reductionist, and theology is rightly suspicious of the interpretation of the 'nothing but' theories present within the discipline. Both disciplines also hold different views on the purpose of human life and human nature, but as Watts suggests, there is still a lot to be gained from engaging with their 'complementary perspectives to elucidate different aspects of [various] phenomena' and there is 'value in bringing them into creative dialogue'.[1]

As a psychologist, working in ministerial formation for the past 15 years, my teaching has sought to establish this dialogue as essential to pastoral theology and practical theology. In the course of analysing a pastoral situation or incident, the insights of psychology have provided an important voice in determining a Christian response which is faithful to the gospel. This response must always be respectful and never diminish the human beings involved by reducing them to a model of the human person which fails to acknowledge their role in creation and the image of God within them. Hence the task has been to interpret the evidence from psychology through the lens of theological understandings of human nature and purpose.

This book aims to document this enterprise. By intersecting human experience and purpose as described by psychology with the description offered in the biblical narrative, I hope to enrich a Christian description and understanding of *human being*. The complexity of the reality of human experience means that this project is by no means complete. However, if it sparks interest to understand more fully what it means to be human by critically engaging with psychological research in a well-informed way then it has been worthwhile. It also aims to be a resource which will transform our understanding of ourselves and others.

We spend a significant amount of our lives listening to the stories of others' experiences and telling our own story. In these narratives human experience is captured, reflected upon, and the process of

---

1 Watts, F., 2010, 'Psychology and theology', in Harrison, P. (ed.), *The Cambridge Companion to Science and Religion*, Cambridge: Cambridge University Press, pp. 191–3.

meaning-making occurs. We live within our personal story, and this in turn intersects with numerous stories of others which are part of the web of relationships that constitute our social world. Into this web, the stories of our community, society, and ultimately the story of God are woven. They have a varying amount of influence on the narrative of our lives, but they shape and sometimes transform our narrative. The relationship between narrative, human experience and identity is a constant theme in the book. By offering psychological reflection on stories from the biblical narrative and setting this in dialogue with a theological reflection, resonances between the two approaches emerge which I hope will deepen our understanding of the transformative power of the gospel at work in people's lives.

There are many people who deserve my thanks for their support during the process of conceiving and writing this book. My colleagues at Cranmer Hall and The Wesley Study Centre have graciously made space for a psychologist in a community of theologians. They have listened to my different questions and enriched my theological knowledge and understanding. This book would not have been possible without them. Natalie Watson has encouraged me over the past five years to write the book I wanted to write, and has never ceased in her support. Many students have wanted this book to accompany my teaching; their enthusiasm for the creative interface between psychology and the Christian faith, and their stories of its impact on their ministry, have also sustained my belief in the enterprise. Also, thanks to Rachel for reading the draft and offering such helpful comment and critique. As always, I am eternally grateful to my husband Steve and my children, Will, Rachel and Ed. More than anyone else, you four have taught me so much about myself and the power of love to sustain, enrich and ultimately transform human experience. This is for you.

JMB
Epiphany 2016

I

Introduction: Human Beings

In the month and year of my birth, the city of Berlin was carved in two. Overnight it became host to a wall that would mark the division between two global political ideologies for the next 28 years. Newsreel footage from the time shows the desperation of the citizens of Berlin as they literally jump from the windows of houses to freedom in the West. Their everyday lives were dramatically changed in a matter of hours. Families, friends, communities were divided physically and emotionally. The political story of the wall became cruelly entwined with the lives of Berlin's citizens. Of course I have no recollection of the wall being built, but it signified one of the most important social and political divides in my lifetime, the consequences of which are still played out on the world stage today and, however remotely, they have impacted on my life.

Frieda Schulze was 77 years old when she made her attempt to flee into West Berlin. In a dramatic scene, the East German police held onto her through a window in the East while she was being pulled down by her neighbours in the West. Matt Frei,[1] in his BBC series on Berlin, describes Frieda in that moment as *being* Berlin 'suspended between two regimes, two ideologies, two halves of the world'. After she finally fell into the West of the city, Frei notes that 'she slipped quietly into the shadows'. The majority of those who had witnessed the scene would never see or hear of her again. But, for Frieda, it was likely that this episode was *the* self-defining moment for the rest of her life. The intensification of emotion, fear and action would be etched deeply in her memory. It was a life-changing moment, in which not only the map of the city but the

---

1 Frei, M., 2009, *Berlin*, BBC: DVD.

map of her life was redrawn. She, and many others like her, would see and identify themselves in a different way after the trauma of August 1961. Frei suggests that what characterized Freida on that day is also present in the faces of Berliners today 'in their resistance, their determination, and their hope'. He even extends this notion to suggest Berliners 'represent all of us. We are all Berliners.' But how much do each of us represent each other, what are the characteristics which human beings all bear and in what ways are we unique?

Frieda Schulze's actions captured something about human nature which is embodied not only in most individual human beings but also in our social groups: in our families, communities and cities. In her case she displayed her motivation to stay with her family and escape the perceived oppression of the East German regime. Under the effect of a huge surge of adrenaline, a fundamental human biological response, she courageously struggled and found her way to freedom. Frei's identification of the human characteristics of resistance, determination and hope, as seen in Frieda Schulze, is fitting in the light of the success of human evolution and the history of humankind. Frieda's individual personality resonated strongly with Frei's perception and experience of the generalized character of the people of Berlin; and indeed all people facing the trials of political and social oppression.

But the stories of human beings are multitextured and multilayered. Each episode in the history of the world is played out in the story of countries, cities, families and individuals. Frieda's story was indelibly influenced by the story of her family, her city, her country and its part in the world order at that time; that is and always will be the case. But her story is also unique to her and her unique personality. Her particular response to each event in her life before and after the construction of the wall is a composite of her unique genetic make-up and the variety of relationships and contexts which made up her life. No one is a replica of anyone else, and neither is their story. Every Berliner who made it across the wall will have a different story to tell, even though the same momentous events will have transformed each of their lives. It is true of each of us. Every human being has a different story to tell that grows organically in relationship to their culture's prevailing narrative, their faith narrative (if they have one), and the narratives of others who they relate to. As we witness the millions of Syrian refugees fleeing to Europe or the Umbrella protests in Hong Kong, we are also witnessing how the narrative of international politics becomes entwined in the daily narrative of the experience of individuals.

The story of Frieda, like every human story, illustrates the diversity and commonality between human beings. Every human experience of events or happenings is influenced by numerous factors which make it unique to that person. Some of these we have volition over and others are beyond our control, but all of them in some way or other change us. In the tension between what we can influence and what lies outside this sphere, such as our genetic make-up, gender, and the chance happenings of life, we make our unique response to our experiences in life and this is the expression of our personality. It is our unique variation on what it means to be a human being and it is also our story.

When we reflect on our lives and who we are, we are inevitably drawn to events and episodes which we identify as defining moments in our life story. They are markers in a kaleidoscope of countless experiences. Some of these we remember with clarity, and others we only recall from the stories others have told us about them. My grandmother was orphaned in the first year of her life. She had no recollection of this episode but it profoundly changed who she was and who she became. Tragedies, chance happenings, significant life choices, in fact all manner of experiences, are events which form us. We understand who we are primarily through reflecting on the story of our lives. Every day we share stories about what has happened to us and what we are anticipating or hoping for in our future, but each of these narratives is embedded in the broader stories of our family, the social groups we belong to, society, and beyond that to the unfolding history of the world. The confluence of these multiple narratives is an important source in conveying a sense of who we are, how we became the person we are and who we might become.

Although it is important to stress the uniqueness of every individual person's life, it is also the case that within the infinite diversity of personal narratives there are some common characteristics. We all take an inimitable journey through life, yet it resembles other journeys. The tension between human diversity and our common human nature is deeply engrained in the way we understand and relate to each other. Hence, as often as we correctly anticipate how someone is going to behave, we get it wrong. There are similar personalities and people whose lives follow a similar pattern, but there are considerable individual differences even within the similarities. Indeed, the most notable thing about every human being is that they, and their story, are unique.

My Story and Who Am I?

The probing question of 'who am I?' can be deeply troubling for us, and raises many further questions about what it means to be a human being. How much of my story is determined by my genetics? Am I the same person as I was when I was a child, or twenty, or even five years ago? How much of who I am is due to my parents and their story? I may be like them in some ways, but not in so many others. What are the main events in my story which have contributed to how I feel about myself and how I experience the world? How much influence and control do I have about who I am and the next chapter in my story? What is my core identity and do others really know me? In what ways has God shaped me and been part of my life story?

Christians find the answers to these complex questions in the narrative of Scripture, which affirms that the story of every human life begins with God. We are created and loved by God, and although human beings fail to trust in God and his loving purposes, God continues to reach out to them with love and grace. Furthermore, it is God who knows us better than we know ourselves; it is God who sustains us, and God who through the power of the Holy Spirit is able to transform us. For Christians, personal identity is intimately bound up with an understanding of the ways in which human beings relate to and understand the divine activity of God as a reality in human lives. Here the concept of vocation is important. God calls every human being who he has created to participate in their own unique way in his loving purposes. Therefore an essential part of who we are is rooted in human beings as co-creators and participators in the unending story of God. It is the living story of God which defines who we are and who we become.

Psychology answers the question who am I in a different way. It primarily looks to science and a reductionist approach to find the answer. From psychobiology and evolutionary psychology the answer is that we are a product of evolution and our goal in life is to survive and propagate our genes. Neuropsychology asserts that we are entirely cells, tissue and neurones. Cognitive psychology takes a more mechanistic view, describing human beings as essentially processors of stimuli and information to which they respond. All of these have their limitations when it comes to adequately describing embodied human experience. Knowing the biochemical changes that take place in the brain when a person feels overwhelmingly sad tells us very little about who that person is and why they are so grief-stricken. Their biochemistry is a valuable but limited perspective on who they are and how they experience the world.

Although academic psychology has distanced itself from psychoanalysis, Freud heralded a significant advance in both language and our understanding of who we are. By analysing the stories of his clients' dreams and early experiences, human beings were understood as a product of their early relationships and inner psychic tensions. Freud's model of personality is rejected by many, but psychotherapists and counselling continues to work with the stories people tell of their childhood experiences and life experiences in general to understand who a person is.

More recently, psychology has been drawn increasingly to investigate life stories to understand human identity, personality and behaviour. McAdams[2] has consistently argued that the formation of identity depends on personal narrative which intersects with the personal narratives of others, and the narratives of the society and culture a person is embedded in. The story we construct from our

---

2 McAdams, D. P., 1993, *The Stories We Live By: Personal Myths and the Making of the Self*, New York: Guilford Press; McAdams, D. P., 'What do we know when we know a person?', *Journal of Personality*, 63 (1995), pp. 365–96.

Life story

experience of social relationships, and our experience more generally, typifies the way in which we envisage our lives. This is not static, but rather a 'configuring of personal events into a historical unity which includes not only what one has been but also the anticipations of what one will be'.[3]

Each personal narrative describes the developing and changing self and discovers meaning within the story. But the events of our lives can be read and interpreted through different lenses and from different perspectives. Christians interpret their narrative, and hence themselves, through the narrative of God's salvation. The story of God reveals truths about who they are, and within their story they discover truths about God. Attachment theorists interpret a personal life story through the lens of the nature of early attachment bonds and their influence on the formation of social relationships in later life. Behaviourists interpret personal narratives in terms of positive and negative reinforcement, the key shapers of motivation and goals. Lives are a story of pleasure-seeking and pain avoidance.

The emphasis on the interpretation of story as a source of revelation both in psychology and the Christian faith is the premise of the first part of this book. In what follows, human stories and biblical stories are used to shed light on what it means to be a human being by drawing together insights from personality psychology and theology. Each perspective illuminates different aspects of being human, and by constructing a critical conversation between theology and psychology, significant resonances emerge which can inform the way we understand both ourselves and each other. Scripture speaks to us because it captures the truth about human experience. We feel the pain and fear of Jairus as his young daughter faces death, we hang our heads with shame when we read of Peter's repeated denial of Jesus as the cock crows, and we cry in sorrow with Mary at the foot of the cross. When subjected to rereadings in new situations, the depth of human experience and longing immersed in the life of God in the stories of the Bible continues to reveal fresh insights into what it means to be human. But, in part, these new insights are informed by our ever-increasing knowledge of human experience

3 Polkinghorne, D. E., 1988, *Narrative Knowing and the Human Sciences*, New York: State University of New York Press, p. 150.

and the human condition. We bring this knowledge to the texts and probe the narrative in different ways as we interpret and analyse these biblical stories in dialogue with human experience.

The Significance of Narratives: A Common Theme

he four narratives of Jesus

The Bible epitomizes the importance of narrative for conveying theological truth. The Old Testament chronicles the story of the people of Israel and their relationship with God primarily through stories and history. By reading and analysing these stories, insights into the nature of God and the human condition are disclosed. Likewise, the New Testament includes four narratives of the life of Jesus. Each story offers a different interpretation to suit a different purpose, but each seeks to reveal the truth concerning Jesus' identity as God's son and the Messiah. Furthermore, in each Gospel we read of Jesus telling stories and parables as an important medium by which to communicate truth about human beings and God's kingdom. The capacity of these ancient texts to connect with people's lives today and transform the way they understand who they are and their purpose in life is indicative of the narrative power of Scripture. There is a profound resonance between the narrative quality of human lives and the commonality of our shared journeys through life which enables us to recognize and respond to the God-given truth in the biblical narratives.

In psychology for many years the use of story was treated with suspicion and confined to psychotherapy and counselling, but since McAdams[4] life-story model of identity and the observation by Sarbin[5] that narrative might possibly be the root metaphor for the discipline of psychology, the significance of narratives for uncovering what it is to be human has led to an increasing focus on the stories of individuals' lives. Personality psychology has moved to

---

4 McAdams, D. P., 1985, *Power, Intimacy, and the Life Story: Personological Inquiries into Identity*, New York: Guilford Press; McAdams, 'What do we know when we know a person?'

5 Sarbin, T., 1986, 'The narrative as root metaphor for psychology', in Sarbin, T. (ed.), *Narrative Psychology: The Storied Nature of Human Conduct*, New York: Praeger, pp. 3–21.

make comparisons not only between psychological characteristics such as traits, intelligence, motives, but also between evolving life narratives: their complexity, themes and emotional tone. Our developing, ever-changing life story is recognized as an essential part of our individuality and the construction of our identity embedded in a particular family, with a particular network of relationships, in a particular society, in a particular historical moment. Furthermore, our life story is conceived as the medium through which we discover meaning and unity in our lives. Hence, the psychology of life stories is now emerging as an effective means of integrating the science of human behaviour and lived experience.[6]

Relating a Christian perspective to psychological science or vice versa is not without its challenges. There has been a history of mutual suspicion.[7] Psychology is the science of human behaviour and its interest in religion has primarily focused on studying religious experience and behaviour in the same way as it approaches any other kind of human experience. The Christian faith is a faith founded on the relationship between the divine creator and creation encapsulated in the biblical narrative. Yet this story of human beings' relationship with God and each other also offers a rich description for a psychological analysis of human personality and experience in the context of faith with its complexity and diversity. Human lived experience is at the heart of psychology and the Christian faith is rooted in the human experience of God and creation. Examining the narratives of human experience and Scripture throws back questions for both psychology and theology.

The method in this book is a modification of the critical conversation as outlined by Pattison.[8] In each chapter, a story or human characteristic is analysed through the lenses of psychology and theology, and from this analysis a mutually informed distillation of what is revealed about a particular aspect of the nature of being

6 McAdams, D. P., 'The psychology of life stories', *Review of General Psychology*, 5 (2001), pp. 100–22.

7 Watts, F., 2002, *Theology and Psychology*, Aldershot: Ashgate.

8 Pattison, S. J., 1989, 'Some straw for the bricks: a basic introduction to theological reflection', in Woodward, J. and Pattison, S. J. (eds), 2000, *The Blackwell Reader in Pastoral and Practical Theology*, Oxford: Blackwell, pp. 135–45.

human and embodying the Christian faith is outlined. Our beliefs about God and the faith we live are part of human experience. Therefore, this book seeks to discover the common ground and the resonances which ring true in both the psychological and theological realm. Often this raises more questions than answers. It necessarily involves engaging with a different way of describing human lives and experience from what some of us may be familiar with. But it is hoped that through setting up these new conversations between fundamental aspects of being human, new insights might emerge for practical and pastoral theology.

Narrative, Human Experience and Meaning-Making

In Chapters 2 and 3 the common theme of narrative is examined within theology and psychology. I contend that human experience is best described in narrative form and that without story experience lacks context and temporality. In short, isolated descriptions of experience hold limited and inadequate explanatory power. For this reason, Chapter 2 begins by examining the storied nature of human experience and how narrative has been used to inform both theological and psychological understandings of being human. It lays the foundation for the psychological and theological approach to the nature of human experience which I have adopted, and sets up the context for the critical conversations which follow by outlining the different approaches to narrative in psychology and theology.

Chapter 3 develops the use of narrative further, and examines its importance for meaning-making. Human lives are immersed in meaning-making: from understanding the world, which is essential for coping, to searching for meaning or a sense of purpose in life. Both of these are important for human flourishing. Our search for meaning characterizes human beings, and psychologically it is described as a desire or, in more extreme cases, as an addiction. We are restless until we have understood or made sense of our experience of life with all its apparent contradictions and complexity. Frequently we use narratives to help us understand what has happened or to explain things. They help us identify the relationship between things in a sequence of causes and effects. They provide a temporal order to events; and through constructing a story we can sometimes connect seemingly diverse happenings into an integrated scheme that has coherence and illustrates how human actions and events are related to one another. Hence, a story is a meaning structure which facilitates our understanding of all aspects of life by organizing events and human responses into a coherent account; one which attributes them significance, acknowledges their effect and draws this into a conclusion.[9]

The use of narrative in meaning-making takes many forms. We use stories to understanding personal experiences. We listen to the stories of others and construct a sense of who they are from the way they tell their stories of their lives. Moreover, we use our personal story to understand ourselves and we tell the story of our life to construct our identity and make sense of who we are. We use narratives to reveal the purpose and direction of our life and the lives of others. We express who we are to others by telling stories about ourselves. But as we have already noted, who we are is also influenced by the stories of others: society's story, culture's story and, for Christians, God's story. The narrative of God and God's relationship with creation and human beings in particular is the ultimate story and source of meaning. Hence the search and desire for meaning in a Christian context can be defined as a search and desire for God. But Christianity is not a meaning-making system as psychology would claim, rather it is faith in God, the one in whom we discover all meaning and who reveals to us the truth of all things through the power of the Holy Spirit.

The centrality of human need for meaning has been conceived as meeting other human needs which, if left unsatisfied, cause distress. Baumeister and Wilson[10] identify these as the need for purpose, value and justification, efficacy and self-worth, and claim that fulfilling these needs shapes the stories we tell about ourselves

---

9 Polkinghorne, *Narrative Knowing*, p. 36.

10 Baumeister, R. F. and Wilson, B., 'Life stories and the four needs for meaning', *Psychological Enquiry*, 7 (1996), pp. 322–5.

and hence our personal identity. It is interesting that each of these needs can be met by adopting the Christian faith. By integrating the gospel narrative with a personal narrative, personal identity and meaning-making are transformed in a positive and life-giving way which can be demonstrated psychologically as well as theologically. The suggestion that religion is a way of meeting unmet psychological needs has aroused suspicion in both theology and psychology. There is danger in focusing on psychological problems arising from a distorted or obsessive adoption of faith and ignoring the positive mental health effects of religion and how the Christian faith has a positive influence on the development of personality and well-being. In part, these positive influences are associated with the power of the Christian story to provide meaning and purpose to life.

However, the relationship between narrative and meaning-making is dynamic. When we experience trauma, our meaning-making system can become disorganized and there is a discrepancy between what we believed to be true about the world and human beings and our actual experience. This dramatic upheaval in the meaning of life and personal identity can have devastating effects on psychological well-being and faith. The story someone lives by is violated. The process of telling and listening to the story of trauma is crucial for the construction of new meaning. Here again, psychology and theology find common ground in the significance of narrative and meaning-making to reappraise and reconstruct meaning in the process of personal recovery and transformation. At what level within a person transformation occurs is a matter of debate; but thinking, feeling and a person's behaviour patterns may all be changed. Hence, meaning-making and narrative are significant factors in development and change in our personalities. When our narrative is ruptured, or we cannot conceive of or dare to contemplate our narrative's future, then often our personality undergoes significant change. Others experience us differently as we struggle to reappraise our narrative and construct a new sense of meaning to sustain us. Understanding the complex relationship between narrative, identity and personality continues to present a considerable challenge to psychology, but these are essential components in understanding what it is to be human and are at the heart of personality psychology.

Personality Psychology

The relationship between personal identity and narrative is one way among many of describing and explaining the uniqueness of every human story and every human being. Personality psychology studies the individual differences and similarities between human beings and how these might help to explain the kinds of lives we lead. It strives to give 'an account of an individual person's life',[11] to understand what it is to be a human being and embody a particular story. On the one hand it strives to provide an account of individual differences, and on the other provide a psychological framework for understanding an individual human being: who they are, how they came to be that person, and who they might become. In other words – what a person is like, how they think, feel and behave, and how they developed into the person they are. Epistemologically, this requires both description and explanation, and to meet these requirements the study of personality has augmented its traditional methodologies of case studies, psychometrics, and experimental research with analysing life stories and autobiographical recollections. Reflecting on and comparing life stories gives a coherent overview of differences and similarities between human beings, but it does not replace the need for the more traditional research methods.

The science of personality has been dominated by trait theories that describe how someone compares with others on a number of characteristics, such as the Big Five model[12] which includes the traits – extroversion, neuroticism, openness to experience, conscientiousness and agreeableness. But a person is more than their traits or dispositions. To gain a fuller picture of a human being, we need to know something about what motivates them, their values, their

11 McAdams, D. P., 2002, *The Person: An Integrated Introduction to Personality Psychology*, New York: John Wiley & Sons, p. 3.

12 McCrae, R. R. and John, O. P., 'An introduction to the five factor model and its applications', *Journal of Personality*, 60 (1992), pp. 175–215.

concerns, their ways of relating to others, their attitudes and habits. McAdams[13] describes this as a different level of personality which he calls personal concerns or adaptations. But even this is insufficient for fully describing a person. McAdams asserts that a further level of description is required which describes what a person's life means overall and how their relationships and social development is organized to provide them with some sense of unity and purpose in life. It concerns a person's identity, which he argues refers to 'a particular quality or flavoring of people's self-understandings, a way in which the self can be arranged or configured'.[14] This takes the form of an inner story which is self-defining, and integrates the many often conflicting roles and relationships and experiences which make up our lives. It evolves during our lifetime, beginning in adolescence, and contains our sense of personal unity, purpose and meaning in life.

McAdams claims that these levels are conceptually and epistemologically independent. They are not arranged in a hierarchy and they are not derivatives from one another. However, it is fair to assume that they exist in a system of mutual influence. Hence, our inner story is likely to reflect our traits, and what concerns us might well determine our inner narrative and identity. But the exact nature of the relationship between these three levels has yet to be fully explored. Nonetheless, this theory provides one of the most promising psychological descriptions of human being available, and begins to capture not only the complexity, but the richness of each unique human life. As a model of personality it understands human beings as a unique pattern of traits, personal adaptations and stories. Furthermore, it does not reduce a person to a personality profile of traits and dispositions, but rather seeks to understand their motives, concerns, values and relationships and the story in which these are enacted and embedded. Chapter 4 gives an overview of the psychology of personality and then examines different psychological approaches and theories of personality before considering how Christian faith can influence, or even change, personality, as

---

13 McAdams, 'What do we know when we know a person?'
14 McAdams, 'The psychology of life stories', p. 102.

it transforms what we are like, how we behave and respond to our life's experiences.

The process of the transformation by faith can take many forms, and is understood, psychologically, in different ways. One approach is to consider how a new faith perspective and interpretative framework brings about the reordering or adoption of new life goals which change behaviour, thinking and feelings. Goals and motivation are the first features of personality to be considered in the second half of the book. Here we look at related components of personality in more detail, before revisiting narrative as a unifying concept in personality and identity in the final chapter.

Human Goals and Motivation

The interaction of faith on personality can be evidenced in the different levels of personality as described by McAdams.[15] Chapter 5 focuses on level 2 of the model and presents the psychology of goals and motivation, placing this in dialogue with our understanding of the sinful nature of human beings. Using the example of the disciple Judas, it seeks to offer a more nuanced understanding of how goals and motives influence our personality and our behaviour.

Our goals are informed by our needs, desires and concerns. All human beings have a need for competence, autonomy and being in relationships with others.[16] We are motivated to meet these needs. But beyond these needs we set a seemingly infinite variety of other goals. The energy which drives our being may be intrinsic when we do something because it is rewarding in itself, or extrinsic when we do something only for the sake of the reward or the separable outcome which is anticipated as a consequence of this behaviour or activity.[17] When our motivation is intrinsic we experience a sense

---

15 McAdams, 'What do we know when we know a person?'

16 Deci, E. L. and Ryan, R. M., 2012, 'Motivation, personality and development within embedded social contexts: an overview of self-determination theory', in Ryan, R. M. (ed.), *The Oxford Handbook of Human Motivation*, Oxford: Oxford University Press.

17 Deci, E. L. and Ryan, R. M., 1985, *Intrinsic Motivation and Self-determination in Human Behavior*, New York: Plenum.

of autonomy, but when we are overwhelmed by demands and goals which we perceive as being set by forces outside ourselves, for example other people's expectations of us, society's expectations or even the demands of discipleship, we can become anxious and distressed and lose our sense of being in control of our lives. In this way, our goals and the type of motivation we are experiencing have a significant impact on our well-being and our personal development. Any consideration of human experience and personality must include our personal strivings and motivations. From our early years, they are integrated into our personality and influence the plot of our personal narrative. They orientate our lives.

Within the Christian tradition, a set of goals and concerns are prescribed which shape our lives. These goals are deeply embedded in the Bible and are a constant theme in Jesus' ministry and teaching. To do what is pleasing in the sight of God is one of the ultimate concerns of living the Christian life.[18] However, as human beings our needs and concerns are complex. They have their roots in our biological nature with a desire for self-preservation, for pleasure and avoidance of pain; nevertheless, the desire for power, intimacy and achievement, among others, can take priority over other needs and goals. Our goals and motivations exist in a moral framework and are subjected to judgement by God, others and ourselves. The spiritual and psychological tension between meeting the goals of a Christian life and succumbing to selfish motives and self-gratification is a matter of Christian character formation. We live out our faith knowing that we are in need of grace and forgiveness, regularly confessing our sins and examining our motives, desires and actions. Our beliefs and goals shape who we are, how we behave and who we become. But human formation does not take place in a vacuum. The significance of others and their influence on the formation of our goals and motivations, as well as other aspects of our personality, occupies a central place in developmental psychology; it also has a distinctive place in the Christian faith, as expressed in the importance of the community of the Church and the relational aspects of discipleship.

18 Emmons, R. A., 1999, *The Psychology of Ultimate Concerns*, New York: Guilford Press.

Relationships

From the beginning of the creation of humankind, God realized that it was not good for man to be alone (Gen. 2.18). This echoes profoundly with human lived experience. When we are isolated and alone for long periods of time we become distressed. Chapter 6 is an exploration of how our relationships from the first stages of our lives affect the development of our personalities and personal narrative. We are participators in a living human web[19] of relationships, and each participant bears a narrative which is entangled with the narratives of significant others in their lives. Every relationship we engage in involves a mutual participation in the personal narratives of others. Sometimes this participation is brief and has little impact on us, but on other occasions it occupies distinctive periods or even a lifetime, and influences both personality development and the life-course of one or more individuals.

The relationship between a child and its parents or caregivers is considered to have a lifelong impact on personality. The nature of this relationship, described as an attachment bond, provides the template for the human experience of trust, security and love. From the perspective of psychology and theology, the mystery and power of love is recognized in the profound impact it has on human well-being and flourishing. Love transforms personal narratives and identity. The ministry and life of Jesus is the embodiment of the affirming and transformative love of God for every human being. Evidence of the human need for love is well documented in neurophysiology and developmental psychology.[20] Without secure, loving relationships we become distressed and our personality may become disordered.

Our relationships are also important for providing us with information from which we construct our personal identity. I have little sense of who I am unless people respond to me. Our personal identity is forged by our experience in relationships, particularly

19 Miller-McLemore, B., 2012, *Christian Theology in Practice: Discovering a Discipline*, Grand Rapids, MI: Eerdmans, pp. 25–110.

20 Gerhardt, S., 2004, *Why Love Matters: How Affection Shapes a Baby's Brain*, Hove, Sussex: Routledge.

in our early years but continuing throughout life. But we are not passive recipients of the responses of others. Even in the first year of life, infants exert influence on their parents or caregivers: both participants being formed by each other in a mutual, reciprocal relationship. The social context of human life has a primary influence on our formation. Of particular importance is the family context. We generally spend a large proportion of our time with family members, and these relationships are most likely to be significant to us for most of our lives. Within the family culture, values, belief systems, and the nature and expression of love and care are learned. The Internal Working Model constructed from these experiences becomes the template of love for our future life. Abuse, neglect or authoritarian parenting may lead to a distorted model which creates negative expectations of others and the self which alter, and may have a long-lasting damaging impact on, relationships and self-perception. As social beings, relationships shape our personalities and constitute a large part of our personal narrative, providing essential information for the construction of our personal identity. Our stories are stories about ourselves in the company of others and what we have shared together. They reveal how we feel about others, and how they make us feel about ourselves. The emotional impact of our relationships and experience more generally provide the colour and tone of our narrative. Emotions are a potent source of information revealing the significance of experiences to us and communicating our feelings to others. They determine how others respond to us and provide us with life's joys and sorrows. The peaks and troughs of our narrative are contingent on our emotional responses to the events of our lives, and these are influenced by our personality. Our emotions cannot be dissociated from our personality traits, goals, desires, values and concerns. To know someone is to be able to predict their emotional responses.

Emotions

It is a surprise that the study of emotions has existed predominantly outside the psychology of personality. Even a cursory analysis of the ways in which we describe the personality of others reveals that many of the adjectives used are associated with emotions. We may describe somebody as being contented, anxious or angry in their person and we take this to represent their character disposition. The emotions we express are fundamental to how others experience us, but they also reveal our goals and what matters to us. Nussbaum describes them in this way: 'They reveal the world to the creature, the creature's deepest goals to itself, and all of this to the astute observer.'[21] The multifunctional nature of emotions has spawned a variety of psychological theories. The instinctive emotional responses of fright and flight reveal the world to be dangerous, before we can understand the source of the danger. Emotions have an evolutionary function and are important for our survival. The comfort and love experienced by an infant in the presence of her parents elicits the emotion of contentment, and reveals the world to be a place of security and warmth. When an infant is separated from her parents, she becomes distressed and anxious. Her cries attract attention, and are intended to re-establish the closeness of her source of food, protection and warmth. An alternative explanation is that emotions are 'action tendencies' which prepare us to respond in particular ways: when frightened we have a tendency to escape, when threatened we have a tendency to fight, and when distressed we have tendency to cry.

Cognitive theories of emotion focus on the second of Nussbaum's functions as they reveal to us our deepest goals. We only have feelings for what matters to us. To experience an emotion, cognitive theories suggest that we first appraise the situation and then decide the significance of it in relation to our goals. Hence, we feel anger or frustration when we are obstructed or thwarted in what we want to do or achieve, we feel sadness and grief when we have lost someone or something which is important to us, and we feel

---

21 Nussbaum, M. C., 2001, *Upheavals of Thought: The Intelligence of Emotions*, Cambridge: Cambridge University Press, p. 108.

joy when something we strived for is achieved. The association between personality traits, which predispose us to expressing some emotions more readily than others, and our desires, integrates them firmly into personality. They invigorate our personal narrative and identity.

Emotions also offer the possibility of a fruitful dialogue between psychology and theology. Christianity has been characterized by its suspicion of emotions and passion. Emotions have been considered as disruptions, irrational and in need of control. However, the Old Testament narrative contains many stories which are effusive in their emotional characterization of protagonists, and throughout the psalms the rawness of human emotion is expressed untamed before God. In contrast, the Gospels contain few explicit references to Jesus's emotions or those of his disciples. It is from their actions that we are left to infer how they felt. The relationship between how we interpret a situation, what we feel, and how we respond provides a focus for a helpful dialogue between theology and psychology which is examined in Chapter 7. It strikes at the heart of the transformative impact of faith. Belief in God presents a new interpretation of the self and purpose and meaning in life. Our goals and motivations reflect this belief, and as such it has significant consequences for how we interpret what we encounter and experience in life. The emotions we feel and our responses are thus also changed by faith.

Roberts[22] develops this idea in his conception of spiritual emotions which he defines as Christian construals, by which he means our perceptions of situations in terms of 'the Christian teaching of what the world is like, who we are and what God has done for us'.[23] By extension, Christian character is made up of the disposition to experience Christian emotions, and is described both as a passion and habitual way of seeing and interpreting the world in Christian terms. He chooses joy, gratitude, fear, hope and peace as the spiritual emotions. These are some of the 'fruit of the Spirit' (Gal. 5.22–23) as identified by Paul, and characterize Christian maturity.

---

22 Roberts, R. C., 2007, *Spiritual Emotions: A Psychology of Christian Virtues*, Grand Rapids, MI/Cambridge, UK: Eerdmans.

23 Roberts, *Spiritual Emotions*, p. 31.

However, negative emotions such as guilt, disgust, pride, sadness and shame are excluded in Roberts's selection of spiritual emotions, but they can all be demonstrated to have some psychological benefit and have evolutionary purpose. To portray these as vices or entirely negative feelings is unhelpful both spiritually and psychologically. For example, being able to rejoice even in the face of suffering as Paul suggests in Romans 5.3 is very laudable and of good character, but equally to feel grief and sadness in the face of suffering is also important for well-being and healing. Psychologically, when we experience hurt and lament this can facilitate the process of facing and dealing with our experience of the world which is part of the process of moving towards rehabilitation and healing.[24] The challenge of a constructive conversation between the disciplines lies in understanding how life purpose, goals and motivations relate to character and influence the emotions we feel as well as how we regulate them. Growth in Christian holiness can be informed by a psychological understanding of the impact of reordering our goals and motivations on our emotions and our ability to regulate or manage our behaviour in accordance with these.

Self-Regulation and Self-Esteem

Baumeister, Hetherton and Tice claim that 'self-regulation failure is the major social pathology of the present time'.[25] Regulating our behaviour in response to emotions is a persistent challenge to every human being. We are tempted by many things and we spend most of our time pursuing the things we think will make us happy and trying to avoid anything which will cause us anxiety or distress. Our failure in managing negative emotions such as anger and frustration can result in violence and abuse. Likewise our inability to regulate our passions and urges, especially sexual ones, can also have a destructive effect on interpersonal relationships. An impaired

---

24 Swinton, J., 2007, *Raging with Compassion*, Grand Rapids, MI/Cambridge, UK: Eerdmans, pp. 107–9.

25 Baumeister, R. F., Heatherton, T. F. and Tice, D., 1994, *Losing Control: How and Why People Fail at Self-Regulation*, San Diego, CA: Academic Press.

ability to self-regulate predisposes us to behave in ways which not only harm others, but also ourselves. It is failures in self-regulation that lead to sin.

Self-regulation is psychologically necessary for human flourishing and the functioning of society; without it there would be anarchy. We could not live in the way we do. A basic characteristic of human beings is that they have the capability to control their behaviour within the moral framework they have adopted in their culture to enable them to gain the advantages of living and thriving in social groups. Human beings can regulate and determine their behaviour, and as such have a degree of responsibility for their actions. Human beings are free to choose what they do. They act with autonomy and have agency.

Theology and psychology share a common interest in self-regulation. It is interesting that psychologists have analysed human vices and virtues as a function of self-regulation.[26] In the Christian tradition, followers of Jesus are expected to adopt a disciplined life and confess before God when they have failed to obey his commandments and allowed their selfish desires to determine their actions. Augustine described this tension in human experience as due to a faulty will causing us not to do the good we know about and become enslaved to sin. He believed that our will and desires require reorientation through the grace of God. Managing the self against self-indulgence and gratification is a necessary virtue in the struggle against sin and striving to live a holy and godly life. Psychology is interested in how we achieve self-control and individual differences in people's ability to achieve it. Furthermore, it is also interested in the way in which religious beliefs and behaviours facilitate self-regulation. Hence, it takes a utilitarian view of this aspect of human functioning. In contrast, Christian approaches recognize self-control as one of the fruits of the spirit. It is a necessary part of the Christian life in the battle against temptation and sin.

Chapter 8 examines the psychology of self-regulation and reflects on it as the divided self, described in Paul's letter to the Romans

---

26 Baumeister, R. F. and Exline, J. J., 'Virtue, personality and social relations: self control as the moral muscle', *Journal of Personality*, 67 (1999), pp. 1165–94.

(7.24b–25a) and echoed by Augustine in his writings as the division of the will. The ability to exercise self-control is considered by psychologists Baumeister and Exline[27] to be the master virtue. When the inner tussle described by Paul is lost, we are aware not only of our sinfulness, but carry a sense of letting ourselves and God down. Hence, self-regulation failure is commonly associated with compounded guilt and a lowering of self-esteem. The inner world of the self is characterized by a negative emotion towards the self. In the psychology of self-esteem, the evaluation of the self by the self arouses an appositive or negative emotional response which is focused inwardly. Goals, desire and aspirations and emotions are integrated in the process of self-appraisal which raises or lowers our level of self-esteem. This subjective evaluation influences our well-being and our behaviour as we strive to protect our self-esteem or raise it. Like self-regulation, it concerns both an evaluation of the self and an emotional response, but why this subjective opinion of the self has come to be regarded as so important for psychological well-being and what is its primary function is widely debated in psychology.

The importance of affirmation and love in human flourishing from the first days of life has been well documented.[28] Praise, attention, affirmation and being loved, all contribute positively to the level of self-esteem we feel. Loving our self is one of the three components of the greatest commandments given by Jesus (Luke 10.27), but this is tempered by the command to deny one's self and empty oneself. An awareness of human weakness and sinfulness, and the consequential need for redemption, is also a strong theme in the biblical narrative. Hence, self-esteem requires a careful theological critique.

In psychology, the function of self-esteem is widely disputed. Self-acceptance and self-love is a significant strand in humanist psychology that functions to motivate a person to achieve autonomy and self-actualization. It is considered important in facilitating the achievement of goals, protecting us from anxiety and is a monitor

---

27 Baumeister and Exline, 'Virtue, personality and social relations'.

28 Gerhardt, *Why Love Matters*; Bowlby, J., 1965, *Child Care and the Growth of Love* (2nd edn), London: Penguin.

of the quality of our social relationships. William James viewed it as a fundamental aspect of human nature, and suggested that it 'depends entirely on what we back ourselves to be and do'.[29] But psychology, like theology, recognizes that the pursuit of self-esteem can lead to negative outcomes. When self-esteem is pursued at the expense of other goals and needs, it can damage relationships, physical and mental health and is also associated with a resistance to learning.[30]

The caution apparent in both theology and psychology provides the potential for a productive conversation relating the two disciplines which is explored in Chapter 9. The theory of optimal self-esteem suggests that a healthy level of self-esteem is characterized by goals larger than the self and self-worth, which are rooted in inner values. This can easily be related to the goals and purposes of the Christian life, which are outward-facing and centred on God's loving purposes for all creation. The adoption of this orientation also necessitates facing the fear of being worthless, answered in God's abundant love for all human beings and foundational to the Christian understanding of God's relationship with creation. As creatures created by God, we have value and inherent worth. Love is at the heart of our existence and '[e]ach created thing is loved into being, fashioned to depend upon and be part of a larger, interconnected whole, the fabric of which is relational through and through'.[31] Furthermore, optimal self-esteem also includes a respect for others and their gifts and a deeper appreciation of that which is beyond oneself, such as the wonder of creation.[32] This bears close resemblance to the Christian understanding of the virtue of humility, which entails the recognition of our dependency on God and others. Humility is an attitude of heart which, through an awareness of relationship and connectedness in the world and the

---

29 James, W., 1890, *The Principles of Psychology. Vol. 1.*, New York: Dover Publications, p. 45.

30 Crocker, J. and Nuer, N., 'The insatiable quest for self worth', *Psychological Inquiry*, 14 (1) (2003), pp. 31-4.

31 Reynolds, T. E., 'Love without bounds: theological reflections on parenting a child with disabilities', *Theology Today*, 62 (2005), pp. 193-209, p. 206.

32 Crocker and Nuer, 'The insatiable quest for self worth'.

interdependencies of human life, draws us away from a self-centred orientation to one which looks beyond the self and our subordinate goals to a higher goal. Rather than thinking about oneself in any grandiose way, or inflating one's self-esteem, a humble orientation is grounded and engages in realistic self-appraisal which is unpretentious and grasps the personal limits to any success that might have been achieved. Hence, the insights of psychology and the Christian tradition in a creative conversation can deepen our understanding of the nature of being human and living a Christian life which enables human flourishing.

These reflections on the different components of personality and characteristics of human emotion and experience are hugely informative, but they always need to be integrated into a personal narrative to gain a fuller picture of how they are operating and influencing the life and experience of a person. It is by returning to the personal narrative that we gain a richer description and explanation of who a person is and a fuller understanding of the configuration of their personal identity. Goals, motivations, emotions, self-regulation and self-esteem are all influenced by a person's overall meaning of life and sense of unity and purpose and become integrated into their inner story. Our story evolves through our lives and when we enter the later stages of life we reflect upon it to draw wisdom from our experience and give more attention to the meaning-making process to cope with the losses and changes accompanying ageing.

The Return to Narrative

Freida Schulze was 77 years old when she jumped to freedom in West Berlin. At this point in her life there was a dramatic change in her narrative, her city and country. We are always subject to change, sometimes momentous, but mostly mundane. The final chapter of this book focuses on memory, narrative and identity in the later stages of life. The episodes in our life are held in our memory and we draw upon them as we construct and internalize our inner narrative. During our later years we read and reread our narrative as part of the process of self-evaluation when we ask such questions as 'have I lived my life well?', 'is my story a good story?' At this point the temporal modalities of the past and the future are emphasized, and in the present reminiscence becomes increasingly important in the shadow of an appreciation of approaching death. Our past goals, motivations, successes and failures are all under review. A particular challenge at any stage of life is how to narrate the negative events of our life and explain or construct meaning from them. Sometimes this never takes place or it is only in the last years of life that tragedy, traumas and other negative experiences become assimilated into the personal narrative. In this process a new relationship is created between the past and present, but this is also influenced by what we anticipate in the future, which is a particular challenge at this stage of life.

The appreciation of a good future as death approaches sustains a hopeful story. The Christian narrative of salvation offers this hope and sets each personal narrative within the context of God's narrative, which provides a glorious and meaningful end to every story. By integrating psychological and theological perspectives on the role of narrative in older life, psychological perspectives on ageing and memory and the eschatological hope of God's story, new light is shed on how human experience is transformed from a narrative permeated with the emotions of fear and loss, to one of hope and a continued participation in the narrative of God.

To be a human being is to have a personality shaped by traits, goals, motivation and values, expressed and experienced in our thoughts, actions and feelings. It is to live a story in a web of stories which mutually influence each other. It is how this psychological story of what it is to be human intersects with the living story of God active in the lives of human beings that is the subject of this book.

2

Living Narratives: Psychology, Theology and Human Experience

Elizabeth Bowen's short story 'Look at All Those Roses'[1] tells the tale of a couple – Edward and Lou – stranded in rural Suffolk with their broken-down car. They call for help at a house with a beautiful rose garden belonging to a Mrs Mather. The story relates Lou's growing unease in the company of Mrs Mather and her invalid daughter Josephine, who has a back injury as a result of some untold act of her father. Mr Mather never appears in the tale; yet his deeds and the past they are imprisoned in continue to haunt Bowen's characters. The couple eventually escape the Mathers and make for the garage to recover their car. Edward, who has subsequently received some information about the mother and daughter from a conversation at the local pub, discloses his discovery that, 'Not a soul round here will go near the [Mathers' house]. I must say – discounting gossip – there's a story there.' Bowen's tale ends with the commencement of its unuttered narrative: 'Edward began to tell Lou the story that he had heard in the village about the abrupt disappearance of Mr Mather.'

We all love a good story especially one that keeps us guessing. In just ten pages Bowen has captured a distinct episode in the lives of characters of her story, but she has set this carefully within the context of the past narratives of her characters' lives. Edward and Lou are not married, they live as a couple, but Edward has a wife from whom he is separated. The Mathers have a past narrative of trauma. Mr Mather has evidently departed after his daughter

---

1 Bowen, E., 1999, *The Collected Stories of Elizabeth Bowen*, London: Vintage Books, pp. 571–81.

Josephine's back injury caused her to be severely physically disabled. It is implied that he was responsible for this catastrophe. The past narratives are not explicitly told in the present narrative, but their influence is powerful. This is also true of the characters' anticipation of their future; we sense their fear of the plot of their yet to be lived narratives. So we are told that 'Lou saw life in terms of ideal moments'. She never liked to be left and feared Edward might one day return to his wife. For the invalid Josephine, the monotony of the present makes futurity seem barely of note. 'Nobody comes to see us', she tells Lou, 'they used to, they don't now', or ever will it seems. These fears of future possibilities clearly shape and influence what is experienced in the present by both Lou and Josephine. Bowen, a supreme storyteller, pens an episode in which she captures the successive temporal moments of human experience in the lives she describes and, in doing so, alludes to both their past and possible future narratives. The haunting episode she describes exists in a tensed temporal modality; both past and future are inseparable from lived present experience.

Many of the stories which constitute the gospel narratives also capture successive temporal moments of human experience, and allude to past and future narratives for the main characters. In the story of the man lying by the Bethzatha pool (John 5.2–18) Jesus approaches a man who has been lying there for 38 years. He asks the man, 'Do you want to be made well?' The man does not answer this question directly but instead tells Jesus that he has no one to put him in the pool when the water stirs up. Jesus responds with a command, 'Stand up, take your mat and walk.' The man does this at once. He is healed. But there is a twist to the story. It is the Sabbath and the man has been seen by the Jews carrying his mat. They challenge him and he pleads that he is only doing what the man who healed him told him to do. At this point it is important to note that he was not aware who Jesus was. Later, Jesus finds him in the temple and tells him not to sin any more. The man goes away and tells the Jews it was Jesus who healed him and from then onwards they begin persecuting Jesus.

The lame man's 38 years of suffering, isolation and repeating cycle of hope and hopelessness sets the context of the story. It has a powerful influence on the impact of Jesus' actions and the actions of the man described in the story. Why did Jesus ask whether the man wanted to be healed, when he had been lying for years by a pool which had powers of healing? Was there something Jesus perceived which made him question the man's desire for a recovery? Perhaps the man's past was so integrated into his being that healing was both what he wanted most and feared most. What is more, his future hope of healing has been thwarted by his past narrative of isolation and abandonment. He has no one to carry him to the pool. Yet his possible future narrative is one of a changed life and inclusion in the society which has marginalized him.

Jesus enters the man's present narrative as a stranger; his story, like his identity, remains unknown. The man is ignorant of who Jesus is, what he has done or can do. Jesus approaches him. The power of this story hinges on the dramatic intervention of Jesus who heals him without even touching him, transforming the present and future narrative of the lame man's life. The story captures these temporal events in the experience of the main characters in a manner which encompasses not only the present, but also the past and possible future narratives of each of them. But for Jesus, the consequences of this healing are more explicit. John is preparing us for Jesus' death; we watch as the Jews strive to persecute Jesus and their desire to kill him is heightened by this episode. Knowledge of Calvary haunts us as the Jews turn on Jesus for his breaking of the Sabbath. The story continues with Jesus' response to the Jews in which he asserts the authority of the Son of God, and woven into his response is a vision of the future which includes eternal life for those who believe his word and the coming hour when the dead will hear the voice of the Son of God (John 5.19–29). In both Bowen's story and this Gospel story past, present and future are woven intimately in the lived experience of the characters. The significance of the present moment can only be grasped in the context of the past and the anticipated future. In each story, time and its sequence are fundamental to our understanding of the narrative.

Stories pervade our lives. Both in fiction and life, stories order the flow of events and help organize them. Whether we are the author or audience, narratives are a fundamental medium for meaning-making. We spend hours telling stories to our children, we recall our day by sharing its events in story form with our partner and friends. If our story is too painful or disturbing to share with those we love we seek out professionals who listen to our story and will help us to deconstruct and reconstruct it. It is also the case that we readily become the audience of stories. Our conversations are an exchange of stories, we read stories in books, newspapers and magazines, the entertainment industry is a storytelling industry; it seems that for human beings stories are an essential part of our cognitive architecture.

From the examples of the narratives from Elizabeth Bowen and John's Gospel, it is evident that typically stories provide temporal order to experience. They draw on the past and weave it into the present drama, as well as suggesting the consequences of present actions for the future. To author a story is to conjure with the past, present and future and try to capture the living truth of human experience.

The narrative nature of human life has gained considerable attention in recent years. Human lives are told as stories. We fashion our life up to a point and each of our stories is unique, but all of our lives have some common themes. They resemble one another in a number of ways as human beings have learned to adapt and flourish in the world. Each human being is a variation on the theme of human nature. Psychology as a discipline seeks to identify the major themes in the story of human beings as well as account for our individual differences. In the study of personality it recognizes the significance of narrative in understanding the formation of identity and personhood. However, the personal narrative is not the only narrative which shapes us as human beings. Social narratives of family, society and culture also intersect with and influence our personal stories and become integrated into who we are and become.

For Christians, the narrative of the story of salvation inspires and transforms personal narratives. It sustains and directs our personal story: shaping our present experience, revealing new meaning in our past and offering the promise of eternal life as our future. Through the lens of the story of salvation the narratives of all human lives are changed. The power of God's continued activity in the narrative of human beings, experienced and described in the stories of Christian lives, bears witness to the continuing story of God. For the disciplines of psychology and theology narrative captures the essence of human experience and identity, which makes narrative a promising metaphor for deepening our understanding of human beings whose narrative begins with their creation by God. Disciplines as pluriform as psychology and theology approach the concept of narrative in a number of different ways; yet such multiplicity of perspective holds the promise of an enriching interdisciplinary conversation.

Narrative in Psychology and Theology: Relating the Disciplines

The appeal of narrative[2] to enlighten, describe and entertain has always been part of human experience, but within the past 30 years it has extended its reach to academic circles. The human sciences, theology and ethics have all adopted and adapted narrative to describe and explain both human and divine experience. In psychology it has been used to explain both human action and experience, to describe the construction of self-identity, and to identify what constitutes consciousness and how we impose order on what might be described as a chaotic or seemingly infinite stream of stimuli and experiences. Theology has also engaged with narrative in a variety of ways. In particular it has been used as a motif for human and divine agency, to explain reading strategies and the hermeneutics applied to biblical texts. It has also been employed to demonstrate the significance of the act of storytelling in the development of myths and fables and account for how narrative functions in the development of traditions. In another vein, practical theology has developed canonical narrative theology as a method of theological reflection.[3] Boisen's *living human document*

---

2 I use narrative and story interchangeably throughout the text.

3 Graham, E., Walton, H. and Ward, F., 2007, *Theological Reflection: Sources*, London: SCM Press, pp. 151–222.

motif[4] believed to be taken from William James's term '*documents humains*' in his text *The Varieties of Religious Experience*[5] and reclaimed by Gerkin[6] adopts narrative as the means by which human experience is captured and then interpreted as it is 'read' by those engaged in pastoral counselling or care. Thus pastoral care and counselling is understood by some as largely a hermeneutical exercise, in which the listener to the story becomes an interpreter tasked with offering a new meaning to the 'living human document' before them.

This list is not to suggest that those who delight in the adoption of narrative as a scholarly device are supportive of all of its uses. There is controversy in both the human sciences, theology and ethics regarding the validity of the contribution narrative has and can make. Hauerwas and Jones in their introduction to *Why Narrative?* helpfully warn of the danger of oversimplification of the 'variety of ways in which the category of narrative has been used ... [from which] a misleading and distorted picture can emerge of what is at stake in appeals to narrative'.[7]

Introducing Psychology and Narrative

In psychology the explanatory power of a metaphor from the humanities has perhaps unsurprisingly elicited some suspicion. The discipline defines itself as 'the science of behaviour and mental processes'.[8] By implication it is a discipline which employs systematic observation and seeks to produce repeatable, verifiable findings. It studies both the external observable actions of a person and their

---

4 Boisen, A. T., 1936, *The Explorations of the Inner World: A Study of Mental Disorder and Religious Experience*, Chicago/New York: Willet, Clark & Company.

5 James, W., 1902, *The Varieties of Religious Experience*, new edn (1985), London: Penguin Classic.

6 Gerkin, C. V., 1984, *The Living Human Document: Revisioning Pastoral Counselling in a Hermeneutical Mode*, Nashville: Abingdon Press.

7 Hauerwas, S. and Gregory Jones, L. (eds), 1989, *Why Narrative? Readings in Narrative Theology*, Grand Rapids, MI: Eerdmans, p. 2.

8 Myers, D. G., 2012, *Psychology* (10th edn), New York: Worth Publishers.

mental processes or internal functioning and attempts to understand the relationship between the two. In this way psychology objectifies a person and is correctly viewed by many as reductive in its approach. It is perhaps only in psychoanalysis, humanistic psychology, branches of clinical psychology and counselling where narrative has had any place in the discipline; and some would even contest the assertion that these sub-disciplines can even be included as part of the academic discipline today. But despite significant strides forward in the last 20 years towards integration within the discipline,[9] narrative psychology remains on the margins. There is a deeply engrained suspicion that the use of narrative either as a methodology or as metaphor for the human functioning and experience lacks scientific rigour.

While one might be sympathetic to the need of scientific rigour or indeed academic rigour more generally, the reductionist approach in psychology poses problems especially for any engagement with Christian theology. The predominant 'nothing but' models of what is a human being can be interpreted as reducing human beings to survival machines for their genes or bundles of neurones. The human mind is understood as a sophisticated computer and human reality as a social construction.[10] Furthermore, psychology also has a tendency to abstract behaviours from their context or event sequence and therefore the observations used as part of data collection are detached from the real, lived experience of everyday lives. This is true especially of the research into cognition and memory in which participants are often asked to perform such tasks as recalling lists of words, isolated paragraphs or make reactions to a specified task associated with random images: tasks which can be criticized for being far outside the mundane day-to-day experience of life. Hence, the claims which can be made from these psychological experiments for everyday cognitive experience have frequently been

9 See Mischel, W., 'Toward an integrative science of the person', *Annual Review of Psychology*, 55 (2004), pp. 1–22.

10 See Watts, F., 2010, 'Psychology and theology', in Harrison, P. (ed.), *The Cambridge Companion to Science and Religion*, Cambridge: Cambridge University Press, pp. 191–3.

questioned. This criticism is not to deny the significant contribution this research has made to our understanding of intellectual functioning, but to suggest that it fails to sufficiently take into account the variety and complexity of lived human experience.

However, it is difficult to contest that the mechanistic approach of the great pioneers of learning theory in modern psychology such as B. F. Skinner and I. P. Pavlov were able to identify some important principles of human behaviour. Punishment and reward systems evidently facilitate learning and changes in our behaviour. We associate events and experiences with their consequences or outcomes and respond in accordance to predictable outcomes we have learned through this process of association. If you walk around with your eyes shut or without any light you bump into things. Many teachers and parents use rewards to motivate and affirm children. They also employ punishments to control behaviour. Likewise employers pay workers bonuses if they produce good results and dismiss people who do not conform to the company's expectations and rules of conduct. Our penal system is a system crudely operating on the principle of negative reinforcement. We go to prison for committing certain offences or receive a fine for breaking other laws such as driving over the speed limit. But although this principle enlightens our understanding of how we learn and modify our behaviour, it does not help us to understand what motivates someone to drive over the speed limit despite knowing that if they are caught they would get a fine. To understand that we need to know something about their personality, the reason for the journey, what was their motivation, who was with them, what emotional state they were in, what had maybe happened before the journey and what they were anticipating at their destination. In other words we need to know something of the story of the driver and the journey in order to begin to understand their behaviour of speeding in a more meaningful way. It is the person's narrative which can provide some of this important information. With the proviso that a narrative approach may not have explanatory power regarding some aspects of behaviour such as identifying types of learning or reflexive behaviour, for example the sucking reflex present in all babies and the workings of the nervous system, I suggest that it provides a fruitful way to approach many of the more elusive aspects of studying what it means to be human.

Introducing Theology and Narrative

The place of narrative in theological thinking has assumed greater importance during the more recent past. Following the 'narrative turn' a number of different views on how narratives should be told and engaged with have arisen within the discipline. In pastoral and practical theology storytelling has been adopted as a method of theological reflection and also recognized as an important part of the healing encounter. One of the primary tasks of pastoral care is the interpretation of stories. The conception of human lives as 'living human documents'[11] suggest that we are bearers of stories as well as listeners and interpreters of stories. This has been further developed to encourage pastoral practitioners to hear others into speech and in the telling of their story help the story to be rewritten so that broken or fragmented lives can be reconstituted into a new story of healing.

In a different vein, within biblical studies the New Testament accounts of the life of Jesus form the basis of canonical narrative theology. The Gospel stories are regarded as the means of interpreting the entire life of the creation. They are the ultimate source of meaning and significance for all human stories. In this approach Christian living becomes the faithful outworking of this narrative as we discover our place within it. Hence, the location of our story within the story of Christ is the means of discovering more of the truth of human existence. Our lives are mysteriously written into God's story which is radically inclusive in its nature.[12] Thus, life's meaning is discovered as human stories are intentionally incorporated into the meta-narrative of God's story.

Constructive narrative theology differs from canonical narrative theology in that it is not envisaged as the integration of our

---

11 Gerkin, *The Living Human Document*.

12 Walton, H., 'Speaking in signs: narrative and trauma', *Pastoral Theology. Scottish Journal of Healthcare Chaplaincy*, 5 (2) (2002), pp. 2–5.

individual human or collective stories within the divine story, but rather a creative intertwining of the stories of human experience with the sacred tradition to generate new insight and revelation. The role of parables as provocative, disturbing stories which challenge us, lead to new insights and transformation, points to an understanding within constructive narrative theology that 'stories not only create the world but have the power to change it'. Stories are more than their message; they can be sacred, sites of becoming within our imagination and can facilitate new ways of knowing.[13] Constructive narrative theology takes seriously the storytelling nature of human beings and the power of storytelling to redeem and transform lives. Narratives are understood as the shapers of lives, in much the same way suggested by many of the psychological approaches to narrative. However, constructive narrative theology also acknowledges the storytelling nature of God. The process of revelation through parables, dreams, symbols and the continuing story of creation and redemption is a testament to the richness and mysterious truth which is God, a reminder that we can never fully claim to know completely who God is,[14] but receive moments of insight and glimpses of glory.

Ford, in his reflection on the place of narrative in systematic theology, claims that 'Christian identity can be conceived as system, story and performance ... in Christian systematic theology "story" has a key role, inseparable from the form and content of the Christian stories, especially the Gospels.'[15] For Ford, the Gospels predominantly describe the story of Jesus, but they are written in what he terms the 'middle-distance' perspective which offers 'the detail of how things are'. This means they are not too detailed or close, nor do they contain generalizations. He asserts that it is

13 See Graham, E., Walton, H. and Ward, F., 2007, *Theological Reflection: Sources*, London: SCM Press, pp. 89–90.

14 Graham, Walton and Ward, *Theological Reflection*, p. 89.

15 Ford, D., 1989, 'System, story, performance: a proposal about the role of narrative in Christian systematic theology', in Hauerwas, S. and Gregory Jones, L. (eds), *Why Narrative? Readings in Narrative Theology*, Grand Rapids, MI: Eerdmans, pp. 191–215. Originally published as 'The best apologetics is good systematics: a proposal about the place of narrative in Christian systematic theology', *Anglican Theological Review*, LXVII, 3, pp. 232–54.

important for Christianity that the testimony to Jesus Christ is presented as realistic narratives which emphasize the middle distance identification of Jesus as the key focus of their witness. The Church recognizes these texts as communicating the distinctive message of the incarnation and as having 'primacy over other perspectives on the narrative content of Christian faith'.[16]

For other theologians such as Metz narrative is vital to theology. It ensures that the experience of faith is not reduced to ritual and dogmatic language. Theology is understood to be primarily concerned with direct experience, expressed in narrative form. Scripture bears testament to this beginning with the story of creation and then concluding with the vision of the new heaven and earth portrayed in narrative form. Metz suggests that reason is not the original form of theological expression but narrative.[17]

For many, the question of what the narrative turn has or can achieve remains. What difference does the recognition of the narrative nature of the Christian message make? Does it provide any extra explanatory power? Some like Root[18] suggest narrative skills have been an essential part of theologians' explanation of soteriology for centuries, others are more sceptical. Yet, like psychology, theology continues to draw on narrative to enrich its understanding of experience. Through a narrative approach some theologians claim to discover something deeply significant for human engagement with the events of the life of Jesus and our lived experience as people of faith. It is this identification with lived experience as narratives both written and in the making which draws these disciplines together and enables them to make significant contributions to each other.

---

16 Ford, 'System', p. 199.

17 Metz, J. B., 'A short apology of narrative', *Concilium*, 85 (1973), pp. 84–96.

18 Root, M., 'The narrative structure of soteriology', *Modern Theology*, 2 (2) (1986), pp. 145–57.

The Relationship between Theology and Psychology

The relationship between theology and psychology has never been a comfortable one. Watts, among others, has claimed that both disciplines can make a positive contribution to each other.[19] He suggests that theology can contribute to psychology by critiquing some of the reductionist tendencies in some fields of the discipline and also suggests ways in which it can be broadened beyond its often episodic, practical and individualistic approach. On the other hand, psychology's focus on human beings and how they function in the world provides an obvious intersection of interest with theological interpretations and perspectives on the human person as created by God. The significance of the contribution that psychology can make for the doctrine of human nature has never been fully accepted, let alone realized by theology, and this has led to a tendency in theology to make generalizations concerning human nature which has largely ignored individual differences.[20] But by examining certain fundamental structures and aspects of human nature such as personality, emotions, self-esteem and identity through the application of narrative psychology and its overlap with narrative in theology and pastoral care, we can perhaps conceive of a new integrative framework for deepening our psychological appreciation of human nature and informing our theological perspective and the practice of Christian ministry.

If as I propose, narrative provides a coherent organizing principle and integrative framework for what it means to be human from a Christian perspective, then it is important to begin by understanding what is meant by story before examining the psychological significance of narrative for understanding human experience and the experience of faith in human lives.

19 Watts, 'Psychology and theology', pp. 191–3.
20 Watts, 'Psychology and theology', pp. 195–7.

What is a Narrative?

There are certain characteristics which make a story a story. There is a recognizable difference between reading a help manual for Microsoft Word and a novel by Jane Austen.

First, stories have a context or setting. In order for us to understand a story we are usually given information about the time and place, whether it is a story of an event which happened 200 years ago, recently or in an imagined future. If this information is missing early in the story, then the story is confusing and difficult to engage with. This often happens in conversations. So, I have found myself completely misunderstanding a story, because a friend has assumed that I knew the context which they were referring to and when the events had happened. I then make an inappropriate response which is corrected with, 'No! not when I went to London with Jane in the summer; you know – that time last February when I went down to see Lucy.'

Stories also have a beginning, something happens within the context or setting and that something involves characters either human or usually with human characteristics. We anthropomorphize even inanimate objects in stories, thus cars, trains and even houses become characters in stories. This is particularly true of some children's stories where everything is anthropomorphized from the wind and rain to the entire contents of a toy box. After we begin to get to know the main characters, there normally follows an initiating event which the main protagonist responds to. Something happens, which leads to a set of actions that are intended to achieve a certain outcome in response. As part of the story, the impact of the event and its consequences are usually divulged; different characters might have both different reactions and different intentions behind their responses.

McAdams,[21] in his definition of story draws on Mandler,[22] and claims that each episode of a story may be seen as containing the

---

21 McAdams, D. P., 1993, *The Stories We Live By: Personal Myths and the Making of Self*, New York: Guilford Press, p. 26.

22 Mandler, J. M., 1984, *Stories, Scripts and Scenes: Aspects of Schema Theory*, New York: Erlbaum.

following elements: an initiating event which leads to an attempt, the consequences of which give rise to a reaction. The episodes follow on from each other and build up the story until there is a solution to the plot. All manner of linguistic devices are employed to enhance the dramatic effect of the story and its emotional impact including the revelation of the different motivations, emotions and perspectives of the various characters, but in most cases there is a pivotal point when the plot turns and a resolution follows. This basic structure, although there are various versions of it, describes what we encounter numerous times in our conversations, reading, television entertainment and engagement with current affairs. In our daily lives we are constantly engaging with stories which are presented to us in various media and with which we interact, reflect upon, and respond to in all kinds of different ways.

Narratives: The Language of Human Experience

The very nature of our experience can be described as a living narrative. Through a continuous and sometimes seemingly chaotic intersection and intermingling of stories our lives are given colour and depth. For Crites 'the formal quality of experience through time is inherently narrative'.[23] Hence, it is through telling our stories of falling in love, encountering a scene of breathtaking beauty or being betrayed by a close friend that our lives assume a richness and energy which would otherwise be lost in the relentless mingling of an endless succession of experiences.

Our storied experience with its numerous contexts, characters, initiating events, responses and consequences make up our past and present and direct our future. To understand what it means to be human is to listen attentively to the stories of others and to tell our own story. Human experience characterized in this way assumes that there is a significant relationship between narrative activity and life experience. Bruner summarizes this as, 'narrative imitates life

---

23 Crites, S., 'The narrative quality of experience', *The Journal of the American Academy of Religion*, 39 (1971), pp. 291-7.

Bruner

and life imitates narrative'.[24] In other words the conventions apparent in constructing a narrative mirror life patterns and facilitate a sense of coherence to the myriad of different events which we encounter and negotiate. Life is also storylike with its characters, events, plots, consequences and episodes. This is the fundamental premise of how our quest to understand human experience can be best illuminated by narrative.

The conception of human beings as storied is well documented. We begin our story either at conception or birth and we end it with our death, and in between are the events which constitute our story connected by their temporal sequencing and their cause and effect relationship. Human life construed in this way has a sense of continuity. Stories provide a structure for our perception of time; they link actions over time.

The Significance of Stories

Throughout the literature on narrative in both psychology and theology is the assertion that storytelling is a universal characteristic of human beings. It is something which human beings are predisposed to do. The story is present in some form or other in every culture. As we have already seen, stories make up much of our everyday experience and social activity. Our conversations are usually an exchange of the stories of events which have happened to us. We tell stories to family, friends, colleagues and mere acquaintances. We listen and watch stories unfolding on television and in films. Many of us escape by reading novels, immersing ourselves in fictional stories. We even dream in story form, often recalling their fragmented episodes and then struggling to construct a meaningful narrative from the remembered disconnected images. Likewise, in the process of remembering, as the origin of the word suggests, we re-member the experiences of the past by putting them back together in narrative form.

---

24 Bruner, J., 'Life as narrative', *Social Research*, 54 (1) (1987), pp. 11–32.

The pervasiveness of storytelling has led psychologists to suggest that our minds have an innate narrative structure.[25] Stories help us to structure the constant flow of experiences which constitute our daily lives. Carr extends this to suggest that stories meet our need for a sense of structure and order which is rooted in our practical orientation within the world. He invites us to imagine what life would be like if our experience was a 'mere' or 'pure' sequence of discrete, isolated events, one thing after another, and suggests that to negotiate and achieve everyday tasks and get on with life, we need to make sense of what is happening, to have a sense of connection between episodes, for things to somehow cognitively hang together.[26] So we subconsciously construct narratives to understand our lived experience.

Sarbin identifies this sense-making as a natural psychological phenomenon, labelling it as the narrative principle which he defines as 'emplotment, sense-making through assigning observation to a narrative structure'.[27] In psychotherapy, counselling and pastoral listening we can see how this principle is used to help clients who are confused, or struggling to make sense of what has happened to them. The therapist or listener helps the client to reconstruct their life story and find either *the* meaning or new meaning within it by enabling them to tell or indeed interpret their story differently. This clearly resonates with Boisen who identified the suffering associated with mental illness as located in a blockage or distortion in the process of interpretation and meaning-making regarding the events which happen to us.[28] Often with mental illness ideas and meanings jar with experience and the *living human document* requires the help of an interpreter to find new possible meanings.

---

25 Sarbin, T. R., 1986, 'The narrative as a root metaphor for psychology', in Sarbin, T. R. (ed.) *Narrative Psychology: The Storied Nature of Human Conduct*, New York: Praeger, pp. 3–21.

26 Carr, D., 1986, *Time, Narrative and History*, Bloomington: Indiana University Press.

27 Sarbin, T. R., 'The narrative quality of action', *Theoretical & Philosophical Psychology*, 10(2) (1990), pp. 49–65.

28 Boisen, *The Explorations of the Inner World*.

Stories and Structured Time

An important characteristic of a narrative is how it details events over time. A story has a beginning and an end in time. It is a device for organizing our experience as we piece together discrete episodes to create a unifying story which has temporal coherence. For Crites,[29] narrative as an organizational device is required by the nature of our consciousness which is always in the present. Only the present exists in the moment. Yet, our experience of it is inseparable from our past experiences and those experiences we anticipate in our future. Hence, I experience excitement in the present moment as I wait at the station for the train to arrive with my daughter on it. This present moment with the sights and smells of the station and the emotional tones of anticipated pleasure is what it is because of my memory of who my daughter is and the joy of our relationship, as well as the imagined future narrative of what we will do together once she arrives. Within any experience there is a 'tensed unity' of the modalities of present, past and future which occurs in the experience of the moment. The amalgamation of memory, the momentary present and anticipation of what is to come are held but simultaneously in flux as moment by moment the present changes into the past, and what we had anticipated may or may not have happened. It is our storied engagement with this reality which not only orders our current experience but continually shapes it. Hence both the narratives of our past and those narratives of anticipation influence our experience of the present. They are the 'tensed modalities of the present itself'[30] in which the remembered past and the uncertain future are operating in the present experience. Memory plays a crucial role in this process. It provides the necessary information for us to achieve a sense of coherence in our moment by moment sensations, perceptions, emotions and thoughts. These complex components of our experience are processed and held in an intricate web of associations and then used to reorder, reconstruct or simply reinforce our living narrative. In

---

29 Crites, 'The narrative quality', pp. 291–7.
30 Crites, 'The narrative quality'.

this way our autobiographical narrative is constantly under review and updating.

The confluence of our particular narrative and those of others both past and present determines the construction of our sense of personal identity. Narratives are the threads which we weave together to create a sense of who we are. To develop our identity we depend on our experience of continuity in our lives through time, in which the past is connected to our anticipated future and in which our sense of being and becoming is integrated into a single coherent narrative. As such the stories we tell about ourselves, both to ourselves and others, are seen as capturing the essence of our personal identity.

Personal Identity

For the past 20 years, the notion that we construct our personal identity through the stories we tell about our lives has gathered momentum in the humanities and social sciences.[31] By creating and internalizing a life story the answer to such questions as *Who am I? How did I come to be where I am now?* and *Where is my life going?* begins to take shape. It is not normally until adolescence that our life narratives begin to show coherence with regard to the causal relationships between different events and some identification of the themes or threads which are identifiable in our story. McLean et al. describe this as 'selves creating stories creating selves'.[32]

The development of self-identity will be considered later; however, it is clear that it is the interpretation of one's personal narrative centred on a number of events which are selected as important for an understanding of who one is which forms the basis of personal identity. Ricoeur, extending hermeneutics into the social sciences, argued that our sense of self and personal identity should be understood in terms of a narrative identity, asserting that narrative and

---

31 McAdams, D. P., 'The psychology of life stories', *Review of General Psychology*, 5 (2001), pp. 100–22.

32 McLean, K. C., Pasupathi, M. and Pals, J. L., 'Selves creating stories, stories creating selves: a process model of self-development', *Personality and Social Psychology Review*, 11 (2007), pp. 262–78.

time are fundamental to how the self is defined.[33] Through our imagination Ricoeur argues, we weave together the various elements of our life into a single story, and we maintain a sense of personal identity when we stay true to our promises over time. He sees the self as seeking its identity in many narratives over the 'scale of an entire life'.[34] Ricoeur, like Crites, includes memory as an important component in the process, envisaging memory as maintaining faithfulness to the past and shaping identity in the present and the future.[35]

Our identity story provides a coherent framework which integrates a sense of our persistence through time, who we understand ourselves to be and who we will become and also how we interpret our life so far.[36] It is an autobiography which is an interpretation of our personal history from which the meaning of the whole and its identity is developed. We construct this story of ourselves through our interpretation of selected significant life events. In effect, we tell our story and in doing so we become the main character in the story we are telling.

This is not to say that our personal identity can be reduced to a linguistic construction. The multidimensional nature of the self is recognized in both personality psychology and neuropsychology. But its biological, personal and social aspects have led to an unhelpful separation of the study of personhood in psychology mainly due to methodological differences. However, I claim that narrative can be conceived as a constructive way of drawing these different aspects of the self and the temporality of experience into a unified whole.

We are living narratives. Our stories are both enacted by our actions and composed by our actions. In connecting our activities

---

33 Ricoeur, P., 1992, *Oneself as Another*, Chicago: University of Chicago Press.

34 Ricoeur, *Oneself*, p. 115.

35 Ricoeur, P., 2004, *Memory, History and Forgetting*, Chicago: University of Chicago Press, cited in Wentzel van Huyssteen, J. and Weibe, E. P. (eds), 2011, *In Search of the Self: Interdisciplinary Perspectives on Personhood*, Grand Rapids, MI/Cambridge, UK: Eerdmans, p. 4.

36 Ruffing, J. K., 2011, *To Tell the Sacred Story: Spiritual Direction and Narrative*, Mahwah, NJ: Paulist Press.

together we generate subplots which usually have some consistency with an overarching narrative, and together they produce an internal narrative which sustains the continuity of personal identity. But continuity of identity is also dependent on the extent to which our lives have a sense of integrity and unification. Novak suggests that, '[t]he more integrated a life, the more all things in it work toward a single (perhaps comprehensive) direction'. Discovering a unifying narrative which enables our personal identity to be realized is an essential part of this process as it provides this single direction Novak refers to. Associated with the direction of our lives is the recognition of motivations and goals we identify in order to achieve a progression through life as we intend. These drive our narrative construction and shape both the main storyline and subplots. What we wish to achieve in life, what values we have, the virtues we wish to foster, the meaning we attach to life, all profoundly influence our narrative and identity. Interestingly, Novak also asserts that, '[t]he richer the life, the more subplots the story encompasses'.[37]

Construction of Personal Narrative

The relationship between personal narrative and identity is so close that many use the term interchangeably. However, it is necessary to acknowledge that not everything concerning our identity might be found within our personal narrative. We create our personal narrative selectively. There will always be things which may lie deep within us which influence our identity, but which are never incorporated into our personal narrative. Our knowledge of ourselves is always incomplete, and the possibility that there are influences on our personal identity of which we are unaware remains. The sentiment that God knows us better than we know ourselves, expressed in Psalm 139, acknowledges this fact.

---

37 Novak, M., 1971, *Ascent of the Mountain, Flight of the Dove*, San Francisco: Harper & Row, p. 49, cited in Ruffing, *To Tell the Sacred Story*, p. 71.

It is also the case that we can deconstruct and reconstruct our personal narrative. For many Christians coming to faith is a point when they began to write a new personal narrative. Creating our personal narrative is nothing like as straightforward as writing a novel. We can not filter out or control the events which we find ourselves embroiled in in the way an author does. Rather the reality of life presents us with negotiating, juggling, completing and re-engaging with a vast array of different happenings and projects. There is a need to be aware simultaneously of a variety of different plot lines which may or may not be connected. So my mother's hospital appointment 150 miles from where I am now living does not apparently interfere with writing this book. However, if the outcome of her visit is that she requires an operation, then that might well cause me to have to rearrange my writing schedule. It might also impact on the holiday planned in a few weeks' time and when I have the new kitchen fitted. All of these could be seen as separate episodes in my story, but in life these episodes collide and interfere with one another. We do not have the degree of control over events we so often yearn for.

Our daily life experience locates us somewhere in the middle of our story. We are progressing to an end but we do not know when it will be. There are some factors within it which we can control, such as who I plan to meet today and which books I will read, but for a considerable amount of our time things happen which affect us and we have no way of predicting them or influencing their occurrence. Of course there will always be some episodes we would wish to ignore, avoid or neglect. There are always events we would rather have not happened to us, for example those ones we are ashamed of or cannot make sense of. These are often the events we try to eradicate from our memories and cannot bear to integrate into our identity. But our success at this is inevitably limited. The impact of traumatic and other negative episodes can have psychological devastating effects on our personal identity. These are experiences which cause 'biographical disruption' and profoundly shock us. When these events happen, our whole conception of who we are, what our lives are about and the nature of our world is radically challenged. Frank describes this as 'narrative wreckage' which can dramatically shape the course of a personal narrative.[38] However, for most of the time we continue to create our personal narrative by drawing together plots or storylines which provide meaning to the critical or significant events in our lives so far.

It is easy to conceive of the personal narrative as being self-centred and narcissistic, and of course to some extent it is. To expand one's narrative beyond the individual self to include family, friends, communities to which you belong recognizes the intersection of narratives and how events which might be of significance to others also impact on me. Hence personal identity is not only formed by the plotlines in my story but also by the plotlines of those close to me. By extending the 'I' in the personal narrative to include others who we relate to, as well as the communities of which we are part, a picture of human experience emerges which places it within a web of living narratives. These narratives relate to and influence each other in sometimes subtle and unarticulated ways. To incorporate others and communities into one's identity the temporality of one's story expands beyond birth and death; my past also includes elements of their past, just as my anticipated future includes their future too. The importance of others for a sense of who we are is indisputable. Without the responses of others to us as persons we would have an impoverished conception both of who we are and what we are like. This fundamental aspect of identity formation points to the need for all human beings to be incorporated into the social world and in relationships with others. It also indicates the significance of other people's narratives and community narratives in shaping personal identity.

Other Narratives and Their Influence

McAdams suggests that we define ourselves through fashioning a personal myth, a term he prefers to personal narrative.[39] Myths are the stories which are widely recognized as communicating a

---

38 Frank, A., 1995, *The Wounded Storyteller: Body, Illness and Ethics*, Chicago, IL: University of Chicago Press.

39 McAdams, *The Stories*, p. 35.

fundamental truth about life. They are the stories which become incorporated into a culture and shape it. Hence, myths tell us something about the basic truths about a culture and its people; what concerns them psychologically, socially, spiritually: what has special meaning and is deeply embedded in the consciousness of the people. Drawing on this, McAdams suggests that a personal myth 'delineates an identity, illuminating the values of an individual life. [It is] a sacred story which embodies personal truth.'[40] In his use of the term 'sacred' McAdams is referring to how one deals with the ultimate questions and creates a sense of personal meaning that expresses a profound sense of truth for a person and which they incorporate into the personal myth. He claims that we in the West live in a demythologized world, no longer believing in one just God who created the universe. In this state of 'existential nothingness' we are driven to create our own meanings and discover the truths which govern our lives. In doing so, we construct the personal myths which 'sanctify' our lives.

In the bleak landscape of 'existential nothingness' in which we are no longer told who we are and how we should live, our task in adulthood is to discover this for ourselves. McAdams describes this as a psychological and social responsibility. We are to develop a myth within our particular context which has both ethical and relational implications for the way we live and to which we have a sense of obligation.

In contrast to McAdams' claims of the effect of a demythologized world, Crites does not dismiss the possibility that even in our fragmented and postmodern culture there may be embedded stories which have special resonance.[41] The storied world to which Crites refers infiltrates our very being. These are stories that cannot even be articulated. They are told by our culture and are ubiquitous. They shape our consciousness and our meaning-making in subtle ways which are unrecognized. We live in them and they provide stories which we sense our own lives are part of. For Crites, these are the sacred stories which exist along with the mundane stories we consciously use and tell. In the face of globalization and our evolv-

---

40 McAdams, *The Stories*, p. 34.
41 Crites, 'The narrative quality'.

ing exposure to an array of sacred stories it is possible that we are becoming more aware of our own sacred stories. The current wave of religious extremism and the variety of responses from different regimes and countries to this particular presentation of a sacred story demonstrates the profound influence of sacred stories on both individuals and global relationships. Although it is asserted from the postmodernism perspective that these sacred stories no longer influence contemporary culture, the rise in religious extremism can be seen to contradict this.

Ultimately, it is these sacred stories which help us to create a sense of self and the world. They are stories which orientate us through time. In written form they have a sense of authority which leads people to draw upon them to make sense of their own personal stories in relation to them. This is clearly what we experience in our engagement with Scripture. We open ourselves up to the story of salvation and allow it to bear upon our understanding and interpretation of our own personal narrative.

The complex interweaving of narratives both external and internal to us is both part of who we are, our lived experience and who we become. In the same way as narratives construct personal meaning they also provide significant insight into understanding the lived experience of faith. The transformative power of the gospel narrative can be helpfully understood in terms of an interweaving of narratives which lead to the construction of a hermeneutic lens shaped by a reappraisal of personal identity in the light of the story of Jesus. A psychological analysis of this process in conversation with theological perspectives on human nature and experience should ultimately inform both the theory and practice of pastoral ministry.

Conclusion

The pervasive significance of narrative as an integral part of our lived experience is unquestionable. In this initial survey, the psychological and theological significance of narrative has been developed as a unifying concept through which to explore how these two disciplines might mutually inform our understanding of what it means to be human. Through an analysis of narrative as understood in both disciplines, a picture of the role narrative in creating identity and meaning has begun to emerge.

The reality of human experience can be recognizably described as being storylike. Our lives begin in time with our birth and end in time with our death. The arc of human life is our storied passage between these two poles. But the reach of stories is both present in the overarching realities of experience and its seemingly mundane daily routines. Our conversations are often an exchange of stories. They involve telling, listening to and responding to stories. This seemingly natural activity enables us to process the relentless stream of daily events and experiences in order to construct meaning by interpreting these events in terms of relationships and connections. So, we ask the question: how does this relate to, or is connected to, something else which has happened or might happen, or to someone else or something? In this way we create a story to impose structure on the flow of our experience. Stories about us and the stories we tell about ourselves are the rich material with which we construct our personal narrative and form our personal identity. They are an essential feature of the experience of human beings. Theologically and psychologically, stories are also a means of revelation about the truth of human life and experience.

The interconnectedness of stories and mutual influence of one story on another is indicative of the living human web in which our lives exist. The narratives of others, culture and the sacred narratives of both past and present shape our lived experience. What factors influence the construction of our personal narratives and how do they operate in our lives? If narratives are so powerful in human experience, what can psychology tell us about the nature of this influence, and what resources in theology can we draw upon to shape an appropriate response to the power narratives possess to facilitate human flourishing? Having highlighted the significance of both psychology and theology to inform answers to these questions, the next chapter will examine in detail the meaning-making function of stories, how this has been incorporated into narrative theology, and its importance for pastoral ministry.

3

Narrative and Meaning-Making

On the road to Emmaus, the two disciples who were talking about recent events in Jerusalem failed to recognize the man who had joined them as Jesus (Luke 24.13–15). When Jesus probed their conversation, they were astounded at his apparent ignorance of what had been happening in Jerusalem recently, so they proceeded to tell him the story of the events of Holy Week and Jesus' resurrection. Jesus responded by accusing them of being foolish and slow to believe. He then proceeded to interpret the events about himself in their story through the lens of Old Testament narrative. In this encounter, Jesus overlaid their story with the narrative of Moses and all the prophets to help them discover the meaning of the events in Jerusalem. Despite still not recognizing Jesus in this moment of telling, they later recalled that their hearts burned within them while he opened the scriptures to them.

The conversation the two disciples engaged in on the road to Emmaus was a retelling of the story of the recent events of Jesus' death and resurrection. In among the facts they shared with Jesus were comments about what they had understood and hoped for *in* Jesus. 'But we had hoped he was the one to redeem Israel' (Luke 24.21), and 'moreover some women of our group astounded us ... they had indeed seen a vision of angels who said that he was alive' (Luke 24.22–23). Their unfulfilled hope and confusion at the witness of some of the women indicates that this retelling of the story served as a meaning-making exercise. The disciples were disillusioned, confused and most likely traumatized by all that had happened. By telling and retelling the narrative they searched for meaning in these dramatic events.

The passage of time is also an important aspect in their narration of the past events. They chronicle the sequence and comment 'it is now the third day since these things took place' (Luke 24.21). The storytelling gives the episode structure and a logical frame. In the act of storytelling, the various connections between events and characters become evident and are made explicit. Jesus, the central character in their story, is linked to the travellers both because of their sociological place as among his followers, and because of their emotional investiture of hope in him as the Messiah. The women who visited the tomb were part of their group of disciples, and as such their story is important and woven into the main fabric of the tale. Other members of the group of disciples, who checked that the tomb was empty, were vital witnesses who impacted on the plot of the narrative. Nevertheless, Luke's telling of the incident on the road to Emmaus takes the revelation of meaning into a different realm: that of recognition and memory. It is only in the drama of the breaking of the bread in the present moment of unexpected holiness that the truth of the past and the future is realized and grasped. The re-enactment of the breaking of the bread stirs the two men into recognizing the stranger. They now know it is Jesus. Through his actions they connect the present moment with their past narrative. They recognize Jesus because the present moment activates a trace in their memory of what Jesus had done with them in the past. Among the events stored in their memories of the past was Jesus breaking bread with them, and it is this remembered past which becomes the essential narrative for recognition and meaning-making in the present.

Embedded within the narrative of the disciples on the road to Emmaus is a layering of narrative upon narrative in a search for meaning and truth almost palimpsestic. The disciples share their story to try and fathom what had happened; how and why Jesus was crucified and the mystery of his resurrection. Then Jesus opens their eyes so that they understand the narrative of the recent events in Jerusalem by using the narratives contained within the Scriptures. Finally Luke incorporates all of these narratives into his Gospel narrative, which he describes to Theophilus as 'an orderly account ... so that you may know the truth concerning the things about which you have been instructed' (1.3–4). In each case narrative is employed to convey meaning, and there must be an intersection of different narratives in order for the meaning to be fully grasped.

The use of narrative in the meaning-making process has been acknowledged for centuries. Our experiences are meaningful and the way in which they are made meaningful to both ourselves and others is often in narrative form. In Jesus' use of parables we find him telling the stories of ordinary folk, doing the mundane things of life, and using them as clues to the eternal meaning and truth of the kingdom of God. Through our organization of our human experience into 'temporally meaningful episodes',[1] we are continually making use of narrative to understand both what is going on and the hidden truths which the story might contain. Psychologists largely accept that narrative plays an essential role in our innate need for meaning and understanding. But what does this proposed need for meaning signify, and how does it impact on our well-being? These are questions we must now turn to before examining what theology might contribute to this matter.

The Significance of Meaning-Making

Meaning plays a number of important roles in human experience, but the term is frequently used ambiguously; we struggle to establish the meaning of meaning. There are countless things that we do not understand and will never understand; the world is a place of wonder and intrigue, but we possess a seemingly insatiable desire to uncover its mysteries. From the creation of the universe to the intricate neurology of the human brain, scientific research continues to probe and develop our understanding. The world challenges and excites us, but that which remains strange and unknown can also threaten us. Meaning-making is part of our survival toolkit. While our reflex actions and innate behaviours are vital, the complexity of our physical and social environment requires that we have the ability to understand and anticipate numerous possible events every

---

1 Polkinghorne, D. E., 1988, *Narrative Knowing and the Human Sciences*, New York: State University of New York Press, p. 1.

day. We require a high-level cognitive processing to make sense of our world and to function effectively within it. Meaning, in this context, means to understand the world and the ability to predict what may or may not happen in the world.

Meaning-making is also associated with our sense of purpose in life. Without it we would be reduced to innately reacting to everything that happens to us with our only purpose being to survive and reproduce. It would be instinctive reflexes, rather than any higher level of cognitive processing, that would determine our responses and behaviour. But as human beings we commit ourselves to a number of different goals; goals which extend beyond surviving, avoiding pain, doing what is pleasurable and acquiring knowledge. Rather, we are 'intention generators';[2] we set ourselves personal goals, and these are held within an overarching framework that is based upon our perceived purpose in life. Some of these goals we pursue with great tenacity; others we give up on, or adjust to make them more realistic and attainable. Goals are important factors in directing our responses, what we do and where we invest our time. They are important to us, and in extreme cases can be more important than life itself. Some people are prepared to die rather than abandon their purpose. Their entire sense of life's meaning centres on a particular goal and purpose. Meaning in this context means the subjective understanding of the meaning of life and a personal purpose.

It is naive to suppose that everything we do is always in line with our goals and our sense of meaning in life, but undoubtedly most of the time we behave intentionally and this carries some kind of meaning. We can rationally explain most of our actions. We are aware of our intentions and these are usually associated with goals we have set ourselves. As Christians we regularly confess that we have failed to achieve our main purpose in life of 'being Christlike'. In the act of confession we acknowledge that our actions have conveyed a meaning which is contrary to our expressed intent. As we age this becomes increasingly important to us and we search for meaning and integrity in the story of the life we have lived so far.

---

2 Donaldson, M., 1992, *Human Minds*, London: Penguin.

The desire for congruence between our actions and what we believe life is about is frequently expressed in the concern to have led a meaningful life. In this context meaning refers to living a life that has fulfilled or at least contributed to one's sense of life's purpose.

Each of these expressions of meaning is significant for human flourishing. If we do not have any understanding of the world and the way things operate within our context we are vulnerable and our survival is threatened. Without goals or a sense of purpose our psychological well-being suffers; and when our life lacks meaning we can easily reach a state of despair. Hence psychology has a keen interest in meaning-making and its role in human functioning and experience.

Psychology and Meaning-Making

The notion that human beings are immersed in meaning-making can be found in most areas of psychology. Psychological research by its very nature is seeking knowledge and understanding of who we are. We are creatures who attempt to understand almost everything – unexpected disasters, our family relationships, poetry and great pieces of art, and of course we also strive to make sense of who we are. Our minds are predisposed to meaning-making and narrative enables this process to take place. But narrative is only one way in which we make sense of the world. Bruner[3] argues that we employ two modes of thought which are radically different. The first of these he labels the 'paradigmatic' mode. We operate in this mode when engaged in logical reasoning, reasoned analysis, empirical study. We might think of this as context-free thinking. The other mode is identified as a 'narrative' mode of thought. In the narrative mode, we are seeking coherent stories about particular experiences by making connections between events linked to human wants, needs and intentions. It is the way in which we process the experiential aspect of human life. As Zukier argues, many of the decisions we make and beliefs we hold do not always stand

3 Bruner, J., 1986, *Actual Minds, Possible Worlds*, Cambridge, MA: Harvard University Press, p. 11.

up to formal deductive–inductive scrutiny. Rather, they are justified by being part of a coherent narrative which includes context, intentions, and which we evaluate by a different set of criteria.[4]

The use of the paradigmatic mode is evident in much of academic psychology with its reductionist approach. The desire to understand human thinking, feeling and behaving in terms of neural activity, gene sequencing or evolutionary expediency has led to a number of powerful explanations of human functioning in the world. The narrative mode with its story-making function can easily be criticized for its lack of precision and subjectivity, but despite the huge leaps in our understanding of human nature, the paradigmatic mode has failed to offer a comprehensive explanation of human emotions such as love, jealousy and hate, or human relationships and beliefs. The ambiguity, unpredictability and diversity of human experience continues to challenge these more reductionist approaches. On the other hand, the narrative mode, until recently the province of novelists and poets, captures more faithfully the nature of experience and places it within its temporal sequence. Hence, an account of what had happened previously, what was planned, what actually happened and the consequences for the future, are taken into account in the meaning-making process.

Employing this narrative mode is something we do most of the time, particularly in social interactions. But we do not use either mode exclusively. Factual information about the way things are in the world needs to be included in the narrative for it to have any validity or usefulness. Therefore, the paradigmatic mode and narrative mode must work together to enrich our understanding of events, their origins and consequences, as well as to construct our understanding of the meaning and purpose of our lives.

---

4 Zukier, H., 1986, 'The paradigmatic and narrative modes in goal guided inference', in Sorrentino, R. M. and Higgins, E. T. (eds), *Handbook of Motivation and Cognition*, Vol. 1, New York: Guilford Press, pp. 465–502.

Exploring what Meaning Means

One of the persistent problems with meaning is the assumptions regarding its definition. There is the more obvious definition, which alludes to understanding what is happening, but meaning is often assumed to mean something deeper and more significant: something associated with meaning in life, life's purpose and one's place within the created order. A challenge in the psychological literature is its lack of a clear definition. 'Perceiving patterns', 'comprehension', 'understanding', 'higher level processing' and 'meaning of life' are all terms used in the literature to refer to meaning-making of one sort or another. Two notable, and indeed helpful, applications of meaning-making are making sense of everyday happenings and experience, and meaning of life. Meaning of life, as we have discussed, is a higher level of meaning-making centred on understanding of our existence and its purpose.

For both levels of meaning we draw on a variety of sources. Language, knowledge, symbols, actions, the media, society and many different forms of communication provide the ingredients from which meaning is made. Thinking, reflecting and pondering are all terms referring to processes which we employ in the act of understanding or meaning-making. However, as already suggested, there is a distinction between the everyday task of understanding, or making sense of what is going on around us, and our understanding of the meaning of life. Meaning of life includes our beliefs, goals, motivations and the feelings associated with these aspirational states. It encompasses our overarching sense of who we are and what we understand the purpose of human life to be. While this can be understood as a cognitive script, a fuller comprehension of its significance recognizes its far-reaching impact on our emotional, spiritual and psychological well-being.

The distinction between these two types of meaning-making is important, but they should not be considered as entirely separate. The meaning we construct regarding everyday encounters with people is, as previously suggested, influenced by our overarching meaning of life which includes our goals and sense of purpose in the world. By approaching meaning in this way, meaning of life can be conceived as a different level of meaning from everyday meaning-making. Our daily short-term actions are carriers of meaning, but as meaning of life implies, there is a sense of meaning and purpose which extends onto a much broader canvas and operates at a different and wider level.

But there is a need for caution in assuming that this applies to everyone. Some people would not describe their lives as making sense as a whole. Each day may be planned and have its own implicit meaning, but their lives do not have a clearly defined purpose or goal to provide coherence and a mindful orientation. It is also true that lower-level meanings which are part of our mundane comprehension and functioning do not necessarily contribute to a higher-level meaning. However, if life is attributed with a higher-level meaning then this can influence our interpretation of everyday actions and events. In this way, these two levels of meaning are connected to each other, and each contributes to a sense of personal integrity.[5] Using these two more clearly defined levels of meaning-making, we can now begin to ascertain the contribution of meaning-making to our lives and how this is related to our understanding of narratives of lived experience.

Different Needs for Meaning and the Role of Narrative

Baumeister in his book *Meanings of Life*[6] focuses on the functionality of meaning, concluding that it is essential to our ability to cope in the world. He stresses its importance for all manner of things from making predictions, controlling both our personal and social lives, and transforming our experience from an endless stream of sensory information to episodes we can make sense of. Hence it is an essential component of our everyday living and is part of every thought and action. Meaning-making here is very much understood at a more mundane level, but its importance is nonetheless recognized. However, Baumeister does not limit its effects to adaptive responses

---

5 Baumeister, R. F., 1991, *Meanings of Life*, New York: Guilford Press, pp. 20–3.

6 Baumeister, *Meanings*, pp. 357–8.

but believes meaning is something we crave.[7] It is an addiction, but a positive one. Here is a subtle move in the psychological interpretation of meaning. It no longer is described as an innate adaptive process, but as something we crave, with the implication that we become distressed without it. Frankl, in a slightly different vein, but echoing Baumeister's conviction that meaning-making is an essential part of our human nature, argued that the *will to meaning* is the primary motivating force of human beings. He believed that our main goal in life is to find meaning and value in it. Reflecting on his experiences as a prisoner of war in Nazi Germany, Frankl noted that the prisoners who adapted best to the appalling conditions were those who based their survival on some purpose or meaning in life. Those who suffered most and were more likely to die had no sense of life's meaning.[8]

Implied within both of these understandings is the assertion that human beings are driven to actively seek meaning in life. People can live their lives without having constructed a coherent, overarching notion of the meaning of life, but there remains a need for life to make sense in certain ways.[9] Furthermore, many psychologists assert that the desire for meaning is a prerequisite for mental and physical well-being. It is an evolutionary need which expresses itself in the need to understand life, 'especially its travails, as making sense in serving some worthy purpose'.[10] However, it is important to distinguish between having purpose in life and actively seeking meaning.

Psychologists seem to agree that we are inherently purposeful and inquisitive. In fact, many assert that finding meaning in life is an important human enterprise. Furthermore, evidence also suggests that purposeless living has a negative effect on personal well-being. The feeling which accompanies comprehensibility is determined by

---

7 Baumeister, *Meanings*, p. 359.

8 Frankl, V. E., 1969, *The Will to Meaning: Foundations and Applications of Logotherapy*, New York: New American Library.

9 Baumeister, *Meanings*, p. 29.

10 Frankl, *The Will to Meaning*, quoted in Klinger, E., 1998, 'The search for meaning in evolutionary perspective and its clinical implications', in Wong, P. T. P. and Fry, P. S. (eds) *The Human Quest for Meaning*, Mahwah, NJ: Erlbaum, p. 30.

the extent to which our lives make emotional sense and the demands of life are deemed worthy of energy investment and commitment.[11] Klinger describes it as a feeling that one has a purpose or direction, and noted that it is 'a pervasive quality of a person's whole inner life'.[12] Fundamental to the experience of meaningfulness is the feeling of direction; it is concerned with an orientation to a future goal, but the goal does not have to be attained. When our lives are thrown into confusion and lose their sense of a telos, or events throw us into a feeling of disorientation, then we can easily find ourselves living with a sense of meaninglessness.

Within the study of meaning-making the role of narrative has gained increasing attention. The development of a narrative involves both the selection of the key events which make up the episodes of the story and the interpretative framework into which these events are set and understood. As we construct our personal narrative we are constantly filtering and interpreting events by applying our personal hermeneutic. As we progress through life this might change depending on what happens to us and whether we are successful in achieving what we hoped for in life. There are several dimensions to our interpretation or the meaning we ascribed to our lives, the most significant being our goals, beliefs, moral framework and who we aspire to be. They are also the interpretative needs which contribute to our overall need for meaning, and become major shapers of our personal narrative.

Baumeister and Wilson[13] have identified four main aspects associated with the meanings of life that we construct, related to personal narrative construction and well-being. They argue that people develop meanings of life which are associated with their need for purpose, value and justification, efficacy and self-worth. They suggest that we look to 'work, family, religion and other sources

---

11 Korotkov, D., 1998, 'The sense of coherence: making sense out of chaos', in Wong and Fry (eds), *The Human Quest for Meaning*, p. 55.

12 Klinger, E., 1997, *Meaning and Void*, Minneapolis: University of Minneapolis Press, quoted in Park, C. L., 2005, 'Religion and meaning', in Paloutzian, R. F. and Park, C. L. (eds) *Handbook of the Psychology of Religion and Spirituality*, New York/London: Guilford Press, p. 298.

13 Baumeister, R. F. and Wilson, B., 'Life stories and the four needs for meaning', *Psychological Enquiry*, 7 (1996), pp. 322–5.

in our lives to provide these meanings'.[14] If all of these needs are met then we will view our lives as meaningful, but if one or more of them cannot be satisfied, then we experience emptiness and distress symptomatic of a lack of sufficient meaning in life. The needs can also be seen to shape the construction of stories more generally, and play an influential role in forming the hermeneutic lens through which we interpret the story of our lives. Moreover, they also provide a useful framework for the purpose of understanding both the significance of meaning-making for human flourishing and, in conversation with the Christian faith, they help to illuminate how the gospel can be a transformative force in people's lives.

Purpose

We want to interpret most of the things which happen in our lives as purposeful. But many of us struggle to find or articulate a life-purpose around which we organize our lives. Achieving such a life-purpose permits us to integrate all of the diverse events and narrative threads of life into a coherent story. Nevertheless, many of us tend to organize our lives around a number of distinct but connected main purposes, such as being comfortable financially, having a happy stable marriage and raising a family, achieving success in employment, being fit and healthy. The events and episodes in our lives are ascribed meaning inasmuch as they contribute to or are steps on the way to achieving our *main* purposes.

Value and justification

This need recognizes that for events to have meaning they must be judged against moral standards. It is important to us that the life story we construct presents us as a good person, but we need to provide the evidence to justify this within the narrative. Interpreting our experiences through the lens of our moral framework plays an important role in the construction of our narrative and the sense of meaning our lives have. Negative judgements about ourselves, especially involving unresolved guilt or shame, can have

---

14 Baumeister, *Meanings*, p. 359.

a profoundly damaging effect on constructing our narrative, personal identity and establishing that our life is meaningful. We often seek to justify our past actions in order to assert that our lives have been worthwhile and we are indeed good.

Efficacy

The third dimension of importance is the desire for our narrative to demonstrate positive outcomes for which we have some responsibility. Our lives are not meaningful if we are seen to be entirely passive. Part of the meaning we construct for our lives is one in which we have had an impact, made a difference, contributed in a positive way to the world and lives of others. The need for efficacy is associated with McAdams' development and emphasis on generativity[15] taken from Erikson's idea that, as adults, one of our motivations is to contribute to society and its continuation and improvement (hopefully) through to the next generation. The most obvious expression of this is through bearing and bringing up children, but it needn't be. Endeavours at work, in the voluntary sector, participation in politics, religion and a whole range of social enterprises can be a fulfilment of this desire to leave a positive mark on life in some way or another.

Self-worth

Finally, it appears that affirmation of self-worth is an important need in finding meaning in life. This is met by finding evidence that we have achieved something with our lives, there is something to commend us or admire about us. Baumeister and Wilson[16] suggest that this is not in itself dependent on our narrative in the way that efficacy is, but having self-worth can be construed as a stable property of the self which is evidenced by or conveyed by stories about the self.

---

15 McAdams, D. P., 1993, *The Stories We Live By: Personal Myths and the Making of the Self*, New York: Guilford Press, pp. 227–50.

16 Baumeister and Wilson, 'Life stories'.

Relating the Four Needs to the Christian Faith

Baumeister and Wilson[17] claim that these needs for meaning guide the construction of our personal narrative and our identity. Even when just one of these needs is not met a person feels that their personal story is unsatisfactory. Baumeister also claims that the relationship between religion and the need for meaning is one of cause and effect, with religion being a consequence of this innate need and an extraordinary human phenomenon which grows from this human need.[18] Here psychology is describing faith as a human manifestation of meeting a deep-seated human need, rather than belief in a supernatural God in whom life's meaning is found. Yet I propose that by examining these four needs in the context of Christian faith, the life-giving nature of the Christian narrative when woven into the personal narrative is revealed.

Purpose

The Christian faith undoubtedly offers meaning and purpose to life. In the life and ministry of Jesus we believe that God has revealed his loving purposes for the world and how we might participate in them. The goal for Christians is to seek to discern the will of God and centre their lives on obeying this. They believe they are created and called by God to participate in his divine plan and action. God has created them for this purpose and when they live in accordance with God's will, they experience life in all its fullness. For Christians, God is the source of truth and meaning. Sin is the result of a misalignment of our purposes with those of God, and if self-fulfilment becomes our dominant goal, and we do not live in accordance with God's purposes but our own, then we judge ourselves to not be the person God intends us to be.

The relationship between religion and meaning-making is both 'intimate and complex'.[19] Within our understanding of the overall

---

17 Baumeister and Wilson, 'Life stories'.

18 Baumeister, *Meanings*, p. 359.

19 Park, 'Religion and meaning', in Paloutzian and Park (eds), *Handbook of the Psychology of Religion and Spirituality*.

meaning is held the mystery of the divine and necessity of faith. We place our confidence in a God, who we can never fully know or understand, but who becomes our source of meaning. We somehow absorb this mystery and find our life purpose intimately bound up with the God who not only made the universe, but surprisingly values and loves us. We find meaning in the tension of such paradoxes; and yet through this faith, which involves both knowing and not knowing, meaning is discovered. Somewhat surprisingly this has proved to be one of the most influential sources of meaning in human history. Like other meaning systems, it shapes goals, motivations, the interpretation of experience, emotions and behaviour, and has a profound effect on the lives of believers. However, the distinctiveness of faith as a meaning-making system is chiefly characterized by a focus on the divine or sacred. Meaning, and what it is to be human, is not centred on the physical or material world, personal fulfilment and satisfaction, but in the promises of God and the life in the world to come.[20]

Christian meaning-making stresses the significance of past, present and future in our understanding of the purpose of our lives. Hope in the future and the climatic eschatological event when the kingdom of God will be established is the fulcrum of Christian meaning. This is not simply optimism, or the adoption of a positive attitude to life, but rather a commitment and conviction to a good future; one which orientates Christian goals and the pattern of life towards this coming event.

The purpose of life proclaimed in the Gospels and foreshadowed in the Old Testament is the bedrock of Christian meaning-making, shaping both the lived experience and the interpretation of it. An awareness of a living relationship with God, Jesus Christ and the saints becomes embedded in an understanding of God and his divine purpose in which we are called to participate. Both religious experience and more general experience of life is shaped by Christian teaching regarding the kingdom of God as that which breaks into the present and provides glimpses of the future reign

---

20 Pargament, K. I., Magyar-Russell, G. M. and Murray-Swank, N. A., 'The sacred and the search for meaning', *Journal of Social Issues*, 61(4) (2005), pp. 665–87.

of God. The anticipation of this future provides both purpose and motivation in life.

Many Christians can identify a particular event which has been the catalyst for a more dramatic drive towards meaning-making centred on their newly realized sense of purpose. Often it is part of an overwhelming experience of a personal encounter with God, which becomes the source of a transformation in their understanding of life. Their narrative and personal identity begin afresh, and this is often incarnated in such phrases as 'my new life in Christ', 'dying to my old self' and 'being born again in Christ'. A conversion experience of this nature has a profound effect on self-understanding, life purpose and the future. The power of such a meaning-making event has generated a great deal of debate in psychology concerning the uniqueness of religious experience; particularly whether its distinctiveness means that it cannot be fully explained by the same psychological processes as other aspects of human living and experience. Nevertheless, for Christians it represents the active presence of the Spirit of God in the lives of human beings.

Value and justification

The moral dimension of our lives enables us to justify our actions. It is notable that eight out of the ten commandments tell us what not to do, whereas the new commandments of Jesus are focused on love: '"you shall love the Lord your God with all your heart, and with all your soul, and with all your mind, and with all your strength." The second is this, "You shall love your neighbour as yourself"' (Mark 12.30–31). For the Christian, the main question which relates to leading a life which has coherence and meaning within the confession of their faith is: have I loved God, my neighbours and myself? The likelihood that we fall short of this on numerous occasions suggests that this might well be the need which poses a considerable threat or challenge to our sense of having led a meaningful life. The doctrines of sin and salvation, the place of confession and absolution in our liturgical practice and the rich imagery of judgement, heaven and hell, are all associated with the way we interpret our actions and the value and justification we attribute to them. The requirement in one prayer of confession to 'acknowledge and bewail our manifold sins and wickness',[21] and in a more tempered prayer of confession we say that 'we have sinned against you and against our neighbours, in thought and words and deed',[22] highlights our need to acknowledge our wrongdoing before God and confess that we have not led 'a holy and godly life'. Sin corrupts our relationship with God, one another, and with the world, and with ourselves when we sin in ways contrary to the great commandment of love. Countering the destructive power and grip of sin on human lives is central to the gospel message of salvation. It is through God's decisive act of sending Jesus to deal with sin through his death and resurrection that we are saved. We know through the story of Jesus that God loves us and offers us forgiveness and the opportunity for a new life in Christ. The gospel narrative we live by transforms our personal narrative when we repent and receive God's grace.

Baumeister and Wilson[23] note that the desire to present or construct a good life story which has meaning leads people to justify or interpret the morally questionable things they have done in ways that eliminate, or at least reduce, their experience of guilt. The Christian faith offers people an opportunity to face up to their wrongdoing through the acts of confession and repentance, which then enable them to construct a story which draws on the transformational power of God's forgiveness and the opportunity to begin a new chapter in their story. A temporal boundary is erected between the past wrongs and the future life story. There is a disconnection between the past and future narrated in terms of the old self and the new self. The personal narrative captures the transformation that frees the person from their past sins and demonstrates how powerful positive meaning-making can occur through the interconnection of the personal story with the gospel story.

---

21 Book of Common Prayer, 1928.

22 Prayers of Penitence, Order One Holy Communion, Common Worship, 2000, London: Church House Publishing.

23 Baumeister and Wilson, 'Life stories'.

Efficacy

The desire to respond to God's call and to live according to God's will demands a profound commitment of obedience which is sacrificial in nature. Yet from self-sacrifice and faith in God's promise of a deeply satisfying and joyful life Christians make a commitment to seek and obey God's will. Although it is clear that salvation is not earned through works alone – 'faith ... if it has no works, is dead' (see James 2.14–26), worshipping, reading the scriptures, praying and serving God and their neighbours in the world are essential ingredients of a Christian life. Living faithfully before God is not a passive life, but there is one crucial difference between the need for efficacy as described by Baumeister and Wilson, and that expressed in the Christian life: namely the assertion that people want to show in their narrative that positive outcomes were to some degree a product of their own actions and effort. For the Christian, this is dangerously close to the sin of pride, and as such the need for efficacy is transcended. Positive outcomes are derived from obedience to God's will, acting in God's strength, not one's own, and working for God's glory and not self-edification. Once again, it is apparent that the intersection of personal story and the narrative of Scripture can transform the emphasis of the personal narrative through its understanding of the overall purpose of life.

Self-worth

The need to be admired in some way by others, or feel affirmed for who you are, is an important characteristic of acknowledging that one's life has a positive meaning. Self-esteem will be considered in more detail in Chapter 9, but it is not without controversy and tension in relation to the Christian faith. There are a number of reasons why this is the case. The first is the reality of our sinful nature and propensity to keep on sinning. The acknowledgement of our unworthiness 'even to gather up the crumbs under [the Lord's] table' is expressed regularly by some congregations as part of the liturgy of the Eucharist in the prayer of humble access. Second, there is the command from Jesus that, 'those who want to save their life will lose it, and those who lose their life for my sake will find it' (Matt. 16.25), and 'the last will be first, and the first will be last'[24] (Matt. 20.16). Finally, there is the doctrine of salvation which stresses it is through God's grace that salvation comes and not human achievements and good works. Each of these can be interpreted as undervaluing human endeavour, achievement and even self and the emotional pain of life.

In response, it is helpful to turn to the human desire to love and be loved, both of which are to be found in the nature of the loving relationship between God and humanity. God's love for creation is wilful or intentional love[25] characterized by a determination and faithfulness which affirm the other and proclaims emphatically that the other matters and their presence is desirable. Even in our sinfulness and endless efforts to distort and corrupt our relationship with God, God still finds us worthy of love. The constancy and depth of the everlasting love of God for each human being is the Christian narrative's answer to the need for self-worth. The stability of this aspect of the self is reinforced by the declaration of God found in Jeremiah 1.5 where he says 'Before I formed you in the womb I knew you, and before you were born I consecrated you.' Creation is an act of love by God; what God creates, God loves wilfully and intentionally. The New Testament narrative is the story of God's love embodied in the life, death and resurrection of Jesus. Like the need for purpose, value and justification and efficacy, we can conclude that the need for self-worth is clearly satisfied through the intersecting of the personal and Christian narrative.

It is unsurprising that meaningfulness and the satisfaction of these four identifiable needs are important for our psychological health and well-being. Accompanying a sense of purpose is the capacity to understand and regulate the emotions that we experience in response to life events and the situations we face. It also provides the energy and commitment necessary to deal with the multiple demands we might face. Fundamental to the experience

---

24 Book of Common Prayer and Holy Communion, *Common Worship*, 2000, London: Church House Publishing.

25 Swinton, J., 2012, *Dementia: Living in the Memories of God*, London: SCM Press, p. 180.

of meaningfulness is the feeling of direction and purpose. It is concerned with an orientation to a future goal; this does not have to be attained, but has a profound impact on the fundamental experience of 'lived time'.[26] Most of the time we are hardly aware of experiencing 'lived time', but an important component of this experience is its orientation towards the future. We are constantly projecting our thoughts and actions towards what is coming next, or even further ahead, as we prepare ourselves for what we anticipate in the future. These often hidden assumptions about time and meaning are only brought into sharp relief when we face circumstances which disrupt or shock our projected plans and thoughts regarding the future. On such occasions, the meaningfulness described by Klinger as 'a pervasive quality of a person's whole inner life'[27] may be lost and a person's entire understanding of themselves, their life and their purpose becomes radically challenged. They find themselves in a place of 'narrative wreckage'.[28] It is this to which we now turn as we explore an example of narrative and meaning-making in the context of pastoral ministry.

Returning to the Narrative of Lived Experience

It would be misleading to imply that Christian faith provides and satisfies all our needs for meaning-making and the construction of a positive personal narrative all the time. Critics of the analogy between life experience and narrative highlight that authors of fiction create and control the characters and the plot, but in life we do not have such autonomy; to a considerable extent we construct our narrative from what we have and are faced with. Many of the

---

26 Davies, M. L., 'Shattered assumptions: time and the experiences of long-term HIV positivity', *Social Science and Medicine*, 44 (5) (1997), pp. 561–71, quoted in Crossley, M. L., 'Narrative psychology, trauma and the study of self/identity', *Theory & Psychology*, 10 (4) (2000), pp. 527–46.

27 Klinger, E., 1997, *Meaning and Void*, Minneapolis: University of Minneapolis Press.

28 Frank, A., 1995, *The wounded storyteller: Body, Illness and Ethics*, Chicago, IL: University of Chicago Press, quoted in Crossley, 'Narrative psychology', pp. 527–46.

circumstances we find ourselves in cannot be easily explained, and others we would prefer not to write into our story because of the pain or shame we have experienced in them. They are situations in which we have suffered in some way or other. Baumeister rightly observes 'suffering cries out for meaning'.[29] These events make us more aware of our meaning systems and often everyday concerns fade or seem irrelevant in the light of the need to reappraise our sense of meaning. They can disrupt our sense of purpose, value and justification, efficacy and self-worth. By now turning our attention to trauma, we can gain some further insight into the significance of narrative and meaning-making and its implications for ministry.

Trauma, Narrative and When Meaning-Making is Lost and Found

It may seem surprising that psychologists have found an association between seismic life events and profound personal development.[30] Despite traumatic disruptions to personal worlds of meaning, it seems that positive personal transformation can follow. A helpful way of understanding this is through the impact of trauma on narrative, meaning and identity.[31] Disorganized narratives are when a survivor's self-narrative is substantially or pervasively disorganized after exposure to a traumatic event. In this case, images, and the intense memories of terror, despair and helplessness associated with them, can overwhelm a survivor in such a way so as to disorganize their story of themselves and their life. Their life is invaded by these emotionally charged images that are inconsistent with their previous life's narrative.[32] Furthermore, the thematic assumptions

---

29 Baumeister, *Meanings*, pp. 232–68.

30 Tedeschi, R. G. and Calhoun, L. G., 'Posttraumatic growth: conceptual foundations and empirical evidence', *Psychological Enquiry*, 15 (1) (2004), pp. 1–18.

31 Neimeyer, R. A., 'Fostering posttraumatic growth: a narrative elaboration', *Psychological Enquiry*, 15 (1) (2004), pp. 53–9.

32 Neimeyer, R. A. and Stewart, A. E., 1998, 'Trauma, healing and the narrative employment of loss', in Franklin, C. and Nurius, P. A. (eds), *Constructivism in Practice*, Milwaukee, WI: Families International Press, pp. 165–83.

on which a person has lived their life can be invalidated. This means that their optimistic view of the world, in which it is believed to be safe, life is generally predictable, people are mostly trustworthy and justice eventually prevails, can be turned completely upside down. Often in such cases, a complete revision of the survivor's narrative takes place, which may include a more nuanced world view that comes to include acknowledgement of the complexity of life, preciousness of life and reality of death, as well as a greater existential awareness. As a result a new meaning system can be established.

Following trauma, deliberate meaning-making either involves changing our understanding of the meaning of the trauma, or changing our meaning of life. There are various ways we do this. First, we might reappraise the situation in a more positive light so that we find redeeming value in suffering, or we revise the goals and expectations we have or, as Folkman suggests, we might turn to spiritual beliefs and experiences.[33] All of these strategies are focused on reducing the discrepancy between our narrative and understanding of life, and the traumatic experience, in order that we might restore a sense of meaning. Eventually they may lead us to a point at which we have made sense of the experience, accepted it, or at least come to terms with it.

Pargament has researched the role of religion in this process, and describes the effect of religion as transforming the meaning of events in a graphic way as one sees the sacred working its will in events which at first seemed random, nonsensical and tragic to become 'an opportunity to appreciate life more fully, a chance to be with God, a challenge to help others grow or a loving act meant to prevent something worse from taking place'.[34] In this way, religious beliefs give rise to an obvious reappraisal of meaning which helps

---

33 Folkman, S., 'Positive psychological states and coping with severe stress', *Social Science and Medicine*, 45 (1997), pp. 1207–21.

34 Pargament, K. I., 1997, *The Psychology of Religion and Coping*, New York: Guilford Press, p. 223, quoted in Park, 'Religion and meaning', in Paloutzian and Park, *Handbook of the Psychology of Religion and Spirituality*, p. 304.

to relieve stress.[35] God is incorporated into the personal narrative through the process of engaging with the narrative of God from sources of Scripture, teaching and culture, and creating a new personal narrative and sense of meaning out of the experience of suffering. But not all religious reappraisals are positive. For some, meaning includes the realization that God is cruel, has caused this harm, or has chosen not to intervene and respond to prayer. By incorporating this characterization of God into the personal narrative, meaning-making can lead to anger, mistrust and doubts about God's existence.

Trauma not only causes a dramatic upheaval of life's meaning, but also a fragmentation of the self and loss of agency or efficacy. This disorientation and helplessness causes considerable psychological distress. The reliving of the traumatic experience through memory is in part a search for meaning and reorientation, but frequently the sufferer cannot find any meaning or an ending to this particular part of their life's narrative. The effect of this is to feel locked in time, with no past and no future, 'no direction toward which life unfolds'.[36] Assumptions about the world, the self and others are violated. The sufferer's belief in their personal invulnerability and the world as understandable is destroyed and they struggle to see themselves in a positive light. A sense of meaning and meaningful action is lost.

At the centre of the Christian gospel is the cross, the site of violence and trauma, the site at which Jesus cried 'My God, my God, why have you forsaken me?' (Matt. 27.46). As we meditate on the cross, we bear witness to his questioning of the meaning he has embodied in his ministry and life so far. During the final days of the

---

35 Spilka, B., Hood, R. W. Jr, Hunsberger, B. and Gorsuch, R., 2003, *The Psychology of Religion: An Empirical Approach* (3rd edn), New York: Guilford Press; Pargament, *The Psychology of Religion and Coping*, quoted in Park, 'Religion and meaning', in Paloutzian and Park (eds), *Handbook of the Psychology of Religion and Spirituality*, p. 306.

36 Jones, S. L., 2009, *Trauma and Grace: Theology in a Ruptured World*, Louisville, Kentucky: Westminster John Knox Press.

Passion narrative, we are in the company of those who are frightened, disorientated and have lost their sense of meaning.

The psychological understanding of meaning-making and trauma holds within it the possibility of offering new insights into our theological understanding of the events of Jesus' crucifixion and resurrection. For it is only in the glory of the resurrection that the trauma and seemingly meaninglessness of the cross makes sense. What meaning could we derive from the cross without resurrection? The answer has to be very little. We reappraise the cross through the lens of the truth of the resurrection. Without resurrection there would be no Christian faith or Church. It is the resurrection which ends the trauma and makes a meaning of it. It also enables us to more fully grasp the significance of all of Jesus' life: his birth, ministry and death. It is the ending which pulls it all together. Resurrection provides release from the pain of being caught in the cycle of reliving the trauma and finding no end or meaning. It is the resurrection which ends all struggles to make meaning from all human experience of trauma. Seen in this way, our understanding of meaning-making and its role in traumatic experiences challenges any theology which glorifies the cross or suffering inappropriately. The cross was a place of violence and violation both physical and psychological. It was a place where meaning was ruptured and was only rediscovered through the raising of Jesus in his glorious resurrection. To seek God in the cross is to absorb the darkness and searing pain of violation. It is to realize the agony and helplessness of loss of meaning, efficacy, self-worth and value. It is to wrestle with the evil and suffering of the world and then to find meaning in it through the light of the resurrection.

Conclusion

Human beings have an appetite for meaning. They need to make sense of the world and their lives. Meaning-making is essential for survival in a complex world and for a sense of purpose and well-being. Integral to our meaning-making process are narratives. We tell narratives and use narratives to facilitate our understanding of the world. We also construct a personal narrative in order to understand who we are and a sense of personal identity. Without meaning we become agitated, distressed and depressed.

All human experience is imbibed with meaning or subjected to a meaning-making process. Indeed the process of meaning-making transforms human experience. When we ascribe a meaning to something, the emotions we experience in response to it and the memory of it changes. We saturate our experience with meaning and this satisfies our need for purpose, value and justification, efficacy and self-worth.[37] Each of these needs are met in the Christian life of faith. By responding to these needs through the narrative of the Christian faith this chapter has demonstrated the transformative power of the meaning-making which is offered by the gospel.

When meaning-making is dramatically disrupted by trauma and a person's personal narrative becomes disorganized, the Passion narrative has been shown to be a powerful source of reorientation and meaning-making in the light of Jesus' resurrection. Establishing a discourse between psychology and theology regarding this aspect of human experience will not only enhance pastoral and spiritual care, but also pose questions for both disciplines and how meaning-making is transformative in human experience.

---

37 Baumeister and Wilson, 'Life stories'.

4

Personality: Uncovering the Mystery of Who We Are

When we sit at a funeral service listening to the homily or the reflection on the life of the deceased, we expect to recognize something of the person we have known. Writing or delivering a funeral homily involves the demanding task of describing who a person was, and continues to be, in the memory of those who loved or knew them. By drawing together the characteristics of the deceased, illustrated by a selection of events and stories from their life, the aim is to produce a coherent biographical portrait which resonates with the experiences of those who knew them. It is an attempt to faithfully present the absent person in words so that they can be remembered and psychologically present. Constructed from stories of the deceased's past life, the homily is often a narrative which gives their life meaning and significance.

In the majority of cases, funeral homilies construct a positive portrait of the deceased. They are a favourable and generous description; often carefully omitting to mention any negative personality traits and instead emphasizing the person's more favourable qualities. The task of capturing the essence of another human being and constructing some sense of meaning of them and their life is a considerable challenge. This might seem strange. We spend most of our waking hours in the company of others, striving to understand them in order that we might negotiate and respond appropriately to each unique personality and maintain our relationship with them. Yet other human beings continue to puzzle us, surprise us, frustrate us; and always remain to some extent mysterious to us. We can never fully know another human being however intimate our relationship with them; there will always be something of them beyond our reach. Any description or explanation of another human being is going to be incomplete.

Describing and making sense of people is the ambitious goal of the study of personality. In this chapter we will explore some of the theories in personality psychology used to describe and understand human beings, and consider how the turn to narrative has made a significant contribution to this field. Some theological implications of these understandings of personality are offered in the concluding part of the chapter.

Describing and Understanding Human Beings

An introduction to psychological approaches

Modern psychology's interest in personality blossomed from the early decades of the twentieth century. However, the belief that people were important and unique, bounded by their skin and autonomous, began with the Renaissance and spawned the individualistic approach to personality. The tension between our individual uniqueness and our many similarities has been a paradox which the individualistic perspective has had to confront. Essentially personality psychology is concerned with understanding similarities and individual differences: what is generally true about human beings and how people are different from one another. Personality psychology is not so much interested in cognition but how people differ in their thinking and the impact of these differences on their functioning as human beings in the world. It considers the whole person and how their psychological processes interact to form the person others encounter. One helpful definition is: *Personality represents those characteristics of the person that account for consistent patterns of feeling, thinking and behaving.*[1] From this we can infer that personality psychology attempts to find and explain the regularities in human thinking, emotion and action as we live out our lives. To achieve this it asks the following questions: What

---

1 Pervin, L. A. and John, O. P., 2001, *Personality Theory and Research* (8th edn), New York: John Wiley & Sons.

is a person like? How did they come to be like this? and, Why do they behave like they do? Each of these questions contributes to our overall understanding of another human being. 'What a person is like' is found in the characteristics of a person – are they patient and kind and always keen to give of their best? 'How did they come to be like this?' examines the influence of their genetic make-up and social environment on their character formation. Finally, 'Why do they behave like they do?' explores what motivates them and what goals they set for themselves. It may also include what matters to them and their understanding of the meaning or purpose of their life. Why does someone decide to become a medical doctor? Is it because that was what their father did? In which case, is there a genetic component, or is it to please their parents or because they have a deep sense of vocation to help others? Personality theory attempts to understand the whole person in terms of what, how and why. It provides an understanding of whether, for example, anxiety is a characteristic of a person, how they came to be so anxious and why it is that they experience this in specific contexts and respond in the way they do. It also tries to explain why when two people experience a similar situation one becomes anxious and the other does not. One possible explanation which has received particular attention is that one of them is more predisposed to anxiety. This is explained in part by trait theory.

Trait theory arose out of the desire to measure personality and characterize a person. Traits help us to describe what a person is like and are based upon how they consistently respond to a variety of situations. These traits are identified by psychometric testing, which is still a forceful presence in the study of personality. The term 'trait' refers to a fundamental unit of personality; a person's personality being the sum of their traits. A trait denotes consistent interrelated patterns of behaviour, especially expressive or stylistic behaviour.[2] Both style and expression are difficult to measure, they concern the manner in which someone responds to situations and also the emotional tone that lies beneath it or is expressed within

---

2 Winter, D. G., John, O. P., Stewart, A. J., Klohnen, E. C. and Duncan, L. E., 'Traits and motives: towards an integration of two traditions in personality research', *Psychological Review*, 105 (1998), pp. 230–50.

it. Traits have continued to be important in the description of a person and enable psychologists to predict, modify and even control behaviour. During the past 50 years the number of traits, and scales designed to measure them, has escalated and there is a bewildering array to choose from: often with little evidence of their validity and theoretical basis. But the psychometric tradition is not without criticism. Its focus on traits and individual differences has led to sparse attention being given to the whole person and context in particular. New approaches to personality have emerged in recent years which have broadened the theoretical base beyond trait theory and developed a more integrative approach.[3] These have gone some way towards achieving the ambitious goal of personality psychology to examine 'the total person over the entire life span ... [its] ultimate goal [being] the integration of all aspects of human behaviour into a single theoretical framework'.[4] But even these recent attempts struggle with the seemingly elusive psychological characteristics of human life such as creativity, rationality and spirituality.

From the what, how and why questions of personality psychology it is evident that any attempt to discover the essence of the total person requires engaging in two separate but related processes. The first is description and the second explanation. All epistemological tasks require a rich description of the phenomenon under investigation. What is the person like? What are their characteristics or traits? How do they behave towards others? How do others experience them? What is the quality of their social relationships? It is only after we have a detailed description of a person that we can move towards offering a causal explanation as to why the person is the way they are. In personality psychology, such explanations involve investigating the determinants of behaviour which may be internal, as found in our biological nature, or external, such as our social or environmental context.

---

3 See for example: McAdams, D. P., 'What do we know when we know a person?', *Journal of Personality*, 63 (1995), pp. 365–96; and Mischel, W., 'Toward an integrative science of the person', *Annual Review of Psychology*, 55 (2004), pp. 1–22.

4 Wallace, W., 1993, *Personality Theories*, Boston: Allyn and Bacon.

Consider Julie: Julie is described as assertive, domineering and volatile by her colleagues. She is easily incensed and is impatient. When her plans are met with resistance or she encounters obstacles, her impatience spills over and she becomes indignant and angry. She has a strong sense of what others ought to do and expresses this forcibly and with confidence. If anyone dares to challenge her she either becomes more aggressive or denies there is an issue.

From this description we can begin to construct an impression of Julie as a person. Inevitably this is subjective. It necessarily involves our interpretation of the description, and though we do not always acknowledge it, implicit in our interpretation is our understanding of human nature. Even what we choose to describe about Julie and the way we describe her is influenced by the kind of explanation we presume we will make of who she is and how she behaves.[5]

For example, we might believe that human beings are either innately good or bad. If we adopt the view that human nature is wilful and self-interested, then Julie's behaviour is understood as an expression of this innate tendency. We might also conclude that even when she is being nice to someone there is an ulterior goal of wanting them to do something for her – that she is just softening them up! Her primary motivation is still self-interest. Furthermore, our theory of Julie's behaviour might extend to an explanation in terms of her genetic make-up or early childhood experiences. If we know that her father is characterized as being angry, then we might explain Julie's response to people as a consequence of either her genetic make-up or her upbringing in which she was exposed to angry behaviour and came to see it as a means of getting her own way. The combination of these two theories is also possible and indeed the most likely explanation.

A further question prompted by this analysis concerns how responsible Julie is for her behaviour. Is our human nature passive? In other words, can we change the way we are, or are some of our behaviours so deeply engrained either in our genes or because of our life experiences, that we cannot be held entirely responsible for who we are? The importance of parent–child relationships for later

---

5 McAdams, 'What do we know when we know a person?'

development can be traced to the psychoanalytical school. Critical periods in early life are believed to leave inerasable marks on the person's psychological and social development, and are therefore understood to be major influences on personality development. The belief that the neglected child bears the wounds and scars of childhood into adulthood, and that these experiences have a profound influence on the development of their personality and psychological health in adult life, still carries considerable weight today.

Rapid growth in the fields of genetics and neuropsychology has also made a significant contribution to the nature/nurture debate. The interaction between our biological predispositions and our social environment is undoubtedly complex. Determining which factors are most influential and the dynamics of cause and effect continues to present a considerable challenge to psychology. However, too often responses to difficult behaviours betray a polarization of views around this debate. More positively, researchers such as Rutter[6] advocate a more integrative approach, recognizing the contribution of a number of factors to the formation of personality.

The nature/nurture debate is central to the question of responsibility and change. Theories regarding human agency are hugely contested in personality psychology and within theological anthropology. Responsibility implies making a choice and the ability to act as agents in the world. Choice and responsibility are intertwined with agency. However, choice does not always imply responsibility. Often as children we are asked to choose between options, but it is our parents who hold the ultimate responsibility for the choice, and they might override the child's suggestion as part of that responsibility.

The question of responsibility and agency is approached in different ways in personality psychology. Behaviourists assume that we do not make choices but rather we respond to changes in our environment. Human nature is seen as passive with the environment

---

6 Rutter, M., 'Nature, nurture and development: from evangelism through science toward policy and practice', *Child Development*, 73 (1) (2002), pp. 1–21.

determining our behaviour through the process of instrumental and conditional learning. The experience of reward and punishment and the associations we form as we learn about the world determines our personality. Tendencies in our responses become engrained as habits and are hard to change. It is our environment and our social interactions that determine who we are. Our emotions and responses are a product of the rewards and punishments we have experienced, and not determined by our biological being. Human beings are viewed as response generators in a mechanistic way. In contrast, humanist psychologists assume a high degree of agency in which we can change ourselves and ultimately reach the point of self-actualization. We can influence who we are and who we will become to a point of fully realizing our potential and being all we desire to be.

The terrain of personality is vast and it is inherently complex. Winter and Barenbaum suggest there are two basic claims in personality psychology at present; first, the 'complexity of interaction among elements', and second, that 'earlier experience affects later behaviour in ways that are to some extent irreversible (reversible with greater difficulty than their acquisition)'.[7] This apparent complexity and rigidity of personality in our current understanding should serve as a warning not to claim too much for what we know already, and to remain open to the more descriptive approaches emerging in a field primarily dominated by reductionist approaches. Nonetheless, it is important to take stock of existing scholarship and the theories that underpin our current understanding of personality and its relationship with human experience.

---

7 Winter, D. G. and Barenbaum, N. B., 1999, 'History of modern personality theory and research', in Pervin, L. A. and John, O. P. (eds), *Handbook of Personality: Theory and Research* (2nd edn), New York/London: Guilford Press, p. 20.

Psychological Theories of Personality

Trait theory

Julie can be described as having an aggressive personality or being an angry person. This is how others experience her. Trait theory is not so much a theory but a way of characterizing the traits we are all assumed to have. The most widely used model in trait theory is the five factor model.[8] This was developed by adopting the terms which we use to describe other people. By rating themselves or others on a wide variety of traits taken from a dictionary, five basic personality factors emerged. These were openness, conscientiousness, agreeableness, extraversion and neuroticism. If we gave Julie some psychometric tests using the five factor structure, or 'Big Five', then she would probably score low on agreeableness, high on extraversion, high on neuroticism, maybe high on intellect and conscientiousness. There is some value in this. It gives an informed picture of what Julie is like. It identifies her traits and enables us to make some predictions as to how she might respond in certain circumstances. But this does not tell us *why* Julie has this personality profile. Many trait theorists have the working assumption that traits are genetic: we are born with them and they have predisposed us to behave in certain ways when we find ourselves in certain situations. By adopting this theoretical approach, we interpret Julie's behaviour as an innate characteristic; one which she can learn to manage, but cannot eradicate.

Behaviourism

In contrast to trait theories, a behaviourist approach to personality suggests that our responses are learned by making connections between events and outcomes or stimulus and response. Championed by B. F. Skinner and J. Watson as the discovery of how we learn, and based on the discovery of classical and operant conditioning, this influential theory has been used as a powerfully effective way of changing people's behaviour. The theory claims that connections

---

8 McCrae, R. R. and Costa, P. T. Jr, 1999, 'A five factor theory of personality', in Pervin and John, *Handbook of Personality*.

occur without cognitive processing or analysis. In other words, we are passive in their construction. Even complex behaviours are accounted for by the suggestion that they are produced by adding longer strings of connections between stimuli and responses together. For Skinner we are responders, not thinkers. However, the theory does not limit itself to learning, but extends to a view of the human person as essentially a blank slate which is passively altered by experience. Importantly, behaviourists assert that the same rules for learning as apply in animals apply in humans, and both are motivated by the same motivational goals of avoiding pain and seeking pleasure. Hence, it sees the environment as the determinant of our behaviour, and not our will or any personal goals beyond those of pain avoidance and pleasure seeking. This passive approach at the heart of behaviourism implies a neutral view of human nature. It is neither good nor bad. Our personality is a product of the situational associations we experience and the effect of our perception of consequences. It is these associations which create personal tendencies and further develop into habits. Over time they become difficult to change. However, such a reductive view of personality suggests we are simply response generators. Applying this to Julie, we might conclude that she has learned by association that being aggressive results in her achieving her goals. On many occasions, she has been subtly rewarded for her angry responses and such reinforcement has led to this habitual response any time someone seemingly tries to block her plans or the achievement of her goals.

Cognitive behavioural psychology

Another approach arising from the field of cognitive psychology is a cognitive behavioural psychology understanding of personality, which emphasizes the role of our thinking in the development of who we are. It proposes that we develop patterns of association and thinking which are a combination of our genes, social environment and behaviour patterns called schema. Our schema, or scripts as they are sometimes referred to, influence how we respond to situations, how we respond to others, and how we think about ourselves. In other words, they guide our behaviour and our emotions. Within schema are held connections between actions and goals and likely outcomes. Hence, in a schema for social interaction the connection between being kind and friendly to someone and meeting a goal of establishing good relationships is stored. It contains causal links; the relationship of 'if ... then ...' is programmed into each schema. We hold schema for numerous behaviour patterns, ranging from catching a bus, eating in a restaurant, winning an argument, to how to respond when we feel insulted. As behaviour patterns are learned or frequently repeated, they are activated or accessed more easily. They also develop a large number of links and associations connected to them in memory. This increases the chances of these behaviour patterns being activated across a number of situations. As such, the behaviour becomes generalized across a number of situations through an association network accumulated in the memory system. This builds up over our lifespan, and is characterized by a propensity for stability, with patterns becoming ingrained and increasingly resistant to change. Cognitive behavioural psychology conceives personality as a composite of our schema or scripts. Hence, if we change our thinking patterns the theory suggests our personality can change or develop. There are significant implications here for the way in which coming to faith might lead to an apparent change in someone's personality, as it suggests that by changing the way we think about ourselves and our purpose in the world we change or develop our schema and our personality.

In the case of Julie, it may be that she frequently witnessed aggression in her parents' marriage as a means of establishing power and influence. This parental modelling led to Julie incorporating aggressive patterns of behaviour into a schema which is activated across many situations in her interpersonal and social relationships when her power or influence is threatened. So when she cannot get her own way, the schema is activated and she behaves aggressively towards her peer group. The cue for activating the schema for aggressive behaviour is Julie being obstructed from achieving her goal. Hence, Julie's behaviour pattern of aggression is evoked when she feels threatened or wants to exert power and influence over someone or a particular situation.

This brief introduction to these three basic theories provides a picture of the scope of this highly contested field which occupies a central place in modern psychology. All of the theories have strengths and weaknesses. Each allows for objective investigation, but is also prone to a degree of reductionism that oversimplifies human behaviour, denying the richness and complexity of human experience. They all focus on the specific, individual characteristics of a person and although the influence of social relationships is acknowledged, the focus even in cognitive behavioural approaches is on internal and individual psychological processes. Another problem for both trait approaches and behaviourism is their determinism. Traits are believed to be embedded in our biological and genetic make-up along with early experiences and these lead to the development of fixed personality traits. Behaviourists contest that the associations we form in response to our social environment determine our personality. They look to drives and habits to explain who we are and become. Likewise, cognitive behaviourist approaches suggest that our past experiences drive our future.

More recent theories have begun to acknowledge the complexity of personality and recognize the need to give increased attention to context. For too long, simplified theories have dominated the field. Two theories – social cognitive theory and McAdams's levels theory of personality – provide good examples of complex theories which demonstrate greater explanatory potential for our lived experience.

Social cognitive theory

Social cognitive theory was devised by Bandura in 1986.[9] It views people as self-organizing, proactive, self-reflecting and self-regulating, emphasizing their capacity for agency. People have intentions; they choose what they do and how they do it by regulating their behaviour to achieve certain goals or outcomes. The theory suggests that agency is fundamental to understanding human beings. Our life course is determined by the way we exert agency, and because our actions are predominantly socially situated, they

---

9 Bandura, A., 1986, *Social Foundations of Thought and Action: A Social Cognitive Theory*, Englewood Cliffs, NJ: Prentice-Hall.

are a product of a dynamic interplay between personal and situational factors. We are not passive, experiencing a vast array of internal mechanisms determined by the situations we find ourselves in: we are 'sentient agents of experiences'.[10] It is crucial to acknowledge in any given situation how our behaviour influences, and even changes it; and this in turn affects our thoughts, emotions and subsequent responses.

Although social cognitive theory acknowledges that we have dispositions, these are not understood as traits which are static; rather, they are personal factors such as self-belief, aspirations, and what we anticipate to be the outcome of situations. These are seen as factors which regulate rather than describe us.

An appeal of the theory is its acknowledgement of our social context and its dismissal of dualist approaches within psychology. The dichotomy between agent and object with respect to the self is disputed, because when we are doing something we are also monitoring and analysing the consequences of it and might change our actions in the light of this reflection. Hence, we are just as much an agent in the process of monitoring and reflecting as in the acting out of it. The perspective simply shifts between the person and the situation. It is fair to say that we flip between these two perspectives continuously in everyday life. It is a dynamic system rather than static dichotomy.

The theory also rejects any notion of multiple selves, convincingly arguing that there is one self that can conceive of a number of possible outcomes, evaluate them and choose the appropriate one for whatever the desired goal might be.[11] Any model which splits the self into a number of selves runs into difficulties. Which self co-ordinates or oversees the various selves? How many selves are there and how are they defined? The notion of the divided self might explain a powerful emotional state, but what it really captures is the sense of entertaining competing goals or desires, as Paul in the letter to the Romans states, 'I can will what is right, but I

---

10 Bandura, A., 1999, 'Social cognitive theory', in Pervin and John, *Handbook of Personality*, p. 155.
11 Bandura, 'Social cognitive theory', pp. 161–2.

cannot do it. For I do not do the good I want, but the evil I do not want is what I do' (7.19–20).

Social cognitive theory also dismisses the dichotomy between the social structures with which a person interacts and the person. People are seen as producers as well as products of the social system. There is a 'dynamic interplay between individuals and those who preside over the institutionalized operations of social systems. Social structures are created by human activity.'[12] This is seen in micro as well as macro social systems. In families which are primarily presided over by parents or grandparents, other family members challenge and shape the social system but at the same time continue to be shaped by it.

The model posits a view of human nature which is founded upon human beings' capability to act as agents in the world. They are described as 'contributors to their personal motivation, behaviour and development within a network of reciprocally interacting influences'.[13] This high-level functionality depends on a number of psychological processes which include cognition, self-regulation, self-reflection, and vicarious learning. Our ability to engage in abstract thinking and represent events and their relationships in symbolic form is an essential cognitive capability underpinning this model. Overall, the model offers a positive view of human nature, pointing to its creativity and potentiality within the constraints imposed by our biological physical bodies. It also lauds our capacity to influence our development and future. There is no sense of determinism within such an approach; rather, it suggests that our destiny is in our own hands as we shape the social systems in which we live and set our own goals in line with whatever we wish to become.

From the perspective of this model, Julie's anger is something she can regulate if she chooses to; she has learned what effect it has on social relationships and has the capacity to reflect on the impact of her anger. Others may have influence on her reflection by their response to her. In this way there is a dynamic relationship between Julie and her social environment which is mutually influential.

12 Bandura, 'Social cognitive theory', p. 168.
13 Bandura, 'Social cognitive theory', p. 169.

The key issue with this theory is the primacy of agency and cognitive functioning. If human nature is assumed to incorporate certain capabilities such as high level cognitive functioning, memory, self-reflection and awareness, self-regulation, the ability to set goals and shape our own destinies, then how does it understand those who do not have all of these attributes, such as those with dementia or severe psychological disabilities? Are they deficient in their human nature, or, as would be equally troubling, are they not full persons since they do not fulfil the criteria for personhood? This model with its positive view of human nature focusing on human high-level consciousness, cognition and agency, falls prey to the suggestion that the ones who cannot carry out these processes are non-persons or have defective personalities. The question of how such a model can be applied to personality and personhood of people with any form of cognitive disability impacting on agency and high-level cognitive functioning is neither acknowledged nor discussed in the literature.

McAdams: 3 level model

In contrast to the social cognitive model, McAdams's 3 level model[14] focuses unashamedly on describing rather than explaining personality, thus supporting his assertion that too often psychology has moved towards explanation before carefully identifying the phenomena it is explaining. In a complex model of personality, the use of narrative as a constructive tool for the personality identity is incorporated into a model of personality whereby a person's life story becomes the third of three identified levels. McAdams' use of narrative as a level of personality is important not only because it provides a coherent and integrative framework for addressing his question, 'What do we know when we know a person?', but also because it resonates with how we experience ourselves and others. It has a compelling reality which accounts for features in our personalities beyond those identified in the cognitively bound social cognitive theory discussed earlier. The overstating of rationality and agency might serve to counterbalance the more passive

14 McAdams, 'What do we know when we know a person?'

theories of human nature, but it is nevertheless in grave danger of reducing people and personality to a set of capabilities used to achieve personal goals. The notable omission of both the relational and spiritual aspects of personality is a deficiency in all of the psychological models presented so far. However, it is possible to find within McAdams's 3 level model scope for a more authentic representation and understanding of what it is to be human. By examining this model in more detail we discover a depiction of personality which opens up the possibility of enriching a theological understanding of what it means to be human, as well as developing a positive interdisciplinary approach to pastoral ministry. But first the model needs to be described in some detail.

The first level includes dispositional traits which characterize a person and describe what McAdams calls a 'dispositional signature'. These are adjectives which describe what is termed the overall style of a person's engagement with the social world. This includes how they go about doing things, how they typically think, and how they feel about things.[15] At any one time our thinking, feelings and actions make up our current state; traits are seen as the most common kind of states that someone experiences in a variety of situations and at different times.[16] From traits a recognizable signature is obtained, and although this can be used to suggest the ways in which a person typically expresses themselves in a range of situations and over a significant period of time (a person is generally x in most situations), there are situations in which the response may not conform to this pattern and the signature might change to some extent over a lifetime. Dispositional traits are therefore broad characteristics which are non-conditional, decontextualized and generally linear and bipolar. They are used to compare individuals, such that we can identify ourselves as more or less generally anxious than others for example. Hence they are used

15 McAdams, D. P. and Pals, J. L., 'A new Big Five: fundamental principles for an integrative science of personality', *American Psychologist*, 61 (3) (2006), pp. 204–17.

16 Fleeson, W., 'Toward a structure and process-integrated view of personality: traits as density distributions of states', *Journal of Personality and Social Psychology*, 80 (2001), pp. 1011–27.

to describe individuality using such dimensions as extraversion, dominance, friendliness, neuroticism, tendency to feel vulnerable, optimism and so on. McAdams claims this dispositional signature represents 'the most stable and recognizable aspect of psychological individuality'.[17] It might be interpreted as the core of our uniqueness as individuals, and arises from a complex interaction between our genetic endowment and the environmental changes which are part of the process which brings about evolutionary adaptiveness.

Trait theory has not been without its critics. One key debate concerns how situationally specific (contingent) or cross-situationally consistent our behaviour is. A high score on the trait of neuroticism does not necessarily lead to accurate predictions as to which situations will cause a person to be fearful or anxious. However, there is mounting evidence to suggest that, although for single situations their predictive quality is limited, they are robust predictors of important life-outcomes such as career success, quality of social relationships, and psychological health and well-being. Moreover, there is evidence of stability of traits over time and evidence from studies conducted on twins of a genetic component.[18] Given this compelling evidence, trait theory has re-emerged in personality theory and the Big Five still dominates it.[19] These broad factors of Extraversion 'E', Neuroticism 'N', Openness to Experience 'O', Conscientiousness 'C' and Agreeableness 'A', have a strong consensus as the most robust way of organizing and describing traits. Interestingly, McAdams suggests we make special note of these characteristics of someone when we meet them for the first time as a way of sizing them up.[20] This suggests that traits might provide a good overall impression, but in the relationships which are significant to us we need to develop a far more detailed and nuanced understanding of their personality, beyond the fact that for example a person when compared with others seems more agree-

17 McAdams and Pals, 'A new Big Five', p. 207.

18 See McAdams and Pals, 'A new Big Five', p. 207 for references and discussion.

19 McCrae, R. R. and Costa, P. T. Jr, 1999, 'A five factor theory of personality', in Pervin and John, *Handbook of Personality*.

20 McAdams and Pals, 'A new Big Five', p. 208.

able or less conscientious. In other words, traits have their place in understanding and describing personality, but they are deficient in capturing the complexity of a person's psychological uniqueness as it expresses itself in the variety of contexts and situations which make up their lives, their relationships and various social roles they fulfil. To address this McAdams introduces another level to personality which incorporates goals and motivations. These are derived from our personal concerns in various domains of our life including our work, personal and maybe spiritual lives.

Goals and motivations are incorporated into Level 2, the middle level of the model, which integrates the dispositional signature of Level 1 with personal concerns and changing contexts. Each person develops a characteristic set of goals, plans, strategies, self-images, values, virtues and schemas which make up their *characteristic adaptations*. These are contextualized, non-comparative, conditional, contingent and are related to the motivational, social and developmental concerns of our lives. They are the features of our individuality which, unlike traits, are more likely to change over time or because of a change of perspective, such as coming to faith. It is this aspect of personality that deals with changing situations and everyday personality dynamics which might be described as the 'doing' side of personality, as opposed to traits which are the 'having' side of personality.[21] But it would be incorrect to think of Level 2 as a product of the interaction between traits and the environment. Rather, characteristic adaptations might not be related to traits as such, and develop from other strong influences such as a profound sense of faith, personal mission or vocation, an internalized model of secure relationships, a deep distrust of the opposite sex, or a crisis of sexual identity. These influences are activated in response to the social reality of our everyday lives. They are internal forces and factors which shape and direct how we behave, and despite being situated in particular contexts and subject to change, they are no less important than dispositional traits. It is the impact of these other factors on our lives which give texture and colour to a person.

---

21 McAdams and Pals, 'A new Big Five', p. 208.

In Level 2 McAdams also includes time, place and role as components in the contextualization of our behaviour and responses. Thus, this level of description can be used to begin to explain why someone behaves in the way they do. For example, the components of Level 2 might explain why Julie never displays anger in a church setting, but might be very aggressive at home or in her workplace. This explanation might be concerned with her expectations and learned expression of emotions in these different contexts. It is also at Level 2 that we might begin to understand the effect of faith on coping, health, well-being and life satisfaction as constructs such as goals, strategies, beliefs and values located in this domain can be directly related to faith and an understanding of discipleship. Although Level 2 can appear to contain a number of different concepts and lacks a clearly defined structure, many of the concepts are related and form significant components of personality, and are key determinants in the way we express and regulate our emotions. If traits begin to describe what a person is like, then characteristic adaptations allow an identification of a person's goals and motivations and how these might influence their responses in a variety of situations and change over time.

Knowing a person is more than knowing their traits and characteristic adaptations, valuable though these may be. A full account of human personhood cannot be derived from the most extensive cataloguing of personal traits, strategic goals and motivations. The quest for identifying the essence of another human being remains unsatisfied by these two levels. The mystery of 'personhood' is not solved by a list of traits and motivations however well tested and documented. There is something more to being a person with a unique personality. According to McAdams, if personality only comprises of thinking of oneself in terms of Levels 1 and 2, then one would not have any sense of one's identity, by which he means overall unity and purpose.[22] He asserts that in contemporary Western society, we believe that the self must be constructed in a way which integrates the roles we play, their different values and skills and be organized in a meaningful temporal pattern comprised of

---

22 McAdams, 'What do we know when we know a person?', p. 381.

telling a self...

the past, perceived present and anticipated future. This so called 'challenge of identity' is met by the way we construct a narrative of the self which is Level 3 of his theory – a life story. This is:

A telling of the self that synthesizes synchronic and diachronic elements in such a way as to suggest that a) despite its many facets the self is coherent and unified and b) despite the many changes that attend the passage of time, the self of the past led up to or set the stage for the self of the present, which in turn will lead to the self of the future.[23]

The reference to time is important as it is needed to express the continuity of the self. In the self-narrative, the storied self integrates the self in a particular moment (synchronic self) and the self over time (diachronic self). What this means is by using story, first we hold together conflicting roles and relationships which often make up our lives in the here and now (synchronic self) such as: I might find talking to my parents leaves me depressed and anxious, but being with my children fills me with joy and optimism. These are very different current relationships but both are important to me and form part of my self-configuration. Second, the storied self helps me to integrate diachronically the things which have changed about me over time; for example, during my late teenage years I was passionate about feminist issues, but now I am a wife and mother and have spent a considerable time at home caring for the family. These contrasts are brought into a meaningful configuration of the self by organizing them in a temporal whole which is created through the construction of my narrative.[24] According to McAdams, this is crucial to the creation of identity in that it depends upon the extent that 'the self can be told in a coherent, followable and vivifying narrative that integrates the person into society in a productive, generative way and provides the person with a purposeful self-history that explains

---

23 McAdams, 'What do we know when we know a person?', p. 382.
24 McAdams, D. P. 'The psychology of life stories', *Review of General Psychology*, 5 (2) (2001), pp. 100–22, p. 102.

how the self of yesterday became the self of today and will become the anticipated self of tomorrow'.[25]

McAdams's argument rests upon his conviction that identity takes the form of a story made up of characters, scene setting, plots and themes. The very act of telling the personal narrative is recognized as shaping the process of self-making and identity. Telling a life story not only constructs identity but enables a reflective and coherent account of a person to develop. However, it is important not to use 'identity' and 'self' interchangeably, rather our identity is the storied self – the self as it is made into a story by the person whose self it is.[26] By its very nature this is not an objective portrait of the self, and care needs to be exercised regarding the claims which can be made from such narratives. Personal identity in this model is an internalized story told by the self. Evidently, a description and analysis of the narrative makes a significant contribution to our understanding of personality, but developmental, cognitive, social and cultural psychology may also make important contributions as identifying the factors which have influenced the narrative and their impact on identity formation.

McAdams's model provides three levels of description but does not explain personality. Identifying what is personality as distinct from the factors shaping it can be difficult and must incorporate areas of psychology outside personality psychology. It might be that the explanation for someone's extreme aggressive behaviour is to be found in their genetic endowment and this is an identifiable determinant of this particular trait. The explanation for a person who is very anxious and finds difficulty establishing positive intimate relationships may be found in the sexual abuse she suffered in adolescence. The anxiety and relationship pattern is a feature of her personality, but the sexual abuse is a factor outside her personality. This distinction is important. It is not always easy to discern what is personality and what is outside personality but influencing it. This can become especially difficult at Level 3, because in telling their personal narrative the narrator will inevitably be offering an interpretation of the events which make up their lives. For instance,

---

25 McAdams, 'What do we know when we know a person?', p. 382.
26 McAdams, 'What do we know when we know a person?', p. 385.

a woman who is divorced might tell her story as one of triumph by getting out of a dysfunctional relationship; alternatively she might tell a story of disaster seeing her life ruined by a failed marriage. The divorce itself is outside her personality, but her narration of the story becomes part of her personality at Level 3. The interesting question is why she chose one particular version of identity in her story as opposed to another one. Goals, expectations, beliefs and emotions will have played a part in the process.

It is also important to acknowledge that the narration of the self is an evolving inner story, which changes and is revised over time as other events, new learning and insight mould and shape both our understanding and beliefs. Identity is not fixed, but rather evolves as a person's lived experience constantly changes over time. Key themes will be identifiable within the story emerging in accordance with dispositional traits, goals, motives and significant events. Personal identity, in essence, is the story of negotiating the world and finding one's place within it. The places, roles, positions, opportunities and threats form part of a rich narrative woven into a meaningful pattern which becomes a person's internalized story and identity.

The three levels model of personality offered by McAdams has some limitations especially in its explanatory powers, but it goes a considerable way to inform us of the knowledge needed to establish how well we know a person and what other knowledge might be necessary to give a fuller picture of their personality. For McAdams personality is a complex patterning of traits, adaptations and stories. Three elements are seen as essential to the task of knowing a person: i) the dispositional traits a person has which capture their general behavioural tendencies across situations and over time, ii) their goals, motivations and how they deal with and adapt to the demands and concerns of life in different contexts, and finally, iii) the identity they are constructing through their storied self.

'evolving narrative'

Personality and Faith

In Level 1 of McAdams's theory the distinctive combination of each individual's dispositional traits is recognized. Level 1, and trait theory more generally, stress the significance of our biological inheritance and its role in personality. Personality traits are an important feature of who we are and although they do not define us completely, our inborn predispositions are thought to explain as much as 50 per cent of the variation in human personality.[27] We cannot dismiss our biological inheritance. It is an essential part of who we are and influences who we become. But our biology is not the only important factor in our formation. Our personalities are also shaped by the environments that we inhabit, family, home, school, work and the prevailing social context; all contribute to a varying degree to who we are. Within these contexts, the significant others who we are in relationships with also influence whether they have a share in our genetic inheritance or not. It is easy when reflecting on traits and Level 1 to adopt a deterministic view of personality and it is undoubtedly true that personality traits are difficult to change especially as we get older. However, the Christian faith is emphatic in its proclamation of the gospel as the good news which transforms people's lives. The model of discipleship exemplified in the New Testament narrative begins with a response to the call to repent and believe the good news. Repentance requires an act of change or turning around as it is commonly understood. But this act of change can only take place if the believer truly desires this change and is committed to the personal examination and psychological work necessary to achieve this.

This can be hard and very demanding. But, we do not do this entirely in our own strength. Faith in the power of the Holy Spirit working within and with us to achieve this transformation is an important source of strength in the process. Furthermore, the encouragement and support of fellow believers in a Christian community is also an important factor in sustaining growth in holiness

---

27 Tellegan, A., Lykken, D. T., Bouchard, T. J. Jr, Wilcox, K. J., Segal, N. L. and Rich, S., 'Personality similarity in twins reared apart and together', *Journal of Personality and Social Psychology*, 54 (6) (1988), pp. 1031–9.

and the transformation brought about by the discovery of new life in Christ. Hence, although some changes in our personality traits require considerable work and attention, our personhood is not solely determined by nature or nurture.

Whatever someone's traits might be, knowing these does not always enable us to predict correctly how they are going to respond. A person who scores highly on 'agreeableness' might, in certain situations, be described as stubborn and obstructive. For example, I might be very amenable to my church spending funds on a refurbishment programme, but refuse to participate in this further when they propose to spend several thousands of pounds on a sculpture which I do not like and do not believe adds anything to the mission and ministry of the church. Psychologically, this is explained by my interpretation of the situation interacting with my trait dispositions. Mischel[28] was the first psychologist to draw attention to the significance of the situation in predicting how people will behave. Our experience bears this out. Certain circumstances can ignite anger in a predominantly calm person who is, however, especially sensitive to issues of injustice. The relationship between our interpretation of situations and our emotional response and its place in personality is explored in detail in Chapter 7. In the models examined in this chapter, interpretation is located in Level 2 of McAdams' model which contains our goals and motivations, and it is at this level where we can position the way faith influences what we strive for and what motivates us.

What we believe to be our purpose in life sets our goals and what we desire for ourselves and others. The Christian faith defines these as loving God, our neighbour and ourselves. The expression of this in the lives of each Christian is unique. However, the development of Christian character is founded on this governing principle of the Christian life. Christians also strive to demonstrate the fruit of the Spirit in their lives, namely: love, joy, peace, forbearance, kindness, goodness, faithfulness, gentleness and self-control (Gal. 5.22–23). These characterize Christian maturity and are developed by a prayerful longing for a closer relationship with God and by

---

28 Mischel, 'Toward an integrative science'.

seeking to be obedient to his will in our responses to others and the world. When this becomes the overarching purpose of our lives, it shapes our interpretation of ourselves, others, life events and our behaviour. In this way, faith becomes the defining factor in our personality. The three questions of personality: what a person is like; how they became that person; and why they behave as they do, can be answered by a person's commitment to live a Christian life. Hence, in our description of them we would expect to include some of the fruits of the Spirit and the Christian virtues of faith, hope, love, fortitude, justice, temperance and prudence. Second, 'How they become that person' would be captured by their narrative of coming to faith and their trust and belief in Jesus Christ as the source of their salvation; and 'Why they behave as they do' is answered by striving to obey God and follow his commandments. In this way faith can be demonstrated to have a direct influence on personality or the formation of Christian character.

The development of Christian character is the task of discipleship as we seek to grow into the likeness of Christ. Within this we learn how to regulate our emotional dispositions and traits to reflect the life which we understand God calls us to. This includes not only attending to and refining the dispositions we are born with, but also allowing Christian teaching and the community of the Church to shape us and our personal goals, so that our way of being and behaving in the world reflects the love of God.

Following Jesus involves some kind of personal transformation. Psychologically, this involves changes in our personality. The Gospels contain numerous stories of people responding to the call of Jesus to repent and believe the good news. Metanoia, or repentance, requires a reordering of goals and purpose which is driven by a different motivation. The process of repentance involves Level 2 of personality undergoing a radical change through the adoption of a new way of thinking, being and behaving based on the personal interpretation of what it means to live a Christian life.

Throughout his ministry, Jesus challenged people to adopt a different interpretation of who they were and offers them a place in his kingdom. The hope and promise of the gospel is profoundly significant. Recently the role of teleology in personality and development has emerged as significant.[29] The evaluation of possible futures, known as prospection, as a means of navigating the present is suggested to be just as important as the past in organizing behaviour. What we desire and what we deduce our future might be has a considerable influence on our motivations and how we set about achieving personal goals. The promise of a superabundant life and everlasting life is a powerful transformative feature of Jesus' teaching. Consequently, the impact of faith at Level 2 of personality is demonstrated in the personal narrative and identity constructed by the commitment to faith in Jesus Christ and its integration into our lives. Another way of understanding how faith and personality interact is at the level of narrative or Level 3 of personality. The commitment to Christian discipleship changes the life goals and purpose of our lives and its imagined ending. The plot of our personal narrative is transformed by these, and experiences and situations are interpreted and responded to in new ways. Personal narrative and the gospel narrative interact in the formation of a distinctive Christian character in a process of self-reflection and prayerful discernment as we strive to become more Christlike. Hence, faith is transformational at all of McAdams' levels of personality. Through the power and outworking of the Holy Spirit, a process often described as being born again is witnessed to.

The concept of personality defies a comprehensive description or explanation, yet it is the embodiment of our unique identity and commonality as human beings. This chapter has begun to identify some of the main themes and constituents of personality. In subsequent chapters these will be examined in more detail. The first of these to which we now turn is that of the part played by our goals and motivations in personality and human experience.

---

29 Seligman, M. E. P., Railton, P., Baumeister, R. F. and Chandra, S., 'Navigating into the future or driven by the past', *Perspectives on Psychological Science*, 8 (2) (2013), pp. 119–41.

5

Goals and Motivation

Dostoyevsky's comment that, 'The causes of human actions are usually immeasurably more complex than are our explanations of them and can rarely be distinctly discerned'[1] is suitably apt as we examine why human beings act in the ways they do. What motivates us to do certain things and not others? What determines the goals that we set and the choices we make, and what might these reveal about what ultimately concerns us?

Any attempt to answer such questions must include an examination of some fundamental characteristics of human nature. This is the domain of needs, desires and life goals, and the orientation of the motivation that underlies them. Motivation is also the concern of theology. The response of human beings to God the creator and the source of all life shapes the biblical narrative. It chronicles our selfish desires, motives and actions that fail to be aligned with God's will and vision for all of creation and its flourishing. This profound sense of tension runs throughout the narrative of Scripture. It presents a clear moral code for human beings; one that is rooted in God's mission for the world and the vocation of human beings to participate in the work of God. The biblical narrative also makes clear that both our motivations and actions are subjected to God's judgement. Human behaviour never exists in an ethical vacuum. Not only God, but also others within the social context, be it family, community or society, judge human thought and behaviour and this acts as a powerful control and determinant of our motivation and behaviour and, consequently, our personal identity.

---

1 Dostoyevsky, F., *The Idiot*, 1868, Penguin Classics, new edn (2004), London: Penguin Classics.

The psychological understanding that all human experience and action takes place within a moral framework has developed from our seemingly instinctive response to violations in several areas of social life. Haidt suggests we react instinctively to violations of care, fairness, loyalty, authority and sanctity, and these form the basis of human morality.[2] In his analysis of Haidt's seven moral foundations, McAdams[3] suggests that each of these are reflected in some key biblical texts and other common expressions. They are embedded in our culture. So, for example, our negative response to violations of care, the significance of love and kindness in our lives, our response of caring for those in need and being merciful is signified in Scripture in 'you shall not murder', 'love your neighbour as yourself', and 'love does no wrong to a neighbour'. The moral foundation of fairness can be found in 'an eye for an eye' and 'do to others as you would have them do to you'; it is also echoed in the importance of justice in both the Old and New Testaments and the legal system of most societies. The moral foundation of loyalty is expressed in our negative reactions to breaches of trust or breaking promises, valuing fidelity and commitment, our commitment to a partner as captured in 'till death do us part' as well as biblically in the covenant between God and his people with its emphasis on faithfulness and promise.

It seems quite remarkable, but very young children aged six months to ten months show an awareness of the moral significance of helping and harming. Using a puppet show in which a climber struggled to climb up a hill, Hamlin, Wynn and Bloom[4] showed either a second puppet who helped the struggler up the hill or at other times a second puppet who appeared at the top of the hill and knocked the struggler back down the hill. This was followed shortly by a different puppet show when the struggling puppet looked back and forth between the kind helpful puppet and unkind puppet and

---

2 Haidt, J., 2012, *The Righteous Mind: Why Good People are Divided by Politics and Religion*, New York: Vintage, cited in McAdams, D. P., 2015, *The Art and Science of Personality Development*, New York: Guilford Press, p. 208.

3 McAdams, *The Art and Science of Personality Development*, p. 210.

4 Hamlin, J. K., Wynn, K. and Bloom, P., 'Social evaluation by pre-verbal infants', *Nature*, 450 (2007), pp. 557–60.

then decided to cosy up to the unkind, unhelpful puppet. Infants stare longer at things which surprise them, and during this second puppet show it was evident that these young infants were very surprised that the struggler chose the unkind puppet to cosy up to. Furthermore, when the infants were presented with the puppets in a tray they were far more likely to reach for the helpful puppet. There are several important points arising from this. First, it is no surprise that infants very quickly discern who cares for them and is kind to them. Second, this psychological experiment suggests that infants also watch for how people behave towards each other and develop a preference for those who are nice and kind as opposed to those who are cruel and mean. Third, moral intuitions emerge in human beings very early on and form the basis of our moral development. Infants intuitively know it is better to care for someone in pain than to inflict pain. Likewise, they also are quick to identify injustice and unfairness. They do not like those who cheat or get away with wrongdoing.

As we develop, our judgement is not based entirely on the behaviour per se and the simple binary of right and wrong. Rather, when a person breaks the moral code the motivation and goal behind the transgressing behaviour is also taken into account. It seems that these aspects of the behaviour have as much, if not more, bearing on our judgement than the behaviour itself. Hence, injuring an innocent victim as part of a premeditated vicious attack in order to steal from them is deemed morally unacceptable in terms of both the motive and the action, but injuring another person in self-defence may not be judged harshly or may even be accepted as justifiable. The latter indicates a basic survival motive, while the former suggests a more complex set of motives concerned with power, greed and the release of aggression.

The question of motivation is fundamental to our interpretation of the behaviour of others, yet it is often hidden or disguised. There might be little evidence for our motives, and as such we make assumptions about them in our appraisal of other people. Furthermore, these assumptions frequently belie whether one takes a positive or negative view of human nature and its motivational orientation. It is tempting to interpret the infants' response to the kind/unkind puppets as evidence for a positive view of human nature and the essential goodness in human beings; but we need to guard against such a ready conclusion. Identifying who is more likely to be kind and caring and staying close to them is an important factor in one's survival. The surprise of the infants could be interpreted as a manifestation of an innate selfish need for personal preservation rather than an appreciation of what might seemingly be purely altruistic behaviour.

The dichotomy present in the opposing views of Augustine's doctrine of original sin, and Pelagius' emphasis on human beings made in the image of God and capable of obeying his commandments, continues to be mirrored in contemporary debates on the matter. For example, Richard Dawkins's selfish gene theory argues for a negative view of human nature based on evolutionary theory, whereas the humanist movement presents a more optimistic view of personality and motivation, stressing the importance of striving for self-fulfilment and perfecting the self. Yet, like so many concepts in human life, goals and motivation are difficult to disentangle from other basic characteristics and processes which constitute human behaviour and experience. Indeed there are many times when we are not even conscious of our motivation to do something, let alone aware of the specific goal it is directed towards. Innate motivations and responses operate in human beings as they do in all animals; I, for example, am motivated to eat every day. However, human consciousness and motivation has developed into various powerful subjective experiences. All animals need food, but humans want more than just food for sustenance; they want food to look and taste good. The innate motivation has developed to become part of an expression of other motivations such as our need for relationship as we share a meal with family and friends, or it might be part of a motivation to woo someone for sex or power. The inter-relationships between our different motivations become enmeshed in complex behaviour patterns which can obscure the underlying motivations and at times we are not fully aware of the underlying desires or drives determining our actions, thoughts and feelings.

An awareness of our motivations is fundamental to our character and integrity. Our motivations shape our character. The refining of our desires is an important focus for our spiritual growth. This chapter provides a psychological and theological basis to understand the role of goals and motivation in the lived experience of human life. Our personalities, emotions, self-regulation, self-esteem and spirituality are framed by our goals and motivations. What we want in life and the goals we set for ourselves direct our experience and form the plot of our personal narrative. They make us who we are and direct who we will become.

The Goals and Motivation of Judas

Judas is one of the people in the Gospel narratives whose life story begs an answer to some of these complex questions regarding motivation, goals and character. What motivated Judas to hand over Jesus in the garden of Gethsemane, and what did he hope to achieve? Like many motives, this remains a mystery. In all the Gospels Judas is a man associated with the dark side of humanity. Matthew suggests greed as his motive '"What will you give me if I betray him to you?" They paid him thirty pieces of silver' (26.15). Mark concurs with Matthew, recording that 'they ... promised to give him money' (14.11). For Luke, Judas is a victim of Satan, depicting Satan as entering into him (22.3). But it is John who offers the darkest explanation of his actions by claiming that Judas is indeed the devil (6.70–71). Other proposed motives include Judas' resentment at his exclusion from Jesus' inner trio of Peter, James and John, or his disillusionment and frustration at Jesus' approach to establishing his kingdom.[5]

The apparent goal of Judas' action was ensuring that Jesus would be taken. It is a critical event in the Passion narrative foreshadowed in the account of the Last Supper and then described in the accounts of Jesus' arrest. Judas certainly brought about the arrest of Jesus and received payment for it, but as the events of Holy Week unfolded, his subsequent actions suggest that he deeply regretted his act of betrayal. It is evident from the numerous scholarly works which

---

5 Barton, S., 1994, *People of the Passion*, London: Triangle, SPCK, pp. 15–17.

have examined the character of Judas and his historical influence on the Church that the mystery surrounding his motives continues to haunt our imagination over 2,000 years later.

Each of the Gospel writers in their interpretation of Judas presents different motifs of human nature. In many ways Luke is the most generous, depicting Judas as one who has been entered by Satan. One interpretation of this is that Judas' motives are not at work in the betrayal but those of Satan. If this is the case, then we can conclude that although human beings may be intrinsically good, they can become caught in the grip of the devil who uses them for his actions and purposes. Another possible interpretation is that good human beings can be corrupted by the devil.

Alternately, Matthew and Mark suggest that Judas is responsible for his sinful actions and motivated by greed. But is he *entirely* bad because of his act of betrayal and its consequences? John certainly suggests so by aligning Judas squarely with the devil. He quotes Jesus as saying 'Did I not choose you, the twelve? Yet one of you is a devil' (John 6.70–71). In this extreme view, the possibility that a human being is capable of being motivated by evil goals and embodies evil is recognized. Human beings can become the devil. A further point to reflect upon is the question of whether Jesus by implication suggests that the other disciples are intrinsically good? Jesus certainly demonstrates a conviction that people were able to 'sin no more' and by repenting of their sins they can claim a form of personal cleansing and renewal. However, Judas is not the only disciple who Jesus associates with Satan. Jesus accuses Peter of being Satan and a stumbling block to him in his response to Peter's outburst after Jesus has predicted his death. In the passage Jesus associates Satan with setting one's mind on the interests of man and not those of God. When Jesus describes Judas as the devil, the interpretation he is suggesting, that Judas is one whose interest is on himself and not God, clearly fits.

On many occasions Jesus' understanding of his ministry and his teaching reflects the binary of good and evil in human beings' motives and actions; for example, the parables of the good and bad fruit, the wheat and the tares and the wicked tenants. There is also Jesus' use of the word 'lostness' for sin. Hence, his mission is to restore the lost, to save sinners and to take away the sins of the world. As the second Adam, Jesus is the one who does not sin and is sent to save us from our sin. In the Old Testament narrative too, the sinfulness of human beings is a given but their goodness is also apparent. The notion that good and bad coexist in every human being remains largely uncontested, but the same cannot be said for the question of whether we are predisposed to one or the other. McFadyen's[6] observation that sin talk has disappeared from serious public discourse but still exists in the privatized sphere of personality reality reinforces the notion that each of us is sinful at least to some extent. We all have a predisposition as humans to be tempted, act selfishly and do wrong to others. Whether this can be attributed to the continuing influence of the doctrine of original sin is debatable, but examination of the psychological approaches to motivation, goals and personality needs to recognize that these have not been developed in a secular cultural vacuum which is void of the biblical story of the struggle between good and evil both at a cosmic and personal level. This being the case, it is important to begin by examining the biblical narrative in the first chapters of the book of Genesis as a basis for the psychological theories which are discussed later in this chapter.

The Basis of the Theological Approach to Motivation and Goals

The two creation narratives assert that the heavens and the earth are God's, were created by God, and God saw that they were good. They are part of God's purpose, his divine will, and they are blessed by him. God also created human beings who he empowers to care for the earth, but who are also subjected to certain constraints, the main one being not to eat the fruit of the tree of the knowledge of life. In Genesis chapters 3 and 4 the writer records the resistance of creation to these restrictions and a failure to acquiesce to the purposes of God. It begins with the cunning serpent eliciting the

---

6 McFadyen, A., 2000, *Bound to Sin: Abuse, Holocaust and the Christian Doctrine of Sin*, Cambridge: Cambridge University Press.

first act of disobedience from humankind, and continues through-out the sweep of the entire biblical narrative. The establishment of the dichotomy of good and evil has taken place. As early as Genesis chapter 6, the wickedness of humankind is such that God regrets their creation, and so plans to 'blot out' the human beings from the earth. The flood is God's judgement against creation, but there is one righteous man, Noah, who, with his family, God saves and indeed rescues all that remains of creation, making a covenant of faithfulness to it for all time. But before the covenant is established, God poignantly tells Noah and his sons that, 'Whoever sheds the blood of a human, by a human shall that person's blood be shed; for in his own image God made humankind' (Gen. 9.6). This acts as an important reminder that every human being is made in the image of God. The scene is set for the great narrative drama of God's presence and activity in the world as God deals with the sinfulness of human beings, passes judgement upon them, and offers his gift of rescue and salvation through his son Jesus.

The story of the fall is widely acknowledged as describing an ontological truth of the sinfulness of human beings mainly due to St Augustine's enduring influence. It is also interpreted as an explan-ation of how evil came into the world. But as Brueggemann reminds us, in the text '[t]here is no hint that the serpent is the embodiment of principle of evil'.[7] It is the response of Adam and Eve to the serpent which is paramount. In another vein, Watts[8] suggests that the main thrust of the text concerns the knowledge of good and evil and the ensuing feeling of shame. The apparent change which takes place in Adam and Eve through their interaction with the serpent is an awareness of the possibility of an alternative way from the way which God has decreed. Once they realize this, the safety and trust which has marked their relationship with God and the 'givenness of God's rule' is violated by Adam and Eve as they decide on the alternative way suggested by the serpent. In eating the forbidden

---

7 Brueggemann, W., 2003, *An Introduction to the Old Testament: The Canon and Christian Imagination*, Louisville, Kentucky: Westminster John Knox Press, p. 32.

8 Watts, F., 2002, *Theology and Psychology*, Aldershot: Ashgate, pp. 116–20.

fruit, their motive turns from pleasing God to pleasing themselves, and in effect exercising their freedom. However, once they realized what they had done, in shame and fear they hide themselves. In this reading of the text their response provides evidence of the beginning of human beings' moral consciousness. It is from this point onwards that they know right from wrong, which means that they reflect on their actions, evaluate them and, in doing so, decide whether they are good or not. Furthermore, they experience the consequences of striving after a goal which is not in accordance with God's purposes, amounting to not only their shame, but also their banishment from the garden.

Brueggemann[9] suggests that the opening of Genesis deals with the problem of human autonomy. Adam and Eve no longer want to live within the prohibition of God; their actions are motivated by their pursuit of autonomous freedom. They no longer trust God, and instead desire to be Godlike. The tension between obedience to the will of God and doing what the self desires is a persistent theological theme, culminating in Jesus as the one who demonstrates total obedience to the Father. Jesus' agony in the garden of Gethsemane when he is described as sweating tears of blood represents the most acute incident of the competing desires to please God or to please oneself. Yet, in the end, the difference between Adam and Eve and Jesus as the second Adam is his total trust and obedience to God. But beneath this lies the question – are human beings motivated to behave in ways which are contrary to God's will and God's desire for creation, or are human desires primarily self-seeking and hedonistic? In other words, is human motivation fundamentally good or bad?

If, as Brueggemann suggests, the desire for autonomy, freedom or self-mastery as founded in a lack of trust in God's commandments leads to the fall, then how are we to evaluate this commonly understood need of human beings? Psychologically, it is strongly associated with well-being and positive mental health, and concerns a desire to feel independent of external pressures and to relate to

---

9 Brueggemann, W., 1982, *Genesis: Interpretation: A Bible Commentary for Teaching and Preaching*, Louisville, Kentucky: Westminster John Knox Press, p. 48.

the world as one who has influence rather than being manoeuvred and buffeted by events and people, or even God. Striving for autonomy asserts that human behaviour is consciously purposeful and not innate or shaped entirely by the environment. The issue at stake is the desires which motivate our behaviour and how autonomy is employed. Not all purposeful behaviour is good, but not all purposeful behaviour is bad either. The innocence of Adam and Eve prior to the fall is a state in which they did not have sufficient knowledge of the consequences of disobeying God to exert their autonomy in a purposeful way. Their actions indicate their inability to trust in God's commandment and his good intentions for them. It is a failure of trust which leads to their separation from God, and their sin is not their desire for autonomy as such. There is also a need to be cautious about the evaluation we make regarding Adam and Eve's pre-fall and post-fall states and any motivations we might impose on them. Lash[10] is helpful here, making the point that paradise precedes sin, not to identify which actually came first, but to establish the ontological primacy of goodness in human beings. It is not that we were originally good, but rather that we are inherently good. Therefore it is surely the case that the fall is not so much concerned with the sinfulness of all human beings, but the truth that human beings created in the image of God are corruptible, and this corruptibility is a consequence of the freedom which God's grace affords us. As John Milton in *Paradise Lost* states, quoting God talking about man, 'I made him just and right,/ Sufficient to have stood, though free to fall.'[11] From this perspective, autonomy becomes a sign of the nature of human beings' relationship with God, which is relational and is based on freedom and not coercion. Jesus as the one without sin has absolute trust in the Father and acts in obedience to the Father but he can still be understood as autonomous, being motivated by a desire to do what is pleasing to

---

10 Lash, N., 1985, 'Production and prospect: reflections on Christian hope and original sin', in McMullin, E. (ed.), *Evolution and Creation*, Notre Dame: University of Notre Dame Press quoted in Watts, *Theology and Psychology*, p. 118.

11 Milton, J., 1667, *Paradise Lost Book III*, Penguin Classics (2003), London: Penguin, p. 54.

God. When the desire for autonomy is motivated by a desire to be self-constituting and independent of God and indeed others, then it suggests a motivation to be Godlike and a distortion of the created order. The story of the fall allows for both the acknowledgement of the corruptibility of human motivation and needs, but holds this in tension with the importance of autonomy for human flourishing and well-being.

Within this theological framework, I propose to examine how psychology can contribute to our understanding of what motivates us and how this relates to our needs as human beings and the goals we set for ourselves. As we have already seen in Chapter 4, there are different psychological theories of human nature which underpin psychological explanations of personality and development and hold either a positive, negative or neutral position on human motivation and goals. In all cases human motivation is conceived as the psychological energy for the processes which drive the development of the self. Primarily motivation concerns what we want, but there is an underlying question of what determines our wants and needs in the first place. What are the basic needs and desires that underpin our responses and behaviour? Can they be reduced to pleasure seeking and pain avoidance and, if so, what gives us pleasure or pain? Even such a seemingly straightforward distinction is challenged by the complexity and variety of human beings so that we cannot assume that two people find the same things either pleasurable or painful. But there are some seemingly universal characteristics of human nature which shed light on our motivations, and what was enacted in the Garden of Eden gives some clues to the answer to these questions. Psychology offers a different perspective on human motivation but it resonates with many of the insights we have gleaned from the reflection on Genesis.

Psychological Theories of Motivation

The question of what people want and desire has been approached in a number of different ways in psychology, each reflecting a different view of human nature and the extent to which human beings are able to live good lives, experience happiness and make rational decisions. Theories of human motivation can be broadly aligned with two approaches[12] which place a different emphasis on the body and mind dialectic. The first set of theories emphasize the body and understand motivation as the force which exerts itself in our response to meeting the incessant need for food, water and safety. These theories can be conceived as having a mechanistic approach to human beings as essentially biological creatures whose primary motivation is to survive and procreate. The second approach places an emphasis on human consciousness and our intellectual ability. It stresses our capability to reflect on who we are and our human condition. Our imagination and creativity are integral to the important process of generating new possibilities in our responses to the challenges we face, which includes the challenge of death and our mortality. In this approach, motivation is understood in terms of strivings to meet the goals which seek to extend human experience and capabilities. Theories derived from this place a greater emphasis on the diversity of human goals and the goal-directed nature of human behaviour. They focus on understanding what people strive for and why they respond in the ways they do, and have proved influential in both personality psychology and social psychology. Building on one or other of these two fundamental understandings are four main traditions which have dominated the study of human motivation, namely optimism, pessimism, neutrality and diversity, which we will now consider.[13]

The optimistic approach is one characterized by the assertion that people are basically good, reasonable and can lead happy and fulfilling lives. But more than this, people want to be good and strive to achieve goals which are positive for themselves and others. They approach problems rationally and attempt to make wise, good decisions as well as having a rationale for what they are doing. Such an approach prioritizes cognitive processing, the capabilities of the

---

12 Weiner, B., 1992, *Human Motivation: Metaphors, Theory and Research*, Thousand Oaks, CA: Sage.

13 McAdams, D. P., 2002, *The Person* (3rd edn), New York: John Wiley & Sons, pp. 435–9.

human mind and emphasizes the motivation in human nature for autonomy and self-determination.

The contrasting pessimistic view of motivation suggests that people are generally bad or selfish. They are often miserable and they desire things which are not good for them and can be self-defeating. This resonates with the doctrine of original sin and Freud's conclusion that human beings are motivated by unconscious forces related to sex and aggression which invariably have painful or anxiety-related consequences. It also has significant parallels with evolutionary theories which propose a motivational agenda centred on the propagation of an individual's genes, its species or kinship which suggest that our behaviour responds and adapts to the environmental and evolutionary challenges that threaten this. The view clearly emphasizes the biological nature of the human body as the primary motivational force.

The neutral position posits that in our first years we are unformed and, as we experience the world through relationships and our inter-action with it, we learn what we should and should not want. Our goals and motivations are understood to be primarily shaped by our environment. In this version of motivation, psychology examines the environmental factors which influence our behaviour to understand how they reinforce or reward certain behaviours and punish or neg-atively reinforce others. It is assumed that the desire for positive reward is the primary motivating force in our lives. The goals we set are determined by whatever our environment rewards and so they are as malleable and changeable as the environments we inhabit. Underpinning this approach is a mechanistic model of human nature as exemplified in behaviourism in which punishment and reward are the key influences on our development and behaviour.

Finally, the diversity tradition acknowledges the truth that differ-ent people have different needs and desires which shape and direct who they are and the course their lives take. Rather than look-ing at how people are motivated by basic common motivations, it emphasizes that everyone is different. Our goals and incentives vary considerably. Pervin[14] has classified these into five psychological

---

14 Pervin, L., 1996, *The Science of Personality*, New York: John Wiley & Sons.

goal categories from people's descriptions of what they want in life: relaxation/fun, aggression/power, self-esteem, affection/support and anxiety reduction. According to Pervin, it is the variability in how important each of these goals is to us which characterizes individual differences in human motivation. The diversity approach also emphasizes our ability to choose and make rational decisions about what we want and how we will achieve this. In common with the optimistic position, motivation is seen as the energy which draws us along. It drives progress as we set ambitious goals aligned with our priorities and strive to achieve them. It is therefore our cognitive abilities in devising goals and plans which are given priority in this approach rather than our biological nature.

The dichotomy of conceiving our animal nature or elevated cognitive nature as the primary drivers in human motivation has been debated in psychology for over 100 years. Freud characterized this thinking with his theory that our ultimate motives are sex and aggression. He proposed that the energetic drives for sex and aggression build up over time, struggling to find their expression in more or less socially acceptable behaviour under the constraints imposed by society and its moral framework. When this is not achieved he believed the motivational energy was diverted into psychological symptoms associated with varying degrees of distress or dysfunctionality. Human beings experience the pressure of motivational energy building up inside them and can struggle to manage this appropriately within the constraints of society.

Carl Jung believed that the most significant motive in human behaviour was self-actualization. It became the main cause of his disagreement with Freud and led to their eventual professional separation. Although Jung continued to acknowledge the drive for sex and aggression, he championed the suggestion that we are all driven to be the unique authentic person we were 'created' to be. Jung's term 'individuation' describes the lifelong motivation to develop or actualize the self which laid the foundations for the humanist revolution headed by Rogers and Maslow.

Not all psychologists were convinced by theories which rested on a single motivating force as providing the key to understanding human behaviour, and some looked to identify a range of different types of human motivation. Murray,[15] for example, composed a list of 27 'psychogenic needs' which he believed energized and directed behaviour, whereas Buss[16] proposed that motives energize the problems or conundrums human beings face such as finding a mate, nurturing children, functioning well in social groups, having food and shelter, and defending ourselves. But even among psychologists who advocate multiple motivations, some recognizable general motivation tendencies have been identified, the key ones being achievement, power and intimacy.[17] Achievement is the motive for being effective and doing well in life, the power motive energizes behaviours which give us the experience of feeling that we make an impact and have influence, and the intimacy motive satisfies our need to feel close to someone and experience quality in our relationships. Furthermore, McClelland and colleagues have argued that motives are not all in our consciousness but rather there is a dual system operating, one which is an implicit or unconscious motive system and the other an explicit motive system.[18]

How might this psychological sketch of human motivation inform our understanding of human action? Most of us have a strong desire to do well in a chosen field. For some, this achievement motive is expressed in their career, in academic achievement or a sport. Most of us also are motivated to have some influence or make a difference in the lives of others and in our environment. The power motive might be realized in our working lives where we might like to be in control of people and events, be in an influential role and carry responsibility, it may be in the role of parent or friend, or in the roles we adopt in church or other groups. Finally, for most of us, being in close, warm and safe relationships is an important motivation in our lives. Family, friends and significant others with whom we have good communication and share positive

15 Murray, H. A., 1938, *Explorations in Personality*, New York: Oxford University Press.

16 Buss, D. M., 'Toward a biologically informed psychology of personality', *Journal of Personality*, 58 (1990), pp. 1–16.

17 See McAdams, *The Person*, pp. 458–83.

18 McClelland, D. C., Koestner, R. and Weinberger, J., 'How do self-attributed and implicit motives differ?', *Psychological Review*, 96 (1989), pp. 690–702.

experiences are mutually enriching, directing our behaviour and, for some of us, this motive is more powerful than any other in our lives. Over time our motives might change; in our early adulthood and middle age achievement and power motivation may be most marked, but in later years these motivations might fade and the motive for intimacy become the dominant source of energy in our lives. In this way our motives are different from our personality traits. Motives are directly linked to our goals and desires, and our personality traits describe our behavioural style. While personality traits are understood to become established early in life and associated with our biological predispositions, our motives can change markedly over our lifespan. In fact, they are a reflection of the significant goals and desires during a defined period of a person's life.

The relationship of motives and desires to goals operates in a complex system in which our motivations and desires crystallize as goals. Our goals are the telos, end state or prize for which we strive. They form a personalized agenda for our lives which is distilled from our motivations and desires but has to take cognisance of the different constraints which are operating in our situation, such as our gender, class, financial situation and any personal responsibilities and limitations. The pursuit of our goals shapes our personal identity and provides the structure to our personal narrative. Succeeding or failing to achieve our goals is closely related to how we feel about ourselves. It is one of the primary factors in our sense of self-esteem as discussed in Chapter 9 as well as an authentic sense of self. But before examining goals in more detail it is necessary to engage in some of the finer detail of the processes of autonomy and agency which are necessarily involved in motivation and goal-directed behaviour.

Autonomy and Agency

As creative beings with imagination, human beings are 'intention generators'[19] who devise goals and plans for themselves and others. However, if we do not possess the ability or power to achieve them

---

19 Donaldson, M., 1992, *Human Minds*, London: Penguin.

our goals become hollow or meaningless. Achievement depends on our ability to make choices, exert influence and bring about change to ourselves and the environment, and take responsibility for what we do. The fact that we can create and set our own goals and also achieve them is due to our agency in the world.

In the Garden of Eden Adam and Eve are seen as autonomous agents who made a choice regarding the tree of knowledge and achieved their goal of eating its fruit. The story of Adam and Eve interestingly highlights the fundamental desire to know, to have the knowledge of the tree of life and in knowing to 'be like God' (Gen. 3.5). It is this goal which leads to their shame and expulsion from the Garden of Eden. In this interpretation, the need to exercise agency and autonomy is the motivation behind the fall. Both these characteristics of human beings are considered to be innate and pervasive. Without agency we would not be able to enjoy the freedom to exert our will and achieve what we strive for. Robbed of our agency, we become powerless and deeply distressed. In Western societies the majority of people are able to commit themselves to achieving certain things and becoming a certain kind of adult in the world. This is the fulfilment of what modern psychology understands as the essence of what it means to be human, which is to be active, intentional, goal-directed agents[20] with a basic need for autonomy.

The nurturing of children to become autonomous, making self-determined choices and accomplishing self-determined goals, is important for all societies. But it is also necessary for children and adults to recognize limitations of their autonomy and agency. To function well in society we need to be able to integrate our desires with society's norms at least to some extent. Our decision-making depends upon a dynamic interplay between agency and constraint that resides in the moral framework of society. The very nature of our embodiment, both physically and psychologically, as well as external factors such as time and place, at times impose limits beyond our control. We might set out with a life plan of who we

---

20 Emmons, R. A., 1999, *The Psychology of Ultimate Concerns*, New York: Guilford Press, p. 3.

want to be and what we want to achieve, but our life story is shaped by more than our desires and goals.

Competence, Autonomy and Relatedness

Deci and Ryan[21] claim that all human beings have psychological needs to be competent, autonomous and related to others. Competence refers to our need to assert ourselves effectively in the world and successfully negotiate whatever we face. Autonomy as described above concerns our need 'to behave with a sense of volition, willingness and congruence',[22] and relatedness concerns our need to care for others and to have relationships which bear the marks of authenticity and are mutually supportive. A considerable body of research confirms that satisfying these three psychological needs is essential for our well-being and psychological growth.[23] We are motivated to manage our lives effectively, to make the choices necessary to achieve the goals we set ourselves, and relate to others in caring and mutually supportive ways. These fundamental needs direct and shape our actions and responses to the vast range of experiences making up our lives, and when any one of these needs is not met we become distressed.

Psychological Needs and Intrinsic and Extrinsic Motivation

The psychology of motivation focuses on a meeting of essential needs and the energizing of desires. There are individual differences in both levels of motivation and kinds of motivation. We all know of people who are strongly motivated by their need for power and others whose desire for relatedness is the main motivation in their

---

21 Deci, E..L. and Ryan, R. M., 2012, 'Motivation, personality and development within embedded social contexts: an overview of self-determination theory', in Ryan, R. M. (ed.), *The Oxford Handbook of Human Motivation*, Oxford: Oxford University Press.

22 Deci and Ryan, 'Motivation, personality', p. 85.

23 Deci and Ryan, 'Motivation, personality', p. 87.

lives. We might describe someone as very driven and another as not at all ambitious. Sometimes our needs and desires conflict with one another. I cannot always satisfy my desire for success in my job as well as my desire to spend time with my family. Most days we are juggling our needs and desires and prioritizing them. One of the most well-known models for understanding how we do this is Maslow's hierarchy of needs.[24]

Maslow's hierarchy of needs

According to Maslow, it is possible to group our needs and desires into five categories. The guiding principle of his model was that people do not move on to higher level needs until the lower level needs have been satisfied. The lower needs have the highest priority and these include meeting our bodily needs for physical survival such as food, shelter, sexual release. Above these needs is our need for protection and safety, which implies that people will take risks regarding their safety if they are starving. When our physiological and safety needs are satisfied then our need for belonging and intimate relationships takes precedence above other needs. This is followed by the need for esteem with achievement, competence, status and approval, and then finally the crown is the desire for the fulfilment of one's potential as a human being as self-actualization.

Although it remains influential and has some validity, there are a number of problems with Maslow's approach.[25] First, it over-simplifies the prioritization of needs. There are many counter examples of people pursuing higher needs when the lower ones are not met. Frequently in the pursuit of aestheticism or holiness, higher goals are prioritized over the need for food, sex or intimate relationships; while other people take extraordinary risks regarding their intimate relationships and family life in the pursuit of money, fame and sexual fun. Second, the evidence from question-

24 Maslow, A. H., 1954, *Motivation and Personality*, New York: Harper & Row; Maslow, A. H., 1968, *Toward a Psychology of Being* (2nd edn), New York: D. Van Nostrand.

25 Baumeister, R. F., 2005, *The Cultural Animal: Human Nature, Meaning and Social Life*, Oxford: Oxford University Press, p. 167.

naire studies does not support the hierarchy, but instead it seems that we have a hierarchy of motives and these differ in content and order from Maslow's hierarchy. The key point is that Maslow's model does not fit all. Rather, we construct a personal motivational hierarchy and adopt a particular set of priorities for our various motivations. Hence, for one person the motivation for status and achievement might lead them to sacrifice their intimate relationships, and for another the motivation to fulfil their vocation to the priesthood takes priority over the motivation for sexual relationships and accumulating wealth. We all make different choices regarding our motivations and priorities. It is these differences that contribute to the individual differences expressed in our personalities. Furthermore, our motivations and how we prioritize them is likely to change at different stages of our lives. We might strive for achievement more in our forties than in our sixties. The importance of sexual satisfaction might be a powerful motivation and dominate in our early twenties, but a need for belonging expressed in family life might take priority in our thirties. Each individual hierarchy of motives is subject to the dynamic interplay of life experience and sense of purpose and meaning at any one time.

Intrinsic and Extrinsic Motivation

Motivations are not simply drives associated with a particular need or goal. They are more complex and require a more detailed examination of the experience associated with motivation and the goals associated with it. One of the main distinctions made in the literature is between intrinsic and extrinsic motivation.[26] An intrinsic motivation refers to doing something because it is rewarding in itself. People are motivated by the simple fact that they like doing it; they perceive it as having worth, or worth doing it for its own sake. The reward or reinforcing power of the action is inherent within it. Typically, we are intrinsically motivated to do things

---

26 Deci, E. L. and Ryan, R. M., 1985, *Intrinsic Motivation and Self-Determination in Human Behavior*, New York: Plenum.

connected with love, friendship, family, spirituality, play and other valued areas of human experience. In contrast, extrinsic motivation is defined as doing something for the sake of the reward or the separable outcome which is anticipated as a consequence of our behaviour or activity. I might dislike my job in banking, but because it pays a very high salary I continue to be extrinsically motivated to continue this career path.

Unsurprisingly, there is considerable evidence to suggest that the pursuit of intrinsically motivating goals leads to higher levels of happiness and well-being than extrinsically motivated goals.[27] But a lot of what we do is extrinsically motivated, for example when we strive to reach goals such as social acceptance or approval, prestige, financial gain, material benefit and the like, many of which involve engaging in things we do not find fulfilling. Furthermore, it seems that when we spend most of our time in extrinsically motivated activities, even if we enjoy the success, financial rewards and the affirmation of others, we may not be satisfied overall with our lives. Feelings of enslavement to a set of goals imposed by our perception of social expectations and aims can lead to a compromised or diminished sense of agency, with the external demands exerting an overwhelming power over us. When this happens we not only lose our sense of autonomy, but also our effectiveness in dealing with our lives.

Deci and Ryan[28] suggest that intrinsic motivated behaviour is self-determined behaviour. The energy for it comes from within us rather than some assumed reward or avoidance outside us. We pursue our goals with a sense of choice and doing what we really want to without any coercion from external sources. But the reality of our lived experience is that we deal with a mixture of opportunities and constraints within which we have to manage how to exercise

---

27 Kasser, M. and Ryan, R. M., 'Further examining the American Dream: differential correlates of intrinsic and extrinsic goals', *Personality and Social Psychology Bulletin*, 22 (1996), pp. 280–7.

28 Deci, E. L. and Ryan, R. M., 1991, 'A motivational approach to self: integration in personality', in Diestbier, R. and Ryan, R. M. (eds), *Nebraska Symposium on Motivation: 1990*, Lincoln, NE: University of Nebraska Press, pp. 237–88.

self-determined behaviour of this kind. We all have to do things we do not want to do and we also have to do things which bring little or no reward in themselves but contribute to the achievement of our goals. It can be a struggle to sustain our motivation to reach our goals, especially when we feel overwhelmed by external demands. At this point we may experience helplessness and a loss of control in our lives which may be very distressing and is associated with anxiety and depression. Deci and Ryan suggest that when we reach this particular state, our basic need for autonomy is lost and we no longer feel a sense of responsibility and the author of who we are and who we are to become.

It is undoubtedly true that our home, workplace, wider family, community, church, wider society and even the political and national contexts of our lives to some degree either support or diminish our autonomy. They exert a varying amount of control on what we do, think and feel. And it is the quality of these social contexts in conjunction with our motivations, orientations, experience of our psychological needs being satisfied and goals being achieved which determines our emotional experiences and psychological well-being. All of these things also contribute to our sense of self, in which self-determined behaviour performs a significant role in satisfying our need for competence, autonomy and relatedness.

Deci and Ryan's theory is respected for providing an explanation of how motivated agency works. It also explains how intrinsically motivated behaviour is a source of well-being and satisfaction in life. Their concept of self-determined behaviour with its sense of choice and doing what one wants to do without any sense of coercion or compulsion is also linked to actions which meet the needs for autonomy, competence and relatedness. Thus it is a theory which comprehensively integrates goals, needs and motivation. Furthermore, it has implications for our understanding of selfhood, as they suggest it ultimately enables us to experience our true selves so that we can behave with authenticity which they define as:

> a descriptor for behaviour that is an expression of the true self and for which one accepts full responsibility. When an action is endorsed by its 'author', the experience is that of integrity

and cohesion – the experience is one of being true to one's self. Authenticity is thus self-determination.[29]

There are obvious connections between the needs identified by Deci and Ryan and McClelland's achievement motive, power motive and intimacy motive described earlier. People vary in the strength of these motivations and also the goals they set in association with them, because we set goals within our particular context, which reflect the themes that are central to our lives. These emerge mostly from our interactions with our social world and provide a source of direction and coherence to the patterns of our behaviour. The combination of goals and their associated motivations energize and organize our behaviour and provide the substrate of our personality signature which comprises Level 2 of McAdams's[30] conceptualization of personality. Our beliefs about ourselves, our relationships, our narrative and identity as well as our concerns, tasks, plans and projects are the features of who we are and are integrated into our personality. They are the ingredients of our sense of purpose and meaning. Hence, goals are an important constituent of our personal identity, influencing our experience of the world and our emotional response to it. They are the fulcrum around which our personal narrative is configured. In the remainder of this chapter we will examine the psychology of goals before turning to a theological perspective on motivations and personal goals.

Personal Goals, Strivings and Personality

So far we have acknowledged that human beings devise many different goals associated with a vast array of motivations. Goals are a key source of individual differences and some motivations have a greater impact on our lives than others. Both our goals and motivation shape us profoundly. Motivations are the energetic power behind passions, personal ideologies; a resolute determination to

---

29 Deci and Ryan, 'A motivational approach to self', p. 277.

30 McAdams, D. P., 'What do we know when we know a person?', *Journal of Personality*, 63 (1995), pp. 365–96.

transform, challenge what is, or live a religious life. It is these which form the central themes to a person's life and are related to our overarching purpose and goals. They are embedded in the expression and understanding of our meaning in life.

Goals direct our behaviour: sometimes consciously, and often unconsciously. Life is full of possibilities and incentives, and some of these are related to our goals and others not. I may find making money an incentive because I want to be able to have a comfortable retirement, or I may find attending the next local cricket match an incentive because I anticipate that I will meet up with an old friend there. Incentives are related to our personal goals and have a considerable influence on what occupies our thoughts and our feelings.

Klinger introduced the idea of current concerns to describe the incentives which are most important to us at a particular time.[31] A current concern is a motivational state which we exist in when we have committed to a goal, but have not yet achieved it or decided to abandon it. While I am still committed to losing half a stone in weight I am concerned about what I eat, and while this does not occupy my thoughts all the time, it is a concern which I am conscious of and directs my behaviour. I avoid taking a coffee break with colleagues on the day when cake is provided and ensure that I take a packed lunch into work so I can control my calorific intake. But this is one of a number of my current concerns, all of which are connected to various goals I have committed myself to at present. These range from making an appointment for an eye check-up, planning a holiday in Spain, finishing writing this book on time, and ensuring that I make time to spend with my family over the summer. Hence, concerns might be very specific and narrowly construed, or be broad; they may last several months, years, or only a few minutes. Concerns keep the motivation and pursuit of a goal in focus. Although I may not be conscious of all of them all of the time, they are often triggered by events, conversations and circumstances, and the emotional significance of them leads us to interpret these experiences in the light of them. When a friend mentions that they have just lost over a stone in weight I immediately feel guilty

31 Klinger, E., 1977, *Meaning and Void: Inner Experience and the Incentives in People's Lives*, Minneapolis, MN: University of Minnesota Press.

about my slow rate of progress and am reminded of my goal and my lack of progress towards it. Furthermore, there is often a strong emotional component associated with current concerns. They frequently appear in our dreams and also may provide insight into some of the psychological problems a person is experiencing.

Another conception of the goals which orientate our behaviour and personal narrative are personal projects. Little describes the personal project as a series of activities which are associated with achieving a specific goal.[32] As with current concerns, these projects are wide-ranging and can include anything from cooking dinner this evening to living a holy life. There is an obvious overlap between personal projects and current concerns. The main difference between them being that the content and structure of everyday life is often consciously organized around personal projects whereas current concerns are not always as prominent in our thinking.

Cantor[33] introduced a higher level of goal above personal projects and current concerns classifying some goals as life tasks. These are the challenges and opportunities we face in particular periods of our lives which require considerable time and effort to achieve. An example of a life task in teenage years might be gaining a place at university, in our late 20s or 30s it might be starting a family or establishing ourselves in a career, in later life a life task could be spending more time with grandchildren. These life tasks direct and determine other goals which contribute to meeting the challenge of the life task, so for gaining a place at university there are various goals associated with this such as identifying the right course, engaging in a number of extra curriculum activities, and achieving the necessary grades. Likewise, establishing yourself in a career might entail studying for extra qualifications, gaining particular experience and taking on certain responsibilities.

Concerns, projects, goals and tasks identify what we are trying to achieve, do or be in some way or other. As already noted, these

---

32 Little, B. R., 'Free traits, personal projects and idio-tapes: three tiers for personality psychology', *Psychological Inquiry*, 7 (1996), pp. 340–4.

33 Cantor, N., 'From thought to behavior: "having" and "doing" in the study of personality and cognition', *American Psychologist*, 45 (1990), pp. 735–50.

direct our behaviour and influence the content of our personal narrative and our identity. Emmons[34] introduced the notion of personal strivings to describe what a person is 'trying to do' and broadened this into the field of spirituality. He postulates that each person can be characterized by a set of 'trying to do' tendencies or goals such as trying 'to look after my family', 'to be financially independent', 'to be a good husband'. Personal strivings might be quite broad, positive or negative; for example, trying 'not to lose my temper', 'avoid making a fool of myself' or 'having an improved relationship with my brother'. But they need not be only focused on actions as such, and may involve striving for a particular mode of being, such as 'being at peace with myself'. Hence strivings do not necessarily lead to achievements, but they reveal common qualities in a number of our goals. Therefore, Emmons suggests that it is helpful to view them as equivalent to a motive disposition. They represent a unique configuration unifying what might be 'phenotypically different goals or actions around a common quality or theme'. A bigger claim for them is that they are a valid representation of how we structure and experience our lives and the emotional landscape of our experience.[35] Interestingly, Emmons's initial research into strivings which concerned a transcendental experience found that the frequency of references to God or the divine suggested 'striving for the sacred'[36] warranted closer psychological examination. Given the suggested place of motivations and strivings or goals within personality theory, this suggests that faith becomes an integral part of personality. The significance of this statement for the integration of theology and psychology has yet to be realized, but if this is the case then it can be argued that faith influences every level of personality including the expression of dispositional traits as well as goals and motivations. Moreover, faith is not a cerebral, intellectual activity or a set of behaviours confined to a religious context as so often psychology has approached it, but rather it is an integral part of who we are and our daily lives.

---

34 Emmons, *The Psychology of Ultimate Concerns*.
35 Emmons, *The Psychology of Ultimate Concerns*, p. 27.
36 Emmons, *The Psychology of Ultimate Concerns*, p. 90.

Faith and Personal Goals

Personal strivings become part of who we are. They express what we are trying to do, be and achieve and these reflect our spirituality and religious beliefs. The relationship between goals and faith has always been present in Christianity. From the beginning of creation God's will and purposes have been declared and human beings are called to act in accordance with them. This is the goal of human life – to do the will of God. Psychologically there is no distinction between this and any other human goal. Striving to be obedient to God's will as revealed in Scripture and in the life of Jesus, like all goals, is held as a mental representation of what we desire to be and to do. It represents what is of utmost importance in life and what one commits to working towards. There are a number of outcomes which are associated with this striving, such as those described as the fruits of the Spirit: love, joy, peace, forbearance, kindness, goodness, faithfulness, gentleness and self-control (Gal. 5.22–23). But our spiritual strivings also represent a willingness to embrace a particular perspective on who we are in relation to God, others, self and the world in order that we might progress towards God and become more holy. In other words, our spiritual goals direct our life choices and our chosen experiences, as well as change the way we interpret what happens to us.

Goals have a prominent place in the writing of many devotional and spiritual writings, with the ultimate goal of intimacy with God. St Teresa of Avila in her text *The Interior Castle* describes the journey through the castle to the final room where we achieve union with God. This may happen in our earthly lives but it is more likely to be achieved after death. For Thomas Merton, the goal of human life is to find one's true self in God. By finding God and in God finding our true self, we can fill the void which lies deep within us. Paul writes, 'I press on towards the goal for the prize of the heavenly call of God in Christ Jesus' (Phil. 3.14). These strivings are a strong motivational force associated with a deep desire to be and do what is understood to be pleasing to God. Apter[37] describes the religious state of mind as 'telic', providing a sense of 'the most

---

37 Apter, M. J., 1985, 'Religious states of mind: a reversal theory of interpre-

serious and far-ranging goals there can possibly be'. This reinforces the concept of ultimate concern as a concern that 'above which no other concerns exist – it is literally at the end of the striving line'.[38] This is not to say that everyday concerns are not linked to ultimate concerns, because we can assume that the ultimate concern is a concern with orientating all of one's life around God and, as such, influences everyday goals as well as being at the heart of the ultimate spiritual goal of one's life.

Our goals become or are our concerns. They orientate our lives and affect how we feel about ourselves, others and God. Chapter 7 develops the essential relationship between emotions and goals, but it is important to note here that we often interpret our experience in the light of both our goals and motivation and this can determine the emotional response we experience and express. What we feel is closely related to what matters to us. Many psychological theories of emotion are based on how we evaluate our experiences in relation to our goals and desires. When we are doing well and achieving the goal we aim for, we feel pleasure, pride and happiness. Conversely, if things frustrate us in progressing towards our goal or prevent us from obtaining our goal, we feel angry, frustrated and disappointed. If we anticipate that we will not achieve our goal, then we become anxious or we experience discouragement and even depression. It is these observations which Roberts uses effectively to develop his theory of Christian character based on his understanding of emotions as concerned-based construals.[39] Concerns are what a person cares about, what is of importance to them: in other words, their goals. As Christians, our goals and motivations are shaped by our understanding of the nature of God's relationship with us, the gospel message of the good news of salvation through belief in Jesus Christ as Lord, and our vocation as children of God to share in the life of God's kingdom. It is these goals and motivations as depicted in the narrative of God that

tation', in L. B. Brown (ed.), *Advances in the Psychology of Religion*, Oxford: Pergamon, pp. 62–75.

38 Emmons, *The Psychology of Ultimate Concerns*, p. 95.

39 Roberts, R. C., 2007, *Spiritual Emotions: A Psychology of Christian Virtues*, Grand Rapids, MI/Cambridge, UK: Eerdmans.

reorientate and transform our personal concerns and so work to transform our personality.

The Challenge of Relating the Psychology of Motivation and Goals with the Christian Life

The dialogue between the psychological understandings of goals and motivation and a theological understanding of human motivation must begin with acknowledging how the human condition as portrayed in Scripture connects with human experience. Psychological understandings of motivation and goals suggest that human flourishing and satisfaction in life rests upon the satisfaction of the needs for autonomy, competency and relatedness. It can be argued that in the Garden of Eden, the desire to act with autonomy and be competent motivated the fall. Disobedience is an act which embodies the belief that we know better than the one who makes the rules and are driven by the desire to act in accordance with our will, not anyone else's. It is a lack of respect and trust in authority. The deception of the serpent exposes Adam and Eve's lack of trust in God, and how their relatedness to God falters. After they are cast out of the Garden, the narrative continues to chronicle the consequences of human beings' disobedience. But this negative interpretation of human nature is not the last word. So how might we conceive of our motives and goals in a way which is faithful to the tradition and is informed by current psychological theory and insight?

Sin and Personal Values

Although psychology would not adopt the word 'sin' in its approach to human motivation, there are both positive and negative evaluations of human nature present in the literature. However, it is the human condition to fall short of whatever it deems as virtuous. In the Christian tradition, human nature has the potential for good as well as evil. We exist within the tension of openness to God and our obedience to his holy laws, and attending to the needs of others and our own self-centredness. Our predisposition, whether it is sinful or not, struggles with the reality of our temptations energized by desires for power, achievement and intimacy. Sin is not only present in our actions, but in our thoughts and motivations. Both the object of our striving, and the striving itself, may be sinful and entirely self-serving. We constantly fail to do the good we intend and to be the kind of person we aspire to. Within Christian discipleship, the motivation to follow Jesus and become more like him shapes our desires and sets our overarching goal of growing into the likeness of Christ. The lifelong struggle to know Christ and become Christlike is set within the moral framework which he embodied and pro-claimed as the life of the kingdom of God. Through our prayerful devotion to Christ, attention to God's word as revealed in Scripture and participation in worship, and the Eucharist in particular, we find the means to recognize, address and overcome our predilection to fall short of what God wills and intends for his creation.

Psychology also asserts that human behaviour necessarily takes place within a moral framework, stressing its importance for the social organization and functioning of human beings. Without it there would be anarchy. Human beings are described as moral agents who construct personal value systems which are influenced by parental and social value systems and experience, and express what we believe to be good, of value and right. Our value system in turn influences our motivation and our goals. It orientates us towards that which we deem as good and away from those things which we believe to be unworthy, bad and detrimental to our well-being. Self-control or regulation describes our struggle to do what is right and good for ourselves and for our relationship with others. And although there are different notions of the purpose of our strivings or the goal of human life within the discipline, psy-chology too wrestles with the notion of the intended nature of human beings and how this is fulfilled, or why so few find life-satisfaction or reach self-actualization.

Ultimately, we choose between that which we believe to be vir-tuous and good and the opposite. Our behaviour is purposeful, and we are mostly willing, choosing agents who have responsibility (within certain limits) for the consequences of our actions. But not all behaviour is volitional. There are constraints and limits on our behaviour. Yet, it seems for the most part we are able to control, or at the very least moderate, our instinctive responses. Ultimately, we can decide the purposes to which we wish to commit ourselves, and behave in accordance with these. So, although we are not always entirely responsible for all our actions and thoughts, we can set the overall orientation of our lives. As Christians, we orientate ourselves to God and strive to overcome influences which might lead us to sin as we draw on the help of the Holy Spirit in our aim to be imitators of Christ. In this way, the motivation to love and serve God determines our goals, sets up the moral framework of our lives and becomes our telos.

In McAdams's personality psychology, our personal goals and values are the second layer of personality over the first layer of dispositional traits. But the two should not be thought of as separate layers. Indeed, McAdams suggests that the traits of 'conscientiousness' and 'agreeableness' are both 'laden with moral meanings'. It is also the case that the trait of 'openness' is correlated with many different value dimensions, such as moral reasoning, development of religious values and political liberalism.[40] Our motivations and goals become integrated into who we are and are related to our biological dispositions. They determine our character, our habitus,[41] and therefore how others experience and relate to us.

Erikson[42] located personal ideology in personal identity. Our beliefs shape who we are and who we become. Thus beliefs, motivations and goals drive our personal narrative and identity. The pursuit of personal goals forms the plot of our story and provides the meaning and continuity in the narrative we construct for ourselves. Our story, in McAdams's model, is the layer over our values and goals from which our identity is constructed, and the means through which we know ourselves as integrated human beings. Yet, the origins of our motivation and goals are complex: partly

---

40 McAdams, *The Art and Science of Personality Development*, p. 234.

41 Bourdieu, P., 1998, *Practical Reason: On The Theory of Action*, Stanford: Stanford University Press.

42 Erikson, E. H., 1963, *Childhood and Society* (2nd edn), New York: Norton.

biological, and partly social and cultural. Human beings are by nature relational, and from the time of conception are under the influence of other human beings. It is the social nature of being human and its influence on our personality and our narrative which we turn to in Chapter 6.

—

6

Social Being

In the previous chapter the need for relatedness was identified as one of the three basic human needs along with agency and autonomy. Human beings have an innate social character or disposition. Genesis 2.18 puts it very succinctly: 'It is not good that the man should be alone'. Throughout the Bible the importance of relationship with God and others dominates the narrative. God's purpose not only concerns the relationship between individuals and God, but also the formation of a community bound to God in a covenantal relationship. Human and divine interrelatedness is an essential part of the created order, and can be described as a relational web woven from our relationship with God, with others both individually and in community, and with the world. Our relational existence is fundamental to our understanding of what it means to be a human being. It is a basic and powerful human need. To be alone for any prolonged period of time causes us distress. From the very beginning of human life, an embryo is embedded in its mother, and after birth the relational bonds between an infant and its caregivers ensures survival until independence is achieved: when a young person can meet their own physical and psychological needs within their social context. But more than this, human beings are always dependent on others for their survival and well-being. Adam was incomplete without Eve; we need a complementary 'thou'. Relatedness is a fundamental human striving, an essential characteristic of our humanity. It is also essential to the Christian faith, which is defined by our relationship with God, each other and the world. The image of the body of Christ as the Church proclaims a community bound together by love that God has called to participate in his divine mission. In the community of the Church, together, we bear God's image and build each other up in love as we strive towards Christlike living and the fulfilment of God's loving purposes for creation.

As Christians, we believe that we are always in the company of God. Even when we are alone without another person present, God is with us. Even when we reject him, we remain in his presence. The psalmist captures this in Psalm 139.7, 'Where can I go from your spirit? Or where can I flee from your presence?' The omnipresence of God in the life of the psalmist is an active presence: active in his life, and in the world. This signifies the essential truth of the relationship between all human beings and God from the beginning of creation. We are created to be in relationship with God. In fact, before we are able to know it we are, by our very existence, in relationship with God. Our reality depends on this relationship.

When God created humankind as male and female, he blessed them and spoke to them. From the very start of human life, God initiates the relationship between himself and human beings in the act of blessing and speaking. There is a relational desire expressed in these actions which signifies the love which God has for his creation and especially for humankind. This desire of God for relationship is accompanied by his divine gift of love which defines the value and dignity of human beings. God deems human beings to be worthy of his love, and the importance of love and being in relationship as a source of value and self-worth is also reflected in the innate desire for relationship in human nature. When God says, 'It is not good that the man should be alone, I will make him a helper as his partner', God acknowledges human relationships within the created order as a source of human flourishing and well-being. Thus, human beings are created with a profound longing for relationship which is reflected in their human nature. A longing to love and be loved manifest in the need for intimacy at the very core of what it means to be human.

The New Testament narrative continues the story of divine love begun in God's act of creation and revealed supremely in the life of Jesus. Each Gospel tells the story of Jesus, the embodiment of God's love and how he relates to his heavenly Father and others.

The good news of the gospel primarily concerns the hope to be found in a life-giving relationship between human beings and Jesus. In John 15.1–11, Jesus invites us to abide in him as he abides in us and declares both his Father's love for him and his love for us, commanding that we 'abide in his love'. The intimacy of this language illustrates the depth of relationship which God invites us to share with him through belief in Jesus. In the human embodiment of divine love, Jesus provides us with a model of how we are to relate to God, others and ourselves. His entire ministry and mission is defined by the nature of his relationships. From the choosing of his twelve disciples, to the women who remained at the foot of the cross in his dying moments, the recorded life of Jesus is one which expresses the divine nature of love in human relationships. This is most notably evident in one-to-one encounters with Jesus which are often intimate and personal, probing the person and their deepest desires – such as the Samaritan woman (John 4), the man lying at the Bethzatha gate (John 5), the sinful woman (Luke 7.36–50), and his conversations with Peter (John 21). In relationships such as these, personal transformation occurs and they become a powerful witness to the dramatic effect of faith in Jesus as the Messiah, the Son of God.

Our journey of faith usually begins too with some form of encounter with the living Jesus, as we are drawn into a personal relationship with him as the one who shows us the way, the truth and the life (John 14.6). It is our positive response to his invitation into a relationship which is the basis of the experiential dimension of Christian faith.

But it is not only relationships with individuals and his group of disciples which are significant in the life of Jesus. Social events and hospitality also characterize the Gospels. Jesus at the wedding at Cana, or enjoying supper with friends, is indicative of the significance of spending time with others and its importance for his well-being. He depicts the kingdom of God as a great feast or banquet to which everyone is invited. The promised joy is a shared joy, a relational joy to be found in God. Jesus, it seems, enjoyed parties and feasts. He practised and taught hospitality, always making physical and emotional space for the other. The practice of hospitality to individuals and enjoying company in group settings demonstrates Jesus' recognition of the significance of welcoming, attending to others and the joy of human relating. In inviting others into his space, Jesus affirmed individuals as human beings and enabled them to see themselves in a new way as no longer marginalized, dirty, insignificant, but worthy of love and respect. Their need for positive self-affirming relationship was met in Jesus, as he accepted, forgave, loved and transformed them.

The unassailable significance of human relationships is examined in this chapter. Drawing on the psychological research regarding the relatedness of human life, it considers how this influences the way we understand ourselves and our expectations of the relationships which form the fabric of our lives. Our experience of human relationships also influences our spirituality and formation within the Christian community. Just as we are social beings in the world, we are social beings in the body of Christ, and the complexity of relationships impacts on our nurturing both as individuals and as Christians.

Human nurture is mostly directed towards autonomy, agency and relationship, whereas Christian nurture focuses on the fullness of life found in the loving God, loving others and loving oneself. Both psychology and theology affirm the centrality of love for human fulfilment and satisfaction in life, but approach it in contrasting ways. Our faith is founded on the loving purposes of God who is love and the source of love. The complex nature of love is of interest to psychology and theology. In Christian theology it is the very nature of God who is the source of love. Love is found and experienced through a commitment to follow Jesus. Through being in his company, we grow into an intimate loving relationship with God and participate in the work of loving redemption. In contrast, psychology's interest in love derives from an analysis of relationships, the nature of them, and how they influence us. It measures the outcomes of attachment relationships, identifies what factors determine whether a relationship is enduring and contributes positively to our well-being. It is concerned with the impact of relationships on subsequent social functioning, personality and psychological health. However, both disciplines place significance on our first relationships and the nature of the parent–child relationship in particular. God as father of Jesus and as 'Our Father' is central to the Bible narrative. We are taught to approach God as a parent. Although this can be a problematic image for those who have had difficult experiences of this primary relationship, nonetheless it is the way in which Jesus describes how we should relate to God. Paul notably describes how we are adopted into the family of God and nurtured in our faith as God's children (Eph. 1.5). Psychology also stresses the importance of the parent–child relationship as a source of security, protection and love. It is through the early experience of this relationship with our parents that we develop a sense of who we are, whether we are valued and significant, and what we can expect from others as we emerge into the social world which is the context of the majority of our life experience. For these reasons this chapter will focus mainly on our early relationships and the psychological impact they have for who we are and who we become in our complex social world. It will also offer insight into how this human experience influences our relationship with God and affirms the centrality of love for all human beings.

The Psychological Need for Relationship

Baumeister and Leary[1] claim that the need to belong is a basic and powerful need in human beings. We are motivated to form relationships with other human beings. Forming relationships increases both our chances of reproducing and surviving. From the perspective of evolution, it is a positive strategy. By being in a group, human beings found they could hunt more effectively, share resources, provide care for the weaker members, fight together against their enemies, and share tasks to improve general life efficiency. There were also benefits for ensuring that they could reproduce, since in a group there are increased opportunities for individuals to form couples, and parents stayed together to care for their offspring. In

---

1 Baumeister, R. F. and Leary, M. R., 'The need to belong: desire for interpersonal attachment as a fundamental human motivation', *Psychological Bulletin*, 3 (1995), pp. 497–529.

terms of evolution and personal survival, being with others was far more beneficial than the vulnerable state of being solitary.

The Importance of Social Relationships

The compelling argument from evolutionary psychology is that human beings are inherently social. At a basic level we need social relationships to have children and raise children. But more than this, our personal relationships are important to us at every stage of our lives. Among the myriad events which make up the story of our lives, relationships play a significant part. Some persist throughout most of our personal narrative, such as those with our parents and siblings, and others are part of a particular chapter, such as work colleagues or university friends. The general pattern which emerges in our story can be viewed as one in which our social network has a few significant relationships which are always present and feature as the main characters in our narrative, such as parents, siblings and partners, and a much larger number of other relationships which are more transitory and change over time, maybe featuring only in a distinct episode or chapter of our life story.

Every relationship provides us with various experiences in our social world such as love, care, entertainment, encouragement, demands, support, jealousy, pain and other negative experiences. They also shape our understanding of the world; they educate us and are a significant source of learning about others, ourselves and the meaning of life. In this way, they are essential for the process of human development. We need each other to grow and discover our personal identity.

Relationships and Spirituality

The most obvious place to begin any examination of human relationships is with the first relationship between an infant and its carers, usually the parents. These early experiences of relationships form our unconscious predispositions about ourselves, others and the world. The human baby develops in a social world composed of a complex network of interactions. In the first years of life, our physiological and mental systems are developing rapidly and most intensely. In this early phase of life we experience not only the physical world, but the world of emotions and relationships, and begin the process of learning what emotions are and how to manage them.[2] Our primary relationship with our parents develops into a blueprint which shapes our assumptions about relationships and what we can expect from the other people we relate to throughout our lives. Identified as an attachment relationship between parent and child, Bowlby believed that attachment is present throughout our lives, especially in emergencies.[3] When we are faced with difficult circumstances or feel vulnerable in life, we go to friends or family for comfort and support. These are the people with whom we have a strong enduring social tie and who make us feel safe and secure.

In addition to these relationships with other people, psychological research has begun to examine how the psychological notion of an attachment figure and the centrality of the emotion of love in Christian discourse reinforces attachment dynamics in core aspects of religious experience and spirituality. It is evident that our belief in a personal God with whom we have an interactive relationship acts as a haven of safety and secure base for us in the same way as the parent–child attachment relationship and other attachment relationships do in our lives.[4] Hence, by examining psychology's understanding of relationships, emotions and personality, we can begin to construct a better informed account not only of human relationships, but our relationship with God. Furthermore, if the forming and maintaining of relationships is such a motivational need in human beings, then it is essential that we draw on these psychological insights for any theological description of human nature and human vocation.

---

2 Gerhardt, S., 2004, *Why Love Matters: How Affection Shapes a Baby's Brain*, Hove, Sussex: Routledge, p. 10.

3 Bowlby, J., 1969, *Attachment and Loss. Vol. 1: Attachment*, New York: Basic Books.

4 Kirkpatrick, L. A., 'God as a substitute attachment figure: a longitudinal study of adult attachment style and religious change in college students', *Personality and Social Psychology Bulletin*, 24 (1998), pp. 961–73.

Early Relationships

We begin at the beginning, with a baby's first encounters with the world. By two months of age, a baby shows that they have a preference for the voice and face of their carer, which is a sign that an attachment or personal relationship is forming. By eight months, this attachment has become far stronger. Clearly this first relationship has profound evolutionary significance and is crucial for the survival and development of every child, but even though its formation is considered to be innate, the quality of this attachment bond varies considerably. It is frequently described as a bond of love associated with care, warmth, security and affection, and considered to determine the lens through which our other relationships are interpreted. The recognition of significance of this attachment bond is widely attributed to Bowlby[5] and Ainsworth[6] who developed their influential attachment theory from the late 1960s to the 1990s. They built on the psychoanalyst movement of Freud and others, and perhaps the most important contribution they made was to provide scientific evidence and respectability to the notion that our early relational experiences are more relevant to the development of our adult selves than had been accepted previously. This is now largely uncontested and remains hugely significant in developmental, personality and therapeutic psychology with early relationships receiving significant research attention from the 1960s onwards.

Attachment Theory

Bowlby's attachment theory developed from his understanding of the evolutionary significance of human affectional bonds and the benefits an infant accrues from being attached to a caring adult. By staying close to their protective carer, any risk of harm to the infant is markedly reduced and their chances of survival increases.

---

5 Bowlby, *Attachment and Loss. Vol. 1: Attachment.*

6 Ainsworth, M. D. S., 1973, 'The development of infant-mother attachment', in Caldwell, B. M. and Ricciuti, H. N. (eds), *Review of Child Development Research*, Vol. 3, Chicago: University of Chicago Press.

Bowlby also underscored the significance of the carer's natural concern to care for and protect their infant. This initial bond between infant and carer is an example of the human being's propensity to form deep and long-term relationships which he postulated to be the result of a genetic bias favoured by evolution. In Bowlby's view, human love has an evolutionary basis since the success and maintenance of long-term relationships brings contentment and satisfaction, and guides our behaviour in favour of our survival. He believed that the prototype for all loving relationships is the bond formed between the infant and the caregiver. Its main purpose is to provide safety and enable a child to explore the world. Safety ensures survival, and exploration enables a child to develop the skills and intellectual competencies to manage adult life.[7]

The need for both closeness and tender physical contact as part of attachment behaviour has been observed in a number of studies of non-human primates. The classic study by Harlow and Zimmermann in 1959[8] involved rearing monkeys with two different surrogate mothers: a wire mesh mother and a cloth mother which was wrapped in foam and covered with terrycloth. Half of the monkeys were fed by the wire mesh mother and half by the terrycloth mother. They found that the infant monkeys became attached to the terrycloth mother regardless of which 'mother' had fed them. Those fed by the wire mesh mother spent more time clinging to the terrycloth mother and ran to this mother if they were afraid. This famous experiment demonstrated that contact comfort is a more powerful factor in attachment in monkeys than the provider of food. The terrycloth mother was a source of comfort and a safe haven for the infant, especially when it became frightened, and it was this that was essential for the attachment bond to become established.

The attachment bond ensures that the carer and infant remain in close proximity, and infants have a number of different ways, or infant attachment behaviours, to achieve this, which include suck-

---

7 Bowlby, J., 1988, *A Secure Base*, New York: Basic Books, p. 81.
8 Harlow, H. F. and Zimmermann, R. R., 'Affectional responses in the infant monkey', *Science*, 130 (1959), pp. 421–32.

ing, crying, smiling, clinging and following. When a baby is close to her parent, she feels secure, and it is notable that, by the age of eight months and older, when she is separated from her parent for even a short time, she can show considerable distress, and even suffer from 'separation anxiety'.[9] It is inevitable in everyday life that a parent and infant will be separated for brief periods of time, but it seems that long separations arouse feelings of abandonment which are emotionally very frightening and painful. For any infant, total abandonment results in death, and as such Bowlby suggested that the experience of prolonged separation from a parent might even initiate a process of mourning. He identified three stages which the infant moves through in their response to their perceived loss: protest, despair and detachment.[10] The final stage of detachment signifies a rupturing of the attachment bond when the attachment is emotionally fractured. In cases of child neglect and abuse, this final stage might occur and has been shown to have significant negative effects on subsequent relationships.[11]

As with all human experience, our past experiences of these attachment relationships shape our expectations of relationships with other people in the future and how we experience them in the present. Bowlby proposed that our expectations and experience of attachment make up an Internal Working Model (IWM)[12] which has been described by Shaver and Rubinstein[13] as an internalized template of love. Others have described this unconscious knowledge

---

9 Bowlby, J., 'Separation anxiety', *International Journal of Psychoanalysts*, 61 (1959), pp. 1–25.

10 Bowlby, J., 1973, *Attachment and Loss. Vol. 2: Separation*, London: Pimlico.

11 Lyons-Ruth, K. and Jacobvitz, D., 2008, 'Attachment disorganisation: genetic factors, parenting contexts, and developmental transformation from infancy to adulthood', in Cassidy, J. and Shaver, P. R. (eds), *Handbook of Attachment: Theory, Research and Clinical Applications*, New York and London: Guilford Press.

12 Bowlby, *Attachment and Loss. Vol. 2: Separation*.

13 Shaver, P. R. and Rubinstein, C., 'Childhood attachment experience and adult loneliness', *Review of Personality and Social Psychology*, Beverly Hills, CA: Sage, Vol.1 (1980), pp. 42–73.

as emotional schemas[14] or procedural memory.[15] Whichever term is used, they all affirm that in this early period of our lives, the development of expectations of other people and how they will respond to us takes place and these become the foundation of our relational behaviour throughout our lives. The IWM, or 'love template', in effect acts as a personal representation of our social world of relationships, and we use it to interpret ourselves and others. Hence, if I believe that I am lovable and cared for by others, then when another person is kind to me I am unlikely to be suspicious of them or reject them. These early experiences teach us whether other people are responsive to our needs and our feelings, whether they help us to feel better, or whether they are more likely to disappoint us or hurt us. In this process our repeated experiences become generalized, and the learning becomes established and integrated into our psychological organization.[16] So an infant with responsive parents who has formed a secure attachment will construct an IWM which includes trust and self-confidence, whereas an infant with an insecure attachment might well develop an IWM characterized by uncertainty and rejection which in later life may contribute to low self-esteem and a vulnerability to loneliness.[17]

However, there is no set prototype for the nature of attachment bonds; they differ from one parent and their infant to another. Individual differences in attachment bonds have been analysed in terms of the quality of the attachment relationship. In her pioneering work, Ainsworth[18] focused on the role of security in attachment bonds and how well the attachment figure provides the infant with a secure base from which they can explore the world.

The attachment bond is both a source of anxiety when the baby is separated from her parent or frightened by the appearance of a

14 Bucci, W., 1997, *Psychoanalysis and Cognitive Science*, New York: Guilford Press.

15 Clyman, R., 1991, 'The procedural organisation of emotions', in Sapiro, T. and Emde, R. (eds), *Affect, Psychoanalysis Perspectives*, New York: International Universities Press.

16 Gerhardt, *Why Love Matters*, p. 211.

17 See Shaver and Rubinstein, 'Childhood attachment experience and adult loneliness', pp. 42–73.

18 Ainsworth, The development of infant-mother attachment'.

stranger, and also a source of confidence when the infant draws sufficient security and confidence from it to explore the world. The dynamic of security and anxiety and the quality of the attachment bond was investigated in the influential Strange Situation study set up by Ainsworth and her associates.[19] In a series of different situations the quality of the attachment bond was tested by gradually increasing the stress experienced by infants as a stranger approached them and their caregiver departed and returned. From the study the team were able to identify individual differences in the patterns of behaviour and categorized the response of the infants into four types:

Secure Attachment: A securely attached infant actively explores the room when alone with her mother, indicating the mother is a secure base. She may be upset by separation, but greets her mother when she returns and is outgoing with a stranger when her mother is present.

Resistant Attachment or Insecure Attachment: This is characterized by ambivalent attachment. The infant is quite anxious and does not explore even though her mother is present so we cannot assume that the mother is a secure base. But the infant is very distressed when her mother leaves, showing separation anxiety, as she may doubt whether her mother will return. But when her mother returns she is ambivalent, there seems to be resentment towards her, and she may resist physical contact or even kick or hit her in anger. She is quite wary of strangers even in the presence of her mother. The infant appears to want attention but is unsure if she will receive it.

Avoidant Attachment: The infant appears disinterested in exploring and does not show much distress when separated from her mother and avoids contact with her when reunited. She is not particularly wary of strangers but sometimes will ignore or avoid them. She appears to be distant from her mother and seems to deny her need of affection.

---

19 Ainsworth, M. D. S., Blehar, M., Waters, E. and Wall, S., 1978, *Patterns of Attachment*, Hillsdale, NJ: Erlbaum.

Disorientated Attachment:[20] The behaviour of the infant reflects confusion about whether to approach or avoid her mother. After separation from her mother she appears stunned and may freeze. She may go towards her then suddenly move away. There does not seem to be a consistent or coherent pattern for regulating her negative feelings and even appears frightened of her mother.

Ainsworth claimed these patterns reflect the quality of the attachment bonds. She observed mothers with their children at home and saw that responsive warm mothers were the most likely to have children who were securely attached. They were confident that their mothers would reliably respond to them and were more courageous and confident in the strange situation. In contrast, mothers who were unresponsive and remained aloof from their infant were most likely to have avoidant children who had learned not to expect help and support from their mother. Mothers who were erratic and inconsistent in their behaviour with their infants were most likely to have resistant children whose experience had taught them that sometimes their efforts to gain attention worked and other times they did not.

It is claimed that these different experiences of parenting provide the basis for our IWM, which remains relatively stable after the first year of life, although it may be changed by subsequent relationships. Hence our IWM is believed to guide us in our emotional and behavioural responses to our significant others throughout our lives. So if I have experienced an anxious ambivalent insecure attachment with my mother where any attempts at establishing an intimate relationship have been ignored, then my IWM will interpret the world as disinterested in me and my well-being, and I might be suspicious of the attempts of others to become intimate with me, or may be over-attention-seeking in my attempts to develop an intimate relationship. This suggests that the style of parenting we receive in our early years is a primary influence on our experience as social beings, and our emotional experience of the world.

---

20 Added later by Hesse, E. and Main, M., 'Disorganised infant, child and adult attachment: collapse in behavioral and attentional strategies', *Journal of the American Psychoanalytical Association*, 48 (2000), pp. 1097–127.

Without doubt this interpretation places a heavy emphasis and responsibility on the quality of the attachment bond established by the parent. There is little acknowledgement of the role of genetics or nature in the process; instead nurture is viewed as the main determinant of a child's subsequent relational experience and behaviour. As discussed in personality theory, the nature–nurture dichotomy has been a persistent debate in psychology; one which has far-reaching implications beyond the discipline, raising questions for theology, politics, social theory and practice. Adopting either polemic has important consequences for understanding human development and change. If our genetic make-up is understood as the main determinant of who we are, then it suggests that this blueprint holds the clue to our personalities and life story; whereas if nurture is believed to be the most significant contributor to human behaviour and development, then this has very severe implications for social policy. Both approaches also raise profoundly different questions regarding the theology of the image of God within us, original sin and being transformed through faith.

The work of Michael Rutter[21] has provided a well-evidenced middle way, stressing the significance of gene-environment interactions and the interplay between nature and nurture. Bowlby's theory and Ainsworth's observations provide an example of this, and can be interpreted as an illustration of this interplay at work. An attachment style develops from thousands of interactions between the parent and child over time. Every child has a particular temperament which is part of their genetically endowed personality, and their need for attention will be expressed in ways which are influenced by this. Every parent also has a genetically influenced temperament and responds – or doesn't – depending on a whole range of factors such as how tired she is, what other demands she is juggling, if there are other siblings to attend to, and what she believes about parenting. Each event in itself is not necessarily of particular significance, but over time these responses become generalized by the infant into their IWM of themselves, the relationship, and what to expect from relationships. Every relational experience builds up

21 Rutter, M., 'Nature, nurture and development: from evangelism through science to policy and practice', *Child Development*, 73 (2002), pp. 1–21.

trust or disappointment, frustration or gratification as the pattern of responses becomes predictable and the nature of reciprocal interactions is learned.

A further note of caution must also be highlighted in some earlier writings on attachment and parenting: namely an emphasis on a critical period for development. It is important that this is nuanced by more recent discoveries in neuroplasticity across our lifespan. Thus, the effects of early negative attachment experiences and disruption of attachment bonds do not necessarily destine a child to painful and difficult relationships, but rather they can be improved by subsequent positive, affirming relationships in later life.[22] Meaningful affirming relationships continue to influence our ongoing development throughout our lives and can, and do, become the means of hope and transformation.

Parenting

The role of parents both in psychology and in theology is seen as important in the lives of the next generation. Parenting is much broader than the attachment bond which has been our focus so far. Attitudes and approaches to parenting vary between contexts, and there are significant cross-cultural differences. Psychological approaches have usually been based on investigations which envisage parenting as the practices of the parents, and have a tendency to give little attention to the role and influence of the child in the process. But clearly parenting concerns a dyadic or triadic relationship, and there are systems of mutual emotional influence between the parent and child which consequently influence the nature of the IWM and how the child grows in their awareness of others and of themselves. Any acknowledged mutual influence is also understood by some theorists to imply a levelling of any assumed hierarchy between the parent and child.[23] Ask any new parent about the disruption to their home, and it quickly becomes evident that most

22 Siegel, D. J., 2001, *The Developing Mind: How Relationships and the Brain Interact to Shape who We Are*, New York: Guilford Press.

23 See Siegel, D. J. and Hartzell, M., 2004, *Parenting from the Inside Out*, New York: Jeremy P. Tarcher.

aspects of their lives have been influenced by the arrival of their baby.

Babies assert influence; they are not passive recipients of parenting, but they have some agency even in the first months of life. When they cry they are communicating how they feel and are demanding attention from their parents to change whatever state they are in for the better, whether that is feeding, comforting, warming up or cooling down, or stimulating them in one way or another. From the outset, a baby participates in a dialogical relationship with their parents, and although the early work on parenting styles has been illuminating, it has sometimes ignored this dynamic characteristic of the relationship.

Baumrind's model of four parenting styles is widely cited in the field and assesses children's behaviour in relation to their parents' actions, but fails to recognize any influence the child might have on the style adopted by the parent.[24] To some extent, the same can be said of attachment models where the child is perceived only as the recipient of care and limited attention is given to the two-way nature of the relationship. This means that the focus has tended to be on the responsiveness of the parent to the child as the main determinant of the quality of the relationship and its impact on future relationships.

The effect of parenting styles on children's patterns of relating and behaviour has been widely studied. Baumrind's taxonomy of four styles combined the two dimensions of permissiveness/restrictiveness with warmth/hostility in the following ways:

Authoritarian Parenting (high restrictiveness and high hostility): characterized by the assertion of parental power and a detached attitude.

Permissive Parenting (high warmth/high permissiveness): characterized by love and affection and only limited control.

Authoritative Parenting (high warmth and achievement demands/ high permissiveness with firm control): characterized by firm control but in non-punitive manner and encouragement of verbal give and take and respecting the child's own wishes.

---

24 Baumrind, D., 'Current patterns of parental authority', *Developmental Psychology*, 4 (1971), pp. 1–103.

Rejecting–neglecting Parenting (high hostility/high permissiveness): characterized by disengaged style. They are neither responsive or demanding and not supportive; rejecting or neglecting the child.

Baumrind's research found that the children's behaviour associated with the different parent styles persisted right through childhood and into adolescence, with the most competent and self-regulated adolescents tending to have authoritative parents.[25] However, parenting does not take place in isolation from a particular context and the network of other relationships which each of us is embedded in. This social network also contains relationships which have an impact on our attachments, social ties and personal identity such as siblings, grandparents, other carers, as well as teachers and peers. The larger sociocultural context – which our family experiences, and relationships are also embedded within and influence attitudes towards gender, role, expectations of parents and appropriate relations between parents and their children – must also be taken into account. For every child, the narratives of the parents, family, community and wider culture interact as part of a web of mutually influential factors, all impacting in some way on their IWM of relationships and their self-identity. Children are shaped by the complex interaction of nature and nurture which has yet to be fully understood, but a multitude of factors combine in our development as social beings.

The web of interrelationships is in effect the social context in which a child develops and where they learn to fit within their particular society. Parents induct their children into cultural norms and into their pattern of family life which will mirror society in some, but not all, respects. The family is also a context of emotional learning as well as emotional intensity. Coping with anger, love, disappointment and success is an important part of learning about social relationships. Within the context of family we are nurtured to cope with a seemingly endless stream of human experiences and to successfully negotiate or overcome the challenges of life.

---

25 Baumrind, D., 'The influence of parenting style on adolescent competence and substance use', *Journal of Early Adolescence*, 11 (1991), pp. 56–95.

Families

The importance of families as the first and most significant context for a child's development and social living cannot be overestimated. Within this small intimate group we learn the rules of behaviour and relating from those who care for us and are committed to our well-being. One of the useful ways of approaching the psychological influences within a family is through the application of systems theory, which suggests that all aspects of the child and their context are important to a child's development.[26] A family consists of individuals and the relationships between them. A basic principle of family systems theory is circularity of influence, which basically states that every member of the family affects and is affected by other family members. At its simplest, this means that how a child behaves affects their parents, but at the same time is affected by the parents. It is also the case that the relationship between the parents affects, and is affected by, the child's behaviour, and the parents' relationship also affects and is affected by their parenting style and responses.[27] Unsurprisingly, the quality of the parental relationship and how it relates to a child's development has received most research attention. It has centred on testing the prediction that a good relationship between parents is likely to be correlated with a good parent–child relationship and is the best context for a child to develop and flourish in. There is plenty of evidence in support of this hypothesis,[28] suggesting that relational quality within the family system is a significant factor for a child's development and well-being, both in the present and in the future.

---

26 Cox, M. J. and Paley, B., 'Families as systems', *Annual Review of Psychology*, 48 (1997), pp. 243–67.

27 Schaffer, H. R., 1996, *Social Development*, Oxford: Blackwell, p. 207.

28 Cox and Paley, 'Families', pp. 243–67.

The Lasting Effect of Early Relationships in Adulthood

As already indicated, the template of love or IWM established through the attachment bond remains fairly stable and continues to operate in our adult relationships. Hazan and Shaver[29] discovered that in the same way as secure infants are happier and more well-adjusted than insecure attached ones, so secure adults have happier longer relationships as well as lower divorce rates. Securely attached adults described their love relationships as friendly, warm, trusting and supportive. They stress that intimacy is a core feature of these relationships and believe that romantic love exists and intense love can be maintained over a long period of time. Those who have an avoidant style of attachment described their romantic relationships as low on warmth, emotional involvement and lacking friendly interactions. For them, love fades over time and the romantic love of novels and films does not exist. Anxious-style attachments described their romantic relationships as obsessive and passionate, strong on physical attraction, desire for union and a proneness to fall in love quickly and maybe indiscriminately. They reported intense feelings of jealousy and anger towards their partners, and see them as untrustworthy and non-supportive. They often have anxiety about being abandoned and rejected.

In order to further test whether the same psychological systems operate in adulthood as in our early attachment relationships, Hazan and her colleague investigated how childhood attachment changes with age, and so surveyed hundreds of people aged between six years through to eighty-two.[30] They asked questions related to the four defining features of attachment relationships laid out by Bowlby:[31] 'proximity maintenance' (child wants and strives to be close to the parent), 'separation distress' (child is distressed when separated from her parent), 'safe haven' (when the child is fright-

---

29 Hazan, C. and Shaver, P., 'Romantic love conceptualized as an attachment process', *Journal of Personality and Social Psychology*, 52 (1987), pp. 511–24.

30 Zeifman, D. and Hazan, C., 2008, 'Pair bonds as attachments: re-evaluating the evidence', in Cassidy, J. and Shaver, P. R. (eds), *Handbook of Attachment: Theory, Research and Clinical Applications*, New York/London: Guilford Press.

31 Bowlby, *Attachment and Loss. Vol. 1: Attachment.*

ened or distressed she comes to her parent for comfort) and 'secure base' (the child uses the parent as a base from which to explore the world). Questions such as 'Whom do you like to spend most time with?' and 'Whom do you turn to when you are upset?' were designed to test out whether these defining features changed across the lifespan. They found that from between the age of 8 to 14 a safe haven expands from the parent–child relationship to being satisfied by a peer relationship. However, it is only at the end of adolescence, ages 15 to 17, that all four features of attachment are satisfied by a peer, specifically a romantic partner.

It seems that our romantic partners become attachment figures, and this is also supported by research into how people cope when they are separated from them for long periods of time.[32] Adult partnerships resemble childhood attachment in three ways: in times of stress we want to be with our partner; we associate our partner with comfort and security and when we are separated from them we can become anxious.[33] Love and attachment are profoundly connected. Love takes away fear; it is a source of security, warmth, comfort and protection. This truth is clearly stated in, 'There is no fear in love, but perfect love casts out fear' (1 John 4.18). If our experience of early relationships and love has such a profound effect on who we are and become, then what impact does it have on our relationship with God whom we believe is the source of all love?

Reflections for Spirituality

Kirkpatrick[34] has suggested that there are many similarities between attachment theory and religious beliefs and behaviour. The emphasis on a loving, trusting, warm relationship with an attachment figure characterizes our relationship with God. Some

32 Vormbrock, J. K., 'Attachment theory as applied to war-time and job related marital separation', *Psychological Bulletin*, 114 (1993), pp. 122–44.

33 Weiss, R. S., 1982, 'Attachment in adult life', in Parkes, C. M. and Stevenson-Hinde, J. (eds), *The Place of Attachment in Human Behavior*, New York: Basic Books, pp. 171–84.

34 Kirkpatrick, L. A., 'An attachment-theory approach to the psychology of religion', *Journal for the Psychology of Religion*, 2 (1992), pp. 3–28.

describe their relationship with God in terms which are similar to the way human loving relationships are described, and even use the phrase to 'be in love' with God. The safe haven provided by an attachment figure giving protection and security is also analogous to the protection afforded by God as father who shelters us under his wings like a mother. When we pray, we speak to God who is immediately present to us and close to us, mirroring the feature of proximity in attachment theory in the act of praying. When we are frightened or stressed, God is our haven of safety who cares for us and takes away our fears through our confidence in his love for us and his power to protect us from harm. As an omnipresent and omnipotent God, it is difficult to imagine a more secure base.

The psychology of religious attachment suggests that as with other relationships, our IWMs of relational attachment may also correspond to our relationship with God. We can describe a secure attachment with God as loving, responsive and present, an avoidant attachment as distant and inaccessible, and an ambivalent attachment which involves an experience of God as being inconsistently available and responsive.

We believe that God has created each of us to be in relationship with him and to respond to the fundamental call to love God, love one's neighbour and oneself. Furthermore, we believe that God loves us and his love is the energy behind all that is and is to come. The impact of this truth is quite simply that we are called to participate in a relationship with God in which he constantly reveals his love for us and sees us as worthy of that love. Our identity in God is one of worthiness and attractiveness. It is in our life in relationship with God that we come to know ourselves and others in a process of transformation as we discover our true identity in Christ.

As Jesus interacts with people, he releases them into a new understanding of who they are and who they can become. Their IWM, or corrupted template of love, no longer binds them or holds them in a stagnating spiral of negative relationships and relating, but is rather transformed to encompass a sense of personal worthiness signified by the hospitality and dignity which is embodied in the way Jesus interacts with them. In this way, Jesus surrounds them with love and does not require them to draw on their own limited resources of love, but rather they draw on his love for them as their source of love for themselves and others as it becomes incorporated into their IWM. Our need for intimate loving relationships becomes rooted in God's love shown to us in Jesus.

Social Relationships and Emotions

In *Why Love Matters*, Gerhardt[35] argues that the first years of infancy are a crucial time in our emotional development. The neurological systems which manage emotions, including the neural pathways which encode our understanding of relationships, develop in this concentrated time of development. These crucial biological systems are influenced by our social context and the primary relationships which are present at this rapid developmental time. The link between emotions and relationships is obvious. Our relationships with others are often associated with the most intense emotional experiences in our lives. Overwhelming feelings of joy, happiness, excitement and hope are associated with forming or existing relationships; while a host of negative emotions are experienced when relationships break down, are damaged, or worse still end completely.[36]

New relationships are an especially common source of happiness and positive affect, and anything which intensifies a relationship is also likely to bring about positive feelings. When a couple move from dating to marriage, a baby is baptized or a student graduates, in each case there is a change and intensification of a relationship between individuals or an individual and an organization.[37] When a relationship is damaged or there is separation in a relationship, then sadness, anger, jealousy, fear and grief may be commonly experienced, and depending on the cause accompanied also by anxiety and stress.

---

35 Gerhardt, *Why Love Matters*.

36 Baumeister, R. F. and Leary, M. R., 'The need to belong: desire for interpersonal attachment as a fundamental human motivation', *Psychological Bulletin*, 3 (1995), pp. 497–529.

37 Baumeister, R. F., 2005, *The Cultural Animal*, Oxford: Blackwell, p. 256.

Baumeister and Tice[38] found that a prevalent and powerful source of anxiety was fear of social exclusion or being alone. The fear of being rejected by loved ones, deserted by a lover, or excluded from those who our being in relationship with is important, gives rise to considerable anxiety. Shyness often makes someone avoid social situations because they fear being rejected by those present. The pain of feeling excluded or ostracized is familiar to most of us at some point in our lives. Childhood memories of being the only one not chosen to join a team in a physical education class, or being ignored by a group of friends, can still sting. In studies where people share their emotional reactions to memories or scenes from their personal narratives, the anxiety of social rejection is the most consistent fear reported.[39] There is also considerable evidence supporting the damaging effect on psychological and physical health of being lonely,[40] and it is therefore unsurprising to find happiness being correlated with belongingness and good social relationships. Having a good social network is a robust predictor of happiness even compared with money, health, marital status or place of residence.[41] In fact very happy people have been found to have rich satisfying social relationships and spend little time alone compared with unhappy people who have social relationships which are significantly worse than average.[42] Overwhelming evidence suggests that being social and having affirming, satisfying intimate relationships is an essential part of our human nature on which our well-being and happiness depends. Yet achieving this can to some extent depend on our very early attachment bonds, parental relationships and the way this has influenced our interpretation of

38 Baumeister, R. F. and Tice, D. M., 'Anxiety and social exclusion', *Journal of Social and Clinical Psychology*, 9 (1990), pp. 165–95.

39 Craighead, W. E., Kimball, W. H. and Rehak, P. J., 'Mood changes, physiological responses and self-statements during self-rejection imagery', *Journal of Consulting and Clinical Psychology*, 47 (1979), pp. 385–96.

40 Lynch, J. J., 1979, *The Broken Heart: The Medical Consequences of Loneliness*, New York: Basic Books; see also Sbarra, B. A, 'Taking stock of loneliness: special section', *Perspectives on Psychological Science*, 10 (2) (2015), pp. 200–1.

41 Myers, D., 1992, *The Pursuit of Happiness*, New York: Morrow.

42 Diener, E. and Seligman, M. E. P., 'Very happy people', *Psychological Science*, 13 (1) (2002), pp. 81–4.

ourselves and the expectations we have of relationships stored in our IWMs. This is not to say that our IWMs are not able to change or are inflexible; on the contrary, we continue to engage in social learning throughout our adult life. But the psychological evidence suggests that the nature of these early experiences be given careful attention as should all our relationships if we are to flourish and enable others to flourish.

Reflections on Self with Others and God

The psychological research affirms that human beings have an innate desire to belong. It affirms that the biblical affirmation *it is not good for humans to be alone* is reflected in our human nature. This is not only supported by our evolutionary history, but also by our need for approval from others, and our anxiety concerning social rejection and isolation. We are indeed social creatures created for relationship, and without relationships we can experience a 'terrible feeling of chaos'.[43]

One of the most painful aspects of the development of a negative IWM is its impact on personal identity and our model of self. Much of our understanding of who we are develops from our social experience and relationships. As we have already seen, when these relationships are negative they can have a damaging impact on our personal identity. A child who experiences rejection will incorporate in their IWM that they are unworthy and unlovable. Their template of love becomes corrupted and they struggle to both love themselves and others. In this case their relationality which is fundamental to their personhood is damaged.

It is the Church's calling to be a community of love which builds each of its members up in love, but as we have seen in this chapter, we can only love if we are loved and surrounded by loving relationships that model the nature of love to us. Likewise, if we do not feel accepted and valued then we are unlikely to accept and value others. The same is true of our relationship with God. To

---

43 Vanier, J., 1999, *Becoming Human*, London: Darton, Longman & Todd, p. 7.

feel accepted and loved by God is a difficult step for someone with an insecure attachment, so the challenge for church communities, I believe, is to be places of love, acceptance and belonging where corrupted templates of love can be renewed and realigned through new experiences of love.

Meaningful acceptance and belonging restores trust and facilitates human flourishing. The Church should always be a community we can trust to be inclusive, and one which values being in relation with one another as a gift. Each of its members affirms the existence of others and is committed to their well-being in mutual relationships which are characterized by loving acceptance. It is a community which embodies God's love and so ensures that both its members, and those who come into contact with it, encounter love as a tangible reality. At its heart, the Church is a community of belonging where we are free to discover who we are and grow as children loved and treasured by God.

7

Understanding Emotions:
The Colour of Experience and the
Tone of the Narrative

On the morning of the day of Jesus' resurrection, Luke paints a picture coloured with emotion. He writes how the women were perplexed when they arrived at the empty tomb and that when the men appeared in dazzling clothes the women were terrified and bowed their faces to the ground. After the women had returned to the disciples, who did not believe their story, we are told that Peter runs to the tomb and went home amazed at 'what had happened' (see Luke 24.1–12). The changing emotions of the disciples on Easter Sunday are not so explicit in John's Gospel (John 20.1–19). All he records about Mary Magdalene after she visited the tomb is that she ran to Simon Peter and John, and that they in turn set out running to the empty tomb. In this case we are left to infer Mary's emotions from her response of running to find the disciples. Once the disciples arrive at the tomb, the Gospel tells us that, after seeing the linen wrappings lying in the tomb, the disciple John 'saw and believed' (John 20.8). Once again there is no reference to how he felt in that moment of knowing the truth of the resurrection. In fact, it is only when Mary remains at the tomb that any emotional tone is present in the narrative. Here, Mary is described as weeping, signifying her grief and anxiety at the missing body of her Lord. Moments later, she turns and Jesus is there; yet at the point of recognition there is again no explicit indication of her feelings. We are given but a hint of them in Jesus' instructions for her not to 'hold on' to him. Could it be that her actions reveal a powerful rush of excitement, disbelief and love? This constrained emotional tone on the part of the narrative continues until the end of the day when Mary shares her story with the disciples, who are locked in their house in Jerusalem 'for fear of the Jews' (John 20.19).

In Mark's Gospel (16.1–8) the facts of the discovery of the resurrection are succinctly conveyed. Nevertheless it mentions that the women were instructed not to be alarmed by the young man dressed in white whom they saw in the empty tomb. In a more dramatic tone, the passage ends with the women who 'fled from the tomb, for terror and amazement had seized them' (16.8). Matthew's Gospel (28.1–10) also mentions the fear of the women, and the fear of the guards who, at the earthquake and the appearance of the angel who rolled back the stone, 'shook and became like dead men' (28.4). Matthew too records the women's feelings as they left the tomb, noting their 'fear and great joy' as they ran to tell the disciples (28.8).

It is perhaps surprising that the most startling and dramatic event in the entire gospel narrative is recorded in a way which leaves the reader to mostly imagine the feelings of the women who first witnessed the empty tomb and the risen Christ. All that is recorded is their fear and weeping. Equally, in the case of the male disciples we are told only of their fear and amazement. For the Gospel writers Jesus being raised is paramount. The reactions of his followers add colour and texture to the accounts, but their importance is their witness to the supreme event, not how they felt.

It is not only the emotions of the disciples and followers of Jesus who receive limited attention in the gospel narrative, we are also told very little about Jesus' emotions. However, it must be noted that there are few specific references across the gospel narratives that draw our attention to how Jesus was feeling. John's Gospel contains the most, having 28, Mark has 16, Matthew 10, and finally Luke has just 6.[1] We know he wept over Jerusalem, in the Garden of Gethsemane, and at the death of Lazarus. He shows anger in the temple. He is moved to pity those who come to him for healing, and on the cross he lets out a cry of dereliction. But much of the

---

1 Voorwinde, S., 2011, *Jesus' Emotions in the Gospels*, London: T & T Clark.

emotional aspect of Jesus' personality remains hidden to us; we are left to imagine what he might have felt.

The emotions of the disciples who witnessed the strange and wonderful happenings of Jesus' resurrection tell us not only something about the event beyond the facts of what occurred, but they also reveal important information about their personalities. First, their feelings of fear indicate that the events were so extraordinary that they felt threatened by them. It is important to note that the group of disciples had also experienced the trauma of Jesus' crucifixion and their own safety was in jeopardy because of their association with Jesus. They locked the doors of the house because they were afraid. Hence, they were already in a state of heightened anxiety when the women found the empty tomb. It was evidently beyond their imaginings that Jesus' body would have gone. They had not understood what Jesus had taught them about himself, and so their interpretation of the empty tomb arouses terror and amazement. They were confused and disorientated. It is only when they come to understand the meaning of the empty tomb or when the risen Jesus appears to them, that they experienced a change in their emotional state. This is brought about by the angel and Jesus telling them not to be afraid. These words of reassurance caused their fear to subside, giving way to joy or excitement.

It is fair to assume that during the days of Holy Week, Holy Saturday, Easter Sunday and the days that followed, the women and disciples will have experienced a period of affect intensity. Mark's Gospel describes the emotional intensity most clearly, stating with reference to the women that 'terror and amazement has seized them'. In this description, the emotions which are felt in the moment are recorded, but feelings are also indicative of another dimension of the characters and their personalities in the narrative: namely their goals, motivations and strivings. The women and disciples had believed in Jesus; they had entrusted themselves to him and to work for God's kingdom. For most, if not all of them, this had involved considerable sacrifice and risk. After Holy Week, they were left traumatized by the crucifixion and the loss of Jesus, but they also may have had a profound sense of failure and disillusionment. Their present story was not the one they had believed it would be, or the one they had given up everything for. The intensity of their feelings demonstrates the deep significance of who Jesus was for them and their investment in his enterprise as participators in his mission. The loss of their anticipated future is integrated into their experience of these dramatic happenings. Furthermore, it is important to note that their emotions indicate the nature of their relationship with Jesus; a relationship grounded in love. The emotion of grief, only explicitly mentioned with respect to Mary as she weeps at the tomb, is a constant throughout the narrative, and is one which informs the analysis of all the described responses.

By piecing together the fragments of emotions recorded in the resurrection story, we gain some insight into what the women and disciples felt, and the significance of the events for them, based on their sense of purpose and what is termed their 'ultimate concerns'. But, overall, we have very little evidence in the Gospels on which to build any understanding of the disciples' individual personalities. Simon Peter is revealed as impetuous, devoted, overconfident, assertive and, when challenged, unreliable. Martha and Mary are presented as having contrasting personalities. Personality is understood in what we 'have' as part of who we are and what we 'do' or how we respond. From a close reading of what the disciples did, and our limited knowledge of their emotional responses, it is possible only to gain glimpses of who they were and what they were like.

To know someone, as McAdams asserts, is not only to know their dispositional traits, but also their goals, their concerns and their life stories. Emotions are essential to each of these levels of personality, and it is to them we now turn our attention. As already concluded, the gospel narratives are more concerned with events rather than feelings, but it is important to note that words and actions are frequently a response to an emotion. However, we need to be mindful of misinterpreting or assuming an underlying emotion in association with a behaviour. For example, one person may be running away from an unexpected event through fear, and another through excitement. Voorwinde,[2] in his analysis of Jesus' emotions, restricts his discussion to passages where emotions are

---

2 Voorwinde, *Jesus' Emotions.*

clearly identified and those actions which unequivocally signify an underlying emotion such as weeping or sighing. However, even with these strict criteria, one can assume too much. For example, a sigh may signify frustration, despondency, sadness or exhaustion. Hence the danger of overspeculation remains despite the emotional overtones of the context and characters becoming for many readers an important dimension for their personal engagement with the biblical narrative. Yet, the drama and deep emotional resonances of the Gospels have an evocative power which touches hearts and minds. For Voorwinde, understanding Jesus' emotions holds 'the potential for more authentic Christian living',[3] as becoming Christ-like cannot exclude this central dimension of life. But it is somewhat naive to isolate emotions in this way. Any Christian understanding of emotions has to acknowledge the intimate relationship between emotions and our personality. It is emotions that reveal our pre-dispositions, our goals and motives, and the influence personal narrative and other narratives have on who we are and who we become. More authentic Christian living requires engagement not only with emotions, but what they signify about the person and their personality.

Hence, in order to appreciate more fully the nature and complexity of emotions and their role in the uniqueness of personality and an expression of faith, it is necessary both to examine the psychology of emotions in more detail and their relationship to personality. Without a deeper understanding of the psychological components and function of emotions, Christian anthropology cannot meet its task. To be human is to experience emotion, but the source of such feeling and the factors which influence it reveal far more than is often recognized about the psychological and spiritual life of a person.

A Brief Overview of the Christian Life and Emotions

The emphasis on self-control, rationality and order in early Christianity has left a long legacy of distrust regarding the emotions. Passions, desires or emotions were considered as disruptions.

---

3 Voorwinde, *Jesus' Emotions*, p. 8.

They were thought of as misleading, bringing about disorder leading to a failure in focus on what was good and right. Rooted in the dualistic influences of Greek philosophers such as Plato and Socrates, emotions belonged to the less noble order of body rather than the mind where pure reason resided. Descartes furthered this diminutive dichotomy by likewise placing a high value on reason and giving emotions a much lower place in human functioning.

Augustine was notable in his theological reflection on emotions. He was evidently a very passionate man whose sensual desires are well documented in his *Confessions*. However, he concluded that his appetites for food, sex, beautiful sounds and a number of other things were a threat to his relationship with God, causing disorder in his will and his desire for God. He believed that our desires require reordering from seeking fulfilment in self-satisfying things, to seeking satisfaction in that which is ultimately satisfying. To achieve this we have to orientate ourselves towards the divine will and a desire for God. A practice that necessarily involved both discipline and control. Accordingly, he thought that earthly focused passions and sexual desires were sinful and evidence of humanity's corruption. It was only in worship that passions and desires could have a place. Consistent with this view, Augustine was proud of not crying at his mother's death, but was able to pour out his heart passionately to God.[4] Even today, this pattern of attitudes towards emotions, especially those classified as 'negative', prevails in many sections of the Church.

Watts[5] identifies two approaches to strong emotions in religious life. The first acknowledges the connection between strong emotions and a strong faith. This is apparent from many of the characters in the Bible. The prophets spoke God's word with intensity and passion. Job cries out to God in his suffering as he experiences grief, despair and desperation, and the psalms expose a rich and colourful emotional landscape which demonstrates the heights and depths of human experience, as the psalmist pours out his intense feelings to

---

4 Pattison, S., 2007, *The Challenge of Practical Theology: Selected Essays*, London and Philadelphia: Jessica Kingsley, p. 188.

5 Watts, F., 'Psychological and religious perspectives on emotion', *Zygon*, 32 (1997), pp. 243–60.

God. In a communal setting, the contemporary charismatic movement is an example of a combination of intense positive emotion,
revelation and worship. These traditions stress the active power
of the Holy Spirit, and encourage the expression of emotions in
response to the work of the Holy Spirit and as part of an act of
worshipping God in spirit and in truth.

In contrast to this, Watts suggests there is an alternative tradition
within Christianity which values the calming of emotions in the
contemplative tradition. Emotions are regulated, or quietened, in
order that the voice of God can be attended to. In Buddhism, this
emotionally quiet approach to religious experience is well refined,
whereas the Christian contemplative tradition, though receiving
more widespread attention, is still only followed by a minority.

Undoubtedly, religion gives rise to some emotions. There are
several different ways in which this takes place.[6] Religious belief
presents the opportunity for a unique and powerful emotional
experience of awe, wonder and closeness with God. Within the
tradition, as already mentioned, certain emotions are encouraged
and others discouraged. Feelings of joy, love, gratitude and hope
are affirmed and prescribed, whereas sadness, anger and lust are
viewed as negative. Beliefs about God, God's relationship with the
world and humanity also influence our feelings about the events
and circumstances of our lives. A belief in the goodness of creation
and our role as co-creators is linked with positive emotions and
well-being. An emphasis on the grace, love and forgiveness of God
as opposed to the wrath and judgement of God will inevitably result
in a very different emotional relationship with God. The dominant
image held of God is central to personal spirituality and is reflected
in the variation in the emotional tone of the lived experience of
faith.

There are also more subtle emotional influences. For example,
the belief that God is present and active in everyday events affects
our interpretation of what is happening in the world and influ-

6 Silberman, I., 'Spiritual role modelling: the teaching of meaning systems', The International Journal for the Psychology of Religion, 13 (3) (2003),
pp. 175–95; Silberman, I., 'Religion as a meaning system: implications for the
new millennium', Journal of Social Issues, 61 (4) (2005), pp. 641–63.

ences the intensity of their emotional impact. In the face of world disasters and tragic life-events, anger and despair with God may be experienced. Conversely, this belief concerning God's presence in the world can make believers more accepting of life-events because of their ultimate faith in God's divine purposes for the world.

Context and culture also affect our emotional responses. The influence of historical ideas and more contemporary attitudes to emotions has led to confused, if not conflicting, views and perspectives within a Christian context regarding the place of emotions in personality and in the embodiment of faith. Emotions remain controversial. For over 2,000 years, the conflict between reason and emotion has been fought. To describe someone as emotional or sentimental is often interpreted negatively, and yet it is considered socially important not to 'hurt people's feelings'. Caring for someone does not only mean ensuring they are comfortable physically, but also that their emotional health is attended to. The encouraging emphasis on holistic care in contemporary approaches to health care indicates the significance attached to emotional well-being alongside physical well-being.

During the past 50 years, psychology has come to regard emotions as being functional, purposeful and of evolutionary importance for our social success. There has also been a dramatic increase in research and interest in psychological well-being, counselling and talking therapies which have furthered the academic interest in emotions. It is this interest which has influenced pastoral care, Christian counselling and spiritual direction, leading to a significant shift in Christian approaches to emotions.

However, emotions are prone to misunderstanding and are undoubtedly psychologically complex. Psychology struggles to define emotion. Part of the problem is its range. Moods, passions, temperament, motives, goals and attitudes are all included in ongoing research. In spite of their complexity, our emotions are the barometer of our state of well-being and give colour to our lived experience. It is easy to assume that we know what we are feeling at any one moment, but the cause of the feeling, managing the feeling, and what it reveals to us and to others about who we are, our motives and our goals, necessarily demands the integration of a number of sub-disciplines from psychology. Furthermore, the expression of emotion characterizes a person and their personality. In social relationships, emotions are a vital means of communication through facial expressions, behaviours and verbal volume and tone. Psychology recognizes emotional experience as essential to human functioning from decision-making to negotiating the social world and making meaningful reciprocal social relationships. Emotions are part of the bedrock of positive living and psychological flourishing.

Approaches to Emotions from Social Science

Many of the social sciences have shown an interest in emotions. Anthropologists have examined the relationship between emotions and culture, and emotions and ritual. Emotions can be viewed as a means of communication, social interaction and control. Cross-cultural studies have led to the identification of six universal emotions: happiness, sadness, disgust, fear, surprise and anger.[7] Neuropsychologists reduce emotions to neurological processes with electrochemical changes stimulated by changes in the sensory systems. Evolutionary psychologists seek explanations for emotions in terms of strategies for survival and adaptation, whereas Frijda explains emotions as 'action tendencies': so, for example, disgust is a tendency to expel, and fear a tendency to escape.[8]

A more comprehensive approach to emotion is rooted in the cognitive component of emotions, which stresses feelings as a response to the relevance of a situation to personal goals and values. This cognitive approach emphasizes the appraisal of the situation's significance and its interpretation as major factors in the experience of an emotion. It also leads to a more integrative theory of emotions in which the whole of the person is recognized in the process, such that traits, goals and narrative are taken into account. Many other theories fail to acknowledge the significance of the place of

7 Ekman, P., 1980, *Face of Man: Universal Expression in a New Guinea Village*, New York: Garland.

8 Frijda, N., 1986, *The Emotions*, Cambridge: Cambridge University Press.

emotions in personality, and maintain an unhelpful conceptual fragmentation between the two. To illustrate the relationship between goals, motivation, emotions and personality it is useful to reflect on a pastoral story.

A Pastoral Narrative

Maisie is 86 years old and lives alone. She has two children, both living within a few miles of her home. She invites them both to a meal and tells them that she can no longer cope with maintaining the large family house and has decided to sell up and move into sheltered accommodation. Mary reacts with both shock and sadness, she immediately suggests that her mother does not have to take this course of action and chastises her mother for not talking about it with them sooner. But David shows very little emotion and responds by showing respect for his mother's decision and reflects that if the large house is causing Maisie to be anxious and she is finding it difficult to manage, then her proposal is a wise one. Mary's emotions are connected to a number of things: her denial that her mother is probably fast approaching her last years of life, her attachment to the family home and the positive memories associated with it, her negative perspective of elderly care provision generally, and her sense of betrayal or regret that her mother has made the decision without consulting her. In contrast, David feels relief. He has long since thought the house was becoming a burden to his mother and was aware that her health was now declining more rapidly. He had been fearful of raising the issue with her, and anxious that she would have been hurt or upset by the proposal.

Psychology understands emotions as having a number of components, which include subjective feeling, a physiological reaction, behavioural response, expressive reaction and some form of cognition. An analysis of this example bears out this complexity. First, Maisie is most likely anxious concerning her children's response to her proposal. Her adrenaline levels will be increased. Her heart rate would be increasing, her hands would be sweaty and she might have a sensation of her stomach and her muscles tightening as she awaits their arrival and then begins the conversation. Mary and

David might also have raised anxiety, because Maisie does not usually invite them for a meal without their partners and children. They have both assumed that Maisie has something of significance to share with them, and that it may not be positive. They too might have a raised heart rate, slightly dry mouth and feel muscular tension. After Maisie has disclosed her intentions, Mary will probably have felt a raised intensity in her anxiety and possibly some anger combined with sadness. In contrast, David's anxiety will have decreased.

The different emotions experienced in this episode were due to the contrasting ways in which Maisie and her children appraised or interpreted the situation: it was judged positively by David and negatively by Mary. Their judgement is made on the basis of the different way each appraised Maisie's ability to cope in her home and its impact on them. Mary expresses sadness and some anger to her mother, while David feels relief. Incorporated in their view of the matter will not only be their relationship with their mother, but also their own concerns, values and plans for the future. Mary was quick to show her emotions and experiences them intensely; David might be described as stoical or emotionally cold. Here, the emotional traits or dispositions regarding their regulation or expression of emotion are revealed and add another dimension to the overall emotional tone of the episode. Finally, there may be significant events in their life stories which are also important factors in their response.

Mary is divorced with two children and her mother has been a significant support to her and her two daughters. When she could no longer live in her marital home, she returned to live with her mother for several years before she was able to afford her present house, which is a short distance from her mother. David has always strived for independence. He is a successful businessman and spends several months a year abroad. Ten years ago, he had suggested that his mother might like to think about buying a bungalow, but she reacted strongly against this, and for six months they did not speak to one another. This illustrates that an adequate explanation of the emotions which David and Mary experience must include their narrative, and make reference to all three levels of personality as described by McAdams: traits, goals and adaptations and personal narrative. Our emotions cannot be extricated from our personality. To add additional evidence in support of this position, we need to examine further the role of our goals and motivation in emotions.

Emotion, Judgement and Appraisal

There is a growing consensus that emotions are an important part of human functioning and implicated in the way we understand, apprehend and make decisions regarding the reality which confronts us. During the past 50 years, emotions have undergone a process of revaluation and are no longer considered as an irrational distraction; rather they are viewed as an important source of information and means of communication. The significance of a cognitive component in the experience of an emotion is widely recognized. Cognitive theories dominate the field and have received an increasing amount of attention since Arnold first presented her theory in 1960. But the role of thinking in feelings has its roots much further back in history. Aristotle not only proposed that emotions were linked to actions, but also that they depend on what we believe and our evaluations. This point is echoed in the quotation from Shakespeare's *Hamlet* 'there is nothing either good or bad but thinking makes it so'. Hence emotions over many centuries have been considered to be shaped by our thinking and judgements. The experience of emotion is largely determined by how we appraise our previous experience of a situation, the current situation and what we anticipate will be happening to us. In other words, thoughts and goals affect feelings.

Is the situation positive or negative? Is it something I am attracted to and desire, or do I want to withdraw from it? The conclusion of such evaluations determines whether I feel happy or frightened. Arnold went so far as to say that 'without appraisal there can be no emotion, for all emotions are initiated by an individual's appraisal of his or her circumstances'.[9] Nussbaum also stresses the importance

---

9 Arnold, M., 1960, *Emotion and Personality: Vol. 1 Psychological Aspects*, New York: Columbia University Press, p. 175.

of appraisal, contending that 'emotions always involve thought of an object combined with thought of the object's salience or importance: in that sense they always involve appraisal or evaluation'.[10]

It seems that evaluation is crucial, but this judgement is not a unidimensional evaluation. It involves not only the present moment, but also the person's goals and aspirations. This future dimension is just as significant as the present context. Hence, both the inner and outer world of the person affects the emotional experience. An emotion is a coalescence of the evaluation of a situation in the light of personal goals and desires. The sequence of this evaluation is important. The event or object is perceived, a judgement is made, and then on the basis of this judgement an emotion is experienced. In this way, our emotions can change with an alteration in attitude or goal over time. As we acquire knowledge and experience, what was once threatening and fearful may be no longer so. Likewise, our goals and motives change over time or because of changing circumstances. For example, I may experience charismatic worship as very uncomfortable and a source of anxiety, but if I am studying prayer in charismatic worship for a research project, my emotional response in attending such an event will be completely changed because my personal goal has altered.

One of the criticisms of the role of appraisal is the time taken for this cognitive process to occur. Zajonic stressed that emotions prepare a person to respond very quickly to life-threatening events as part of their survival function. Their heat and urgency are important and cannot be overlooked. He emphasized that the effect is basic and fulfils an important evolutionary function. Therefore the sequence has to be emotion then appraisal, and 'it is entirely possible that the first stage of our reaction to anything and also to our memory of it is affective'.[11] So we can like something or be afraid of it before we know precisely what it is or even without knowing what it is. He describes this early response as 'gross and vague'[12] but

---

10 Nussbaum, M. C., 2001, *Upheavals of Thought: The Intelligence of Emotions*, Cambridge: Cambridge University Press, p. 23.

11 Zajonic, R., 'Feeling and thinking: preferences need no inferences', *American Psychologist*, 35 (1980), pp. 151–75, p. 154.

12 Zajonic, 'Feeling and thinking', p. 159.

it can have a significant influence on the way we interpret things. In addition, as we reflect on and consider what we are facing in more depth, our initial emotional response might change.

There are undoubtedly events in our lives to which we have an immediate emotional response, then over time we appraise them differently and the feelings we have about the object or situation change. I disliked my first college room from the time I walked into it and saw the colour of the walls, but over time it became home and I felt sad to leave it at the end of the year. The difference in the way we process situations we find ourselves in led Zajonic[13] to propose that affect can occur with minimal processing and might only involve the perception of special features. He asserts that cognition and emotion are independent systems and emotion can be elicited without any cognitive processing occurring. This is seen to be the case when an immediate unconscious evaluation takes place as to whether an object or situation is good or bad which leads to a rapid response of either approach or avoidance. It is in effect a simple good or bad assessment. Russell[14] has developed this further and claimed that these unconscious evaluations form the foundation of our experience of moods and emotions.

Personal experience recognizes this fundamental categorization process operating subconsciously in our responses to events and objects. I immediately respond to the smell of fresh bread as 'good' and the smell of burning plastic as 'bad'. Although I would also categorize listening to a Mozart opera and reading a novel by Jane Austen as 'good', the experience of these is very different from the instant pleasure of smelling baking bread. But emotional experience is far richer and more complicated than an evaluation of whether an object is good or bad. Emotions such as guilt, love, anger or sadness entail a more sophisticated process of appraisal. This takes us into the reaches of deeper cognitive processing, beyond the automatic primary appraisals which Zajonic has identified, and into the area of what has come to be known as secondary appraisals.

---

13 Zajonic, 'Feeling and thinking', pp. 170–5.

14 Russell, J. A., 'Core affect and the psychological construction of emotion', *Psychological Review*, 110 (1) (2003), pp. 145–72.

Appraisal Theories, Goals and Emotion

Most appraisal theorists agree that we appraise an event or object in terms of its relevance to our personal goals. If the event is relevant, or of significance to us in some way, then an emotion is elicited; if not, then there is no emotional response. Thus relevance is an important part of the interpretation process. Nussbaum[15] agrees, asserting that emotions are always about something, whether it be a building, an event or idea. Emotions have an object and the object has to be of some significance to a person. The emotions that ensue when I meet my daughter are about her and who she is and the importance I attach to our relationship. But more than this, they reflect the interpretation of my daughter and her behaviour as I see her at a particular time and place. Nussbaum calls this the object's 'aboutness' which comes from our active ways of seeing and interpreting. They may or may not be accurate, but there are significant implications which stem from an object's aboutness for the emotion's identity and how we experience it. For example, the distinction between sadness and happiness is not the object per se, but the way the object is seen and its significance to a particular person. One person might be distressed by the removal of the church pews because their family had made a considerable financial contribution to them for the church 60 years ago, and another person will be pleased to have them replaced by more comfortable chairs which give greater flexibility to the use of the worship space. The aboutness of the pews elicits contrasting emotions from these two different perspectives.

Lazarus[16] has elaborated further on the appraisal process, and proposes that we not only evaluate whether the event has value or relevance to us, but also whether it contributes to our goals and aims in life. He suggests that we respond to situations according to their 'relational meaning', which includes their implications for our well-being. This is a function of whether the situation offers us good or ill, and whether it fulfils our expectations, intentions

---

15 Nussbaum, *Upheavals of Thought*, p. 27.

16 Lazarus, R. S., 1991, *Emotion and Adaptation*, New York/Oxford: Oxford University Press.

or goals. Different emotions can also be defined by making reference to the effect on the relationship between the person and their world. Lazarus calls these core-relational themes. Anger is felt when a demeaning offence is made against someone and whatever they consider to belong to them: for example, family, friends or possessions. Anxiety is experienced when facing uncertainty or anticipating a threat, fright when facing danger, and guilt when a moral imperative has been transgressed.[17] What emerges from this understanding of emotions is how the emotional landscape of a person can be seen to present a picture of the way they relate to the world, what their sense of self is, and also their values and goals. Without too much modification, this is a psychological portrait of their personality; indeed Lazarus claims that no other concept in psychology is as richly revealing of the way an individual relates to life and the specifics of the physical and social environment.[18]

Nussbaum's theory is similar to Lazarus' core relational themes, asserting that the significance of the role and relevance of the object or situation in the person's life to the emotion is an important aspect of the appraisal process. What we believe about something affects the way we feel about it. When something is believed to be valuable to us, whether it be a person, principle or thing, we are emotional about it. We grieve and feel deep sadness when someone who we love and who cares for us dies, knowing that our lives will be in some measure impoverished without them. Or we might be frightened of losing our job in the dismal economic climate because we have a mortgage and family who are dependent on our income and the thought of the consequences and damage of being unemployed strikes fear into us. These illustrate that the object or situation is of significance and value, and hence is directly related to how a person feels about themselves and their life in general. They are objects and situations which affect a person's sense of well-being.

All of this suggests that our well-being is contingent upon our emotions, and it is not surprising that they are considered as

17 Oatley, K., Keltner, D. and Jenkins, J. M., 2006, *Understanding Emotions* (2nd edn), Oxford: Blackwell, p. 175, adapted from Lazarus, *Emotion and Adaptation*.

18 Lazarus, *Emotion and Adaptation*, pp. 6–7.

eudaemonistic: that is, concerned with the person's flourishing.[19] Feelings associated with achievement of goals, relationships and meaning-making all contribute to our sense of fulfilment and personal well-being. When we succeed and relationships are good then we experience positive affect and well-being. In contrast, when we fail, or our aspirations and goals are thwarted, then we experience such negative emotions as sadness, frustration, fear, hate, jealousy, guilt and disgust which can be detrimental to our well-being.

The link between plans and goals and emotions is fundamental to Oatley and Johnson-Laird's theory,[20] which claims that personal schemes or goals can bring us happiness, pain and grief; in fact, they claim that all emotions are goal based. Emotions are experienced when plans have been interrupted, thwarted, as well as when they have been fulfilled. The theory suggests that an emotion involves not only the appraisal process described above, but is elicited through an awareness of a change in the chances of plans and goals being achieved. Rooted in an artificial intelligence approach to cognition, they propose that this awareness of a change in the probability of goal achievement activates an alert system and this prompts an appraisal process. For example, when we feel frightened it is because the normal smooth running of our lives has been interrupted by something which we perceive as harmful, and this may prevent us from achieving what we had set out to. Likewise, when we feel grief, life has been interrupted by a loss which has brought about a significant negative change for us. This resonates with Nussbaum's notion that emotions are upheavals of thought marking our lives as uneven, uncertain and prone to reversal.[21] In describing her response to her mother's death she writes:

> When I grieve, I do not first of all coolly embrace the proposition, 'My wonderful mother is dead,' and then set about grieving. No,

19 Nussbaum, *Upheavals of Thought*, pp. 30–3.

20 Oatley, K. and Johnson-Laird, P. N., 1995, 'The communicative theory of emotions: empirical tests, mental models and implications for social interaction', in Martin, L. L. and Tesser, A. (eds), *Striving and Feeling: Interactions among Goals, Affect and Self-regulation*, Mahwah, NJ: Erlbaum, pp. 363–93.

21 Nussbaum, *Upheavals of Thought*, p. 1.

the real full recognition of that terrible event (as many times as I recognize it) is the upheaval. It is as I described it: like putting a nail into my stomach.[22]

It is important to note that the judgement does not precede the grieving. It is once her mother's death is acknowledged that the upheaval occurs. 'The very act of assent is itself a tearing of my self-sufficient condition. Knowing can be violent, given the truths that are there to be known.'[23] So in acknowledging the facts or truth of a situation, it becomes felt as part of who we are both cognitively and physiologically. The judgement itself is the cognitive process which leads to a felt 'violent' conclusion. In this dramatic illustration of how 'knowing can be violent', the outcome of the judgement rips deep into a person's being, and both the complexity and pain of the human experience of the emotion of grief is at once realized. When the judgement alters, so does the emotion. But the emotion related to this particular acknowledgement of truth is nonetheless dramatic and communicates something profound about the person as well as their sense of loss.

It is the combination of cognition, predispositions, goals, motives and judgements which makes emotion so significant in human nature. Each of these elements is part of our unique personalities, and so our emotional expression is an integral part of who we are and our uniqueness as human beings.

Emotions and Narrative

So far we have learned from cognitive theories of emotion that they are a product of a complex appraisal process which involves not only an object or situation, but also its relevance and significance to the achievement of our plans and goals. But to reduce emotions to a product of a cognitive appraisal process is in danger of denying the full extent of their range and the powerful impact they have on our lived experience, personality and how others experience us. Not

---

22 Nussbaum, *Upheavals of Thought*, p. 45.
23 Nussbaum, *Upheavals of Thought*, p. 45.

all of our emotional experiences can be rationalized in this way. Sometimes we have conflicting emotions, sometimes we feel sad when there is no definite event, situation or loss of goal to cause it. Emotions can be contagious, we laugh with others when we are not always sure what they are laughing about. They are the barometer of our sense of well-being and the main concern of our psychological health. To understand the emotional life of a person is to understand the person.

But while emotions are very much part of an experience in the present moment and influence decision-making and response from one situation to another, the anticipation of emotions also play an important role in the choices we make, and are a powerful determinant of the course of a life story. In general, people plan and engineer their lives to maximize pleasurable experiences and avoid negative ones; a point McAdams draws attention to in his claim that emotions are the supreme motivators in life.[24] In recognizing that emotions are motivators, their role in influencing the personal narrative becomes more apparent. The desire to experience positive affect directs not only everyday decision-making but also major life choices. We choose careers, partners, friends, leisure activities and the places to live in primarily on the basis of what we believe will give us contentment and happiness. Furthermore, we base such decisions on our previous experience of happiness and sadness in our lives. In other words, we draw on our personal narrative made up of a sequence of scenes of emotional significance to inform the choices we make regarding our future. This review process begins with our earliest memories and ends with the present.

The role of emotion in determining which scenes are stored and our subsequent decision-making led psychologists to consider the importance of emotional scenes for understanding personality. This was developed in Tomkins'[25] script theory, which proposed that our memory stores the scenes of positive and negative emotion

24 McAdams, D. P., 2002, *The Person* (3rd edn), New York: John Wiley & Sons, p. 638.

25 Tomkins, S. S., 1979, 'Script theory', in Howe Jr, H. E. and Dienstbier, R. A. (eds), *Nebraska Symposium on Motivation* (Vol 26), Lincoln, NE: University of Nebraska Press, pp. 201–36.

which make up the drama of our lives. Each scene is an organized whole which has places, people, time, actions and feelings integrated within it. Tomkins argued that the primary structural elements of personality are these internalized scenes and scripts, with scripts being the patterns we discern between the various scenes. Furthermore, he became convinced that not only were scenes and scripts essential to understanding personality, but that the story itself was 'the thing'. Carlson[26] related the scenes to emotions more explicitly, and proposed that certain kinds of scenes occur repeatedly, and we group and discern families of scenes. As we reflect on these patterns, we begin to make sense of the relations between the different scenes and groupings and develop our individual scripts. These enable us to organize and make sense of our lives and devise the plot of our continuing story according to our own unique script. In Tomkins' model, these internalized scenes and scripts shape our consciousness and determine our behaviour so we might understand the differences between individuals in terms of the kinds of scenes and scripts that each of us internalize.

But it is not only our personal narrative which assumes importance in our pleasure-seeking decision-making process; cultural narratives also influence our choices. One industry which has exploited this pleasure-seeking tendency is advertising, which sets out to convince us that owning certain products, living a particular lifestyle and paying attention to our appearance in a prescribed way guarantees happiness. Faith narratives are also influential in this respect. The Christian narrative of the hope of salvation influences our personal narrative, such that daily decision-making, responses and life choices become a product of the anticipated joy of the kingdom of God. Thus emotions have a constructive role within this account in the creation of a personal narrative directing the plot of our story. But emotions are also influential in the development of cultural narrative and the collective narratives of social groups, as well as being a primary motivator in the adoption and integration of faith narratives.

26 Carlson, R., 'Studies in script theory: I. Adult analogs of a childhood nuclear scene', *Journal of Personality and Social Psychology*, 40 (1981), pp. 501–10.

The adoption and integration of faith narratives can be aligned with the research into commitment scripts. These scripts are defined as a 'life program or goal that promises the reward of intense positive affect'[27] with our tendency to seek positive affect understood as the prime motivator. Adopting a commitment script leads to a life which is focused on an inspirational vision and a lifelong investment in accomplishing this, or at least making a significant contribution to it. The promise of joy, happiness or a better world motivates the person and guides them so that they prioritize one cultural narrative or meta-narrative over another, and integrate this into their personal narrative. Often, people who adopt a commitment script have a strong commitment to an internalized narrative, which suggests that they have a vocation or personal sense of destiny to do good things and make a positive contribution to the world. Even when faced with challenges and repeated episodes of negative affect, a person with this script remains steadfastly orientated to their goal, frequently sustained by a clear and convincing belief system. A commitment script does not ensure immunity from negative affect. How we respond to the negative episodes and setbacks in life has implications for life satisfaction, self-esteem, a sense of coherence in life and risk of depression.[28]

Redemptive sequences are prominent in personal narratives of commitment. These are sequences that transform negative events into good outcomes. It is unsurprising that a redemptive sequence is a powerful thread in the narrative of reformed drug addicts and ex-prisoners. Although this has not been researched with people coming to faith, it is likely that redemptive sequences will be a prominent theme in their narrative of key life story scenes too. In contrast to redemptive sequences, we also experience contamination sequences when an emotionally positive experience goes wrong and then becomes associated with negative emotion. When these sequences are prominent in the life story, then a person is more

27 McAdams, *The Person*, p. 640.
28 McAdams, D. P. and Bowman, P. T., 2001, 'Narrating life's turning points: redemption and contamination' in McAdams, D. P., Josselson, R. and Lieblich, A. (eds), *Turns in the Road: Narrative Studies of Lives in Transition*, Washington, DC: American Psychological Association.

likely to suffer from depression, lower life satisfaction and sense of life coherence, and low self-esteem. The prominence of either of these sequences and the emotional tone associated with them plays a fundamental role in the construction of the life story and also which scripts and scenes constitute a person's personality.[29]

Every personal narrative has a characteristic emotional tone which can range from simply very positive to extreme negativity, with a blend of these extremes in varying proportions in between. However, the overall emotional feel of a personal narrative is not only determined by the events themselves, but by the interpretation of the events by the person constructing their narrative. McAdams suggests that our emotional dispositions influence the emotional tone of our life narrative.[30] A number of studies argue that positive affectivity and negative affectivity are the emotional cores of extraversion and neuroticism respectively. It seems that those who score highly on neuroticism are more likely to have personal narratives with a more negative emotional tone. All of this reinforces the way in which emotions are integrated into our personality, personal identity and our personal narrative. They are part of the core of human being and human functioning, but how we manage and regulate them is another important aspect of being human, for this also determines how others experience us and our personality.

29 McAdams and Bowman, 'Narrating life's turning points'.

30 McAdams, D. P., Anyidoho, N. A., Brown, C. Huang, Y. T., Kaplan, B. and Machado, M. A, 'Traits and stories: links between dispositional and narrative features of personality', *Journal of Personality*, 72 (4) (2004), pp. 761–84.

8

Self-Regulation, Emotion and Narrative

In the story of the prodigal son (Luke 15.11–32), self-regulation, emotion and narrative are key elements. The younger brother is impatient for his inheritance; he both anticipates and desires the pleasure that he believes will come from spending his share of his father's wealth and pursuing a hedonistic lifestyle. He knows his goal and has planned how he will achieve it. His motivation for achieving a new life in a distant country where he can party is most certainly associated with the negative feelings he has about his current situation. In this way, the younger son typifies one of the well-established relationships between emotion and behaviour: that 'behaviour pursues emotion',[1] positive emotion in particular. The younger son wants to do something to make himself *feel* better.

In Luke's Gospel, the phrase 'there he squandered his property in dissolute living' (Luke 15.13) signifies the type of behaviour that the prodigal son indulged in as he pursued his desire for happiness. Apparently he made little, if any, attempt to self-regulate his behaviour. We read that 'he spent everything' (Luke 15.14). However, before long, his hedonistic living has turned sour and he is consumed by the negative emotions of guilt and shame. The son feels unworthy to be called his father's son. In response he again goes in pursuit of a better, more positive life than his current one, this time deciding that he would be better off returning home and offering

---

1 Geyer, A. L. and Baumeister, R. F., 2005, 'Religion, morality and self control', in Paloutzian, R. F. and Park, C. L. (eds), *Handbook of the Psychology of Religion and Spirituality*, New York/London: Guilford Press, pp. 418–27.

himself as one of his father's workers than continuing his life in this foreign land.

Before reflecting on the end of the story, there are a number of significant points to note regarding what it means to be human. First, the parable emphasizes a view of human nature which asserts that people are free to make important choices. The father in the parable grants the prodigal son the freedom to take his inheritance early and to spend it in whichever way he chooses. Second, the parable does not indicate the antecedent to the son's desire to leave his father. It may be due to some difficulty in his relationship with his elder brother, he could be at the point of a late adolescent crisis,[2] or he may feel the need to separate from the family to assert his own identity. Whatever the motivation driving his behaviour, the parable makes it explicit that the son takes responsibility for the state he ends up in as a hired hand feeding pigs. Finally, the son confesses his sinfulness to his father. Human beings have the capacity to engage in self-reflection. The self can objectify and evaluate the self. Moral emotions such as disgust, shame and guilt are aroused in response to this process. As the son reflects on himself, his evaluation of himself is harsh but valid. He has fallen short of the standards he wishes to live by, and not acted in accordance with the moral framework that he believes is acceptable. He has failed to exercise sufficient self-control, having spent his inheritance on instant gratification which has left him in a desperate state.

But the parable is not only a warning about aspects of human nature, it is also a parable of restoration and redemption. What was lost is found. Before the son reaches home, his father has already seen him in the distance and runs towards him to embrace and kiss him. Jesus speaks of the father being filled with compassion. The moving restoration of the relationship between father and son in the narrative highlights the transforming role of grace and forgiveness when people fail to self-regulate. The empathetic father knows the deep struggles of temptation and self-will. In the son's

---

2 Marcia, J. E., 1998, 'Optimal development from an Erikson perspective', in Freidman, H. S. (ed.), *Encyclopaedia of Mental Health* (Vol. 3), San Diego: Academic Press, quoted in Santrock, J. W., 1999, *Life Span Development* (7th edn), McGraw-Hill, p. 372.

confession, it is apparent that he is acutely aware of the discrepancy in his behaviour between both his own standards and those of his father. He feels unworthy of any love or respect. His self-esteem and sense of personal well-being have been damaged by his lack of self-control. In returning home, the experience of his father's love and affirmation underscored by the celebration are key facilitators in the restoration of the son as a person of worth. The miracle of his father's grace and forgiveness enables the son to continue and integrate a redemptive sequence into his personal narrative. In the richness of this familiar parable, significant truths about the divine economy of grace and forgiveness and the very nature of God are revealed; as is one of the universal struggles of human experience, which many claim to be a significant cause of human suffering and society's ills: that of self-regulation.

This chapter will examine psychological approaches to self-regulation. The ability to self-regulate is an important topic for any theological understanding of sin and Christian virtue. The personal struggle to manage and/or control thoughts, feelings, impulses and behaviour is what Paul refers to in his letter to the Romans (7.14–25), 'For I do not do what I want, but I do the very thing I hate'. It leads to the experience of a divided self: torn between what one aspires to or knows to be right, and impulses and temptations which draw the self towards that which holds the promise of positive emotion in the immediate or near future but may lead us awry in the long term. The psychological struggle of the self (the I-self) to keep itself (the Me-self) in check in the Christian tradition is the struggle to be holy and obtain the promise of salvation. However, within Christianity self-control does not depend only upon psychological resources. It is a fruit of the Spirit, which strengthens and directs the self in its pursuit of holiness and Christlike living. Hence, the influence of faith on self-control and its influence on the psychological processes involved has been the subject of recent studies in the psychology of religion.

Self-Regulation in Psychology and Christianity

An analysis of the state of the world might easily conclude that the world's ills are largely due to our inability to self-regulate our behaviour and emotions. Baumeister, Heatherton and Tice go so far as to claim that 'self-regulation failure is the major social pathology of the present time'.[3] The association between self-regulatory factors and destructive and negative outcomes is evident. Alcoholism, cigarette smoking and drug addiction entail an inability to control a desire for pleasure-inducing substances and each result in health problems. Obesity may reflect a failure to manage the eating of sugary or fatty foods and maintain a healthy diet. Failing to regulate the desire to accumulate material possessions and spending money excessively to satisfy immediate wants frequently also exemplifies a lack of the ability to self-regulate and may cause debt and relationship problems.

Self-regulation is not simply concerned with managing desires, there are a number of different causes and effects of poor self-regulation. Our failure to deal adequately with negative or unwanted feelings such as anger, guilt or envy can also lead to a range of negative personal and relationship outcomes. Hence relationships are frequently damaged by a failure to regulate ourselves both emotionally and in our behaviour: poor self-regulation of frustration and anger may lead to violence and abuse. Underachievement in some cases may be associated with a lack of self-discipline regarding study or application. A diminished ability to regulate sexual desire and behaviour is often linked to sexually transmitted disease, abuse and dysfunctional relationships. The list could continue. The inability to self-regulate predisposes us to act in ways which harm ourselves and others. In short, to sin.

An account of self-regulation provides an important point of convergence between psychology and theology. It is regarded as necessary for the ultimate flourishing of human beings and the good functioning of society. Without it, human beings could not

---

3 Baumeister, R. F., Heatherton and Tice, D., 1994, *Losing Control: How and Why People Fail at Self-Regulation*, San Diego, CA: Academic Press.

live as they do, instead we would be living in a state of anarchy or social chaos. Failures in self-regulation are associated with our sense of morality. Human beings are assumed to have the freedom and capability to control themselves and be morally responsible for their behaviour. This assumption is also present in the Christian tradition. The theological understanding of discipleship includes adopting a life of discipline and self-regulation. In the act of confession we acknowledge that we have failed to manage our behaviour and be obedient to God, and instead have allowed our selfish desires to direct our actions. There is an expectation that Christians can manage any inappropriate desires and passions and control their thoughts, feelings and behaviour in accordance with God's will. For Christians, self-management is a necessary virtue in their struggle with sin and a desire to live a holy and godly life.

Psychology has drawn upon the religious understandings of virtue and shown a somewhat surprising interest in the notion that self-control is a virtue. Baumeister and Exline[4] examined the contrast between virtues and vices as a means of establishing the centrality of self-control in moral behaviour. The seven deadly sins provided a framework for the examination of the vices as failures in self-control. Gluttony concerns overeating and indulging in other pleasures to excess; the lack of regulation in eating being a common example of a failure of self-control. Sloth or laziness is a failure to override the urge to stop working or desire to do something other than work. The three sins of greed, lust and envy all involve inappropriate desires for the goals of money and material things, sexual satisfaction and the possessions or advantage of others respectively. The sin of anger when roused also requires managing so that this powerful emotion does not lead to sinful behaviour. Last, pride demonstrates the inability to overcome the urge to think well of oneself. Hence, each sin is explained by an inability to manage behaviour or thinking which leads to transgressing God's commandments and will.

---

4 Baumeister, R. F. and Exline, J. J., 'Virtue, personality and social relations: self control as the moral muscle', *Journal of Personality*, 67 (1999), pp. 1165–94.

In contrast, many virtues are associated with self-control. They can be interpreted as the self stifling some of its impulses and performing socially acceptable or God-pleasing behaviour instead. Thomas Aquinas' cardinal virtues have been used effectively to illustrate the connection between virtue and self-control. Prudence, whereby we weigh up long-term implications and risks before making decisions and acting out behaviours, suggests an ability to forgo immediate gain or satisfaction for the sake of greater benefit later on. The association between delayed gratification and self-control has been well documented in the literature, and will be considered later in the chapter.[5] Justice requires the self-control to do what is morally right and temperance involves moderate rather than excessive behaviour achieved through a measure of self-control. Finally, fortitude concerns holding fast in adversity, pain or passion, which requires overcoming the urge to compromise and reduce or eliminate the pain currently experienced. In this compelling analysis both virtue and sin can be explained by the exercise or not of self-control.

The Significance of Self-Control

At the beginning of their book *Will Power: Rediscovering Our Greatest Strength*, Baumeister and Tierney claim that '[w]hen psychologists isolate the personal qualities that predict "positive outcomes" in life, they consistently find two traits: intelligence and self-control ... We think that research into will power and self-control is psychology's best hope for contributing to human welfare.'[6] It is undoubtedly the case that many people feel overwhelmed by the ever-increasing number of temptations they face. The use of computer technology alone provides numerous distractions from work or any other important task. The lure of social networking, online shopping, sexual gratification, gambling and

---

5 See Mischel, W., Schoda, Y. and Peake, P. K., 'Delay of gratification in children', *Science*, 244 (1988), pp. 933–8.

6 Baumeister, R. F. and Tierney, J., 2012, *Will Power: Rediscovering Our Greatest Strength*, London: Allen Lane, p. 1.

much more is available at our fingertips. The easy availability of alcohol, food and sex signifies a world of temptation. Self-control is necessary for negotiating most of our waking hours.

In a study of 200 men and women in Germany,[7] in which they wore bleepers that sounded randomly seven times a day as a prompt for them to report whether or not they were experiencing some kind of desire at the time or had done so recently, about 50 per cent reported some desire at the moment of the bleeper and another 25 per cent said a desire had been felt in the past few minutes. Many of the desires were ones they were actively trying to resist. The study concluded that people spend at least 20 per cent of their waking day resisting temptations. The most common temptations were the desire to eat, followed by the urge to sleep, and then for leisure – such as taking a break from work. Sexual urges were next on the list of most resisted desires, followed by checking emails, going on social networking sites, surfing the internet and watching television. It is interesting to note that, overall, the participants only succumbed to about a sixth of the temptations and reported using various strategies to resist their desires, from finding a distraction, doing something new or simply toughing it out. This applied to such urges as taking a nap, sex and the urge to spend money, but they were less successful at resisting food and soft drinks. It was also the case that they failed to resist watching television, using the internet and other media nearly half of the time.

One final study is worth noting in evidence for the role of self-control in human flourishing.[8] A longitudinal study of 1,000 children in New Zealand from birth to age 32 revealed that children who scored highly on self-control in a number of different measures, and in reports from parents, teachers and self-reports as adults, had

---

7 Hofmann, W., Baumeister, R. F., Förster, G. and Vohs, K. D., 'Everyday temptations: an experience sampling study of desire, conflict, and self-control', *Journal of Personality and Social Psychology*, 102(6) (2012), pp. 1318–35.

8 Moffitt, T. E., Arseneault, L., Belsky, D., Dickson, N., Hancox, R. J., Harrington, H., Houts, R., Poulton, R. Roberts, B. W., Ross, S., Sears, M. R., Thomson, W. M. and Caspi, A., 'A gradient of childhood self-control predicts health, wealth, and public safety', *Proceedings of the National Academy of Sciences* (2011), www.pnas.org/content/early/2011/01/20/1010076108.

better physical health, which included lower rates of obesity, and fewer sexually transmitted diseases. Self-control was not correlated with lower rates of depression, but a low level of self-control was associated with a proneness to alcohol and drug-related problems. Children with poor self-control were also more likely to be in lower-paid jobs, have more children being brought up in single-parent households, and had a higher probability of spending time in prison. Intelligence, race and social class also correlated with these factors, but the effect was still significant when these were taken into account. Furthermore, in a follow-up study which looked at siblings in the study, the sibling with lower self-control during childhood fared worse in life.

A Psychological Perspective on Self-Control: What is Will Power?

The ability to exercise self-control is viewed as one of the most difficult practical challenges for every human being; Plato noted in *The Republic* that 'the first and best victory is to conquer self'. For the purposes of this discussion the psychological definition, 'Self-regulation involves any effort on the part of an agent to alter its own responses',[9] will be used, because it allows for a broad framework of exploration which can encompass personality and narrative as well as more detailed cognitive and biological approaches. Clearly, there are ambiguities in the term. Is self-regulation regulation of the self or by the self? For the sake of clarity in considering self-regulation, I view the self as having the agency to modify its responses in terms of emotions, thoughts and behaviours. But it is important to bear in mind that the regulation of these responses is integral to person-ality and also shapes personal identity: personality traits, goals and motivation, and personal narrative all influence self-control. Hence the development of our ability to exercise control is influenced by our genes, parenting, moral development and self-awareness.

---

9 Baumeister, Heatherton and Tice, *Losing Control*.

The Basic Components of Self-Regulation

For people to achieve any measure of self-regulation, three things are seen as necessary.[10] First, there has to be a standard or some kind of ideal, or notion, of a moral framework. Any control has to bring us in line with our subjective aspirations in this respect. Generally, we strive to behave in accordance with the protocol set by the standards we want to conform to. Some of these are external to us, for example the law of the country; while others are internal standards we set for ourselves – for example, to maintain a healthy diet, never get into debt, or always be honest. The phrase 'I have let myself down' can apply to falling short of these standards and is accompanied by feelings of guilt and a lowering of self-esteem.

Second, we can only know that we have not regulated ourselves well, or indeed regulated ourselves at all, if we are aware of our thoughts, feelings and actions. In other words, self-regulation depends on self-awareness and self-monitoring. People often fail to regulate their behaviour when their self-awareness is impaired. So, if they are under the influence of alcohol or drugs, tired or stressed, they are less likely to exercise self-control. It is not surprising that it is late at night that diets are often broken and sexual acts which are later regretted occur, as do the most violent and impulsive crimes.[11] The converse is also the case; in situations where self-awareness is increased, self-control is enhanced. Diener and Wallbom found that in the presence of mirrors people were less likely to cheat, as the mirrors increased their self-awareness and had a positive impact on self-control.[12]

Finally, self-regulation requires effort as it involves altering the responses we feel inclined to carry out or the thoughts or feelings we are predisposed to. Our dispositions arise from an amalgamation of a number of factors including physiology, learning,

---

10 Geyer, A. L. and Baumeister, R. F., 2005, 'Religion, morality and self control', in Paloutzian, R. F. and Park, C. L. (eds), *Handbook of the Psychology of Religion and Spirituality*, New York/London: Guilford Press, p. 414.

11 Baumeister, R. F. and Heatherton, T. F., 'Self-regulation failure: an overview', *Psychological Inquiry*, 7 (1) (1996), pp. 1–15.

12 Diener, E. and Wallbom, M., 'Effects of self-awareness on autonormative behaviour', *Journal of Research in Personality*, 10 (1976), pp. 107–11.

socialization and culture. The exercise of self-control requires the ability to change or inhibit these natural tendencies in order to achieve a personal goal. Thus, self-control is a psychological intentional response which is directed from within the self to influence the self and the self's response in a particular situation. Moreover, the success or failure of this attempt to alter a response is entirely subjective. To resist surfing the internet for four hours might rate as highly successful for one person and for another it may be interpreted as just one small step on a long journey which aspires to reduce surfing the internet to one hour a day.

Failure to exercise self-regulation generally takes two forms. We either do not apply sufficient effort to the enterprise (under-regulation) or the effort we make is ineffective or counterproductive (misregulation).[13] An example of misregulation might be when someone attempting to give up alcohol has a lapse because they believe that just one drink will help them relax and feel better. This present concern is more important than quitting alcohol. However, they might subsequently feel guilty about this lapse, which could cause further stress and anxiety.

The underlying assumption in all studies of self-regulation is that human beings have the capacity to change or modify their behaviour. It depends on our ability to set goals and standards for our behaviour, monitor our behaviour against these, and then modify it in order to reach a goal or conform to a particular standard.

How Self-Regulation Functions

How do we do this? Carver proposes that self-regulation can be understood by feedback loop systems which provide us with information regarding the goals which we set ourselves and how we are performing in relation to these.[14] The underpinning model of

---

13 Baumeister, R. F. and Heatherton, T. F., 'Self-regulation failure: past, present and future', *Psychological Inquiry*, 7(1) (1996), pp. 90–8.

14 Carver, C., 2004, 'Self regulation of action and affect', in Baumeister, R. F. and Vohls, K. D. (eds), *The Handbook of Self-Regulation*, New York/London: Guilford Press.

the person in this approach emphasizes that we are essentially goal directed and our lives are structured around a hierarchy of these goals, each of which acts as a standard by which we judge our responses. The relationship between goals in the hierarchy can be illustrated by a personal example, such as I have a goal to be a loving, caring wife and mother, but I also have a goal to be on time when meeting my son from school. My goal of being a caring mother is in some measure attained by the more mundane goal of meeting my son on time. Carver suggests that most of our activities are goal directed and we are constantly evaluating our achievement and then regulating our behaviour in the light of our performance. There is a strong emotional component to this. If our progress in achieving our goal is blocked or impaired then this gives rise to negative emotions, and if progress is better than anticipated then we experience positive feelings. This feedback information influences our self-regulation behaviour with regard to achieving our goals. Furthermore, this information is part of a feedback loop which monitors discrepancies between our response and the standard or goal we have set ourselves. In general, we act to reduce any discrepancy between our performance and the standard or goal we set ourselves. When we achieve this we are described as having success in life. The association between self-control and achieving goals has received considerable attention in the psychological literature, with happiness and well-being noted as being linked to self-control and achieving our personal goals.[15]

Most of us set admirable goals and high standards of behaviour with every intention of meeting them, but on occasions we fail to achieve them. It is also the case that some of us can regulate our behaviour to an impressive extent in some contexts, but not others. This is often demonstrated in public life. For example, in the recent child abuse scandals a priest might have exercised laudable behaviour in meeting the demands of the parish with grace and patience,

---

15 Baumeister, R. F., Leith, K. P., Muraven, M. and Bratslavsky, E., 1998, 'Self-regulation as a key to success in life', in Pushkar, D., Bukowski, W. M., Schwartzman, A. E., Strack, D. M. and White, D. R. (eds), *Improving Competence across the Lifespan*, New York, Boston, Dordrecht, Moscow: Kluwer Academic/Plenum Publishers, pp. 117–32.

but was for many years failing to self-regulate the satisfaction of his sexual desires. This incongruity is described as a difference between the self-regulatory will and self-regulatory competence.[16]

Individual Differences and the Development of Self-Control

Individual differences in willpower and self-control appear early in childhood. Mischel[17] conducted a number of interesting research studies to demonstrate not only the effect of willpower, but also how in children a measure of their willpower can be used to predict a variety of outcomes in later life. Young children were faced with the following dilemma: they were brought into a room and shown a cookie and offered a deal before they were left in the room alone. They could either eat the cookie whenever they liked or resist until the experimenter returned and then get a greater reward. Some children ate the cookie straightaway, but those children who chose to resist and wait until the experimenter returned after a maximum of 20 minutes used distraction as a strategy to control their urge to eat the cookie and were rewarded with two cookies.

Although this might appear a trivial and simple psychological situation, it was found to be surprisingly diagnostic. The number of seconds children waited at four years of age made it possible to predict how well they could self-regulate later in life, as well as their competencies on a number of social, emotional and cognitive competencies. This suggests that our ability to remain patient and obtain the greater prize or achieve our goal remains stable and persists into adulthood.

A final factor in the development of self-control is the ability of the self to be reflexive. In order for regulation to occur we have already established that the self needs to observe the self: the self (the I) observes the self (the Me). A number of contemporary

---

16 Mischel. W. and Aydul, O., 2004, 'Willpower in a cognitive-affective processing system', in Baumeister, R. F. and Vohls, K. D. (eds), *The Handbook of Self-Regulation*, New York/London: Guilford Press.

17 Mischel and Aydul, 'Willpower', pp. 107–8.

psychologists suggest that one of the primary functions of such self-awareness is to regulate behaviour. In particular social interactions when the I can observe the Me as an actor and reflect on it, then the I can start to regulate the way it responds and presents itself to others. This begins to emerge at the age of two years, and is supported by the emotions of pride and shame, as the child feels pride in their actions when others approve of them and shame or guilt when met with disapproval.[18]

The Self-Regulatory System

But how do we operate our self-regulatory system? Mischel and Aydul explain self-regulation in terms of a hot/cool system. The cool system can be thought of as the cognitive, contemplative system, which does not have an emotional component as such and is emotionally neutral. It is the system that reasons, is rational and generates goal orientated and strategic behaviour. It is termed the 'know' system. In other words, this can be interpreted as the voice of conscience. It is our internal reasoning that leads us to regret our behaviour and feel guilty or will set us back in achieving our ultimate desire. In contrast, the hot system is essentially an automatic system which is very responsive and governed by reflexive stimulus-responsive reactions. It is dominated by emotion and generates simple, impulsive and 'quick approach-avoidance responses'.[19] In other words, it is the 'go' system and very much in tune with our urges. This system dominates in young children, but the two systems are interconnected and, as the interconnection between thinking and emotion matures, so the relationship between the two systems becomes more intricate and complex. Self-control is conceived of as possible by the cool system circumventing the hot system through inter-system connections of hot spots to cool nodes. It is important to note that this model explains the impact of stress on self-regulation, as stress is seen to affect the balance between the

18 Rochat, P., 'Five levels of self-awareness as they unfold in early life', *Consciousness and Cognition*, 12 (2003), pp. 717–31.

19 Mischel and Aydul, 'Willpower', p. 109.

two systems. For low to moderate levels of stress, the operation of the cool system is enhanced and we can achieve self-control, but at high stress levels the cool system is attenuated and may even shut down. Hence, the hot system becomes more active as the levels of stress increase and this explains why we find it more difficult to self-regulate when we experience high levels of stress. Although these models may appear formulaic and mechanistic, they have begun to demystify willpower and describe some of the processes which underlie it.

To summarize: from the range of psychological perspectives discussed several points emerge. First, self-control is understood as a capacity which depends on our ability to monitor and modify our behaviour to meet the standards and goals we set ourselves or those set by society. It requires the I self to observe the Me self and make an appraisal of itself. There are individual differences in regulatory strength and this is apparent from an early age, suggesting that self-control is a personality trait with a genetic component and that the strength of the predisposition varies from person to person. The process of self-control involves a feedback loop which provides information concerning any discrepancy between our responses and the standards and goals we set out to maintain or achieve. A hot/cool system is also involved in determining how we respond to the various situations we encounter, with the cool system being rational and cognitive, and the hot system fast and emotional. The system is sensitive to stress but also influenced by how we appraise and construe the situations we are faced with, especially in relation to our goals.

Self-Control as a Limited Resource

There are a number of factors which influence our ability to exercise the self-control necessary to achieve our goals, especially those which are challenging, take time and involve considerable self-investment to achieve. It appears that how much value we put on the reward, how much trust we have in the provider of the reward, and also the level of our self-belief that we can achieve this, influence the level of self-control we exercise. In other words, our beliefs about our self-efficacy influence the level of self-control we exercise. These factors also go some way to explain why it is possible for some people to give up their addictions, or resist the temptations that threaten their cherished values and desires, while there are those who appear to be vulnerable to self-defeating behaviours and rarely achieve their aspirations.

It appears that as we exercise self-control, we use up some of our psychological resources. Although it is replenished, it takes time, and therefore subsequent demands on us might be impaired.[20] Baumeister suggests that this is analogous to a temporary state of muscle fatigue. Studies showed that participants moving from a task or situation which required emotional control to a different kind of task altogether showed a decrease in performance on the subsequent task compared with those who had not been involved in the self-control task. So, for example, participants who were required to suppress forbidden thoughts showed less persistence in solving anagrams than a control group. Likewise, participants who were required to eat radishes while resisting the temptation to eat freshly baked cookies persisted for a shorter time on a problem-solving task than those who had not endured such temptation.

The task involving resisting temptation involved participants making a conscious choice to resist eating the cookies. It seems that making such choices also draws on the reserves used in self-control.[21] These findings provide significant insights into why self-control breaks down in multiple areas at the same time, and also how it can be managed more effectively. It is very common for us to be overambitious in the area of self-improvement. New Year resolutions are often a list of good intentions, such as giving up various vices and taking on new activities and attitudes. If all such projects demand energy from a limited resource, then it follows that the more we intend to address at any one time the more likely we are to fail. This is an important consideration in our discipleship

---

20 Geyer and Baumeister, 'Religion, morality and self control', pp. 415–16.

21 Baumeister, R. F., Bratslavsky, E., Muraven, M. and Tice, D. M., 'Ego depletion: is the active self a limited resource?', *Journal of Personality and Social Psychology*, 74 (1998), pp. 1252–65.

as we seek to become more Christlike. We can so easily be over-whelmed by a sense of failure as we strive to reach several goals in a number of areas of our life all at once, but by focusing on one or two areas for attention and development, we are more likely to succeed and feel encouraged by our progress. If making choices also depletes this resource, then this may have a negative effect on our moral reasoning and subsequent self-control. A demanding day, when physical and psychological resources are low, can easily result in the breakdown of self-regulation; be it in controlling our emotions such as anger, our sexual behaviour or drinking behaviours.

Evidence of the Relationship between Religion and Self-Control

Psychology has recently begun to examine how religious beliefs and behaviours help those who are trying to exercise self-control. Its approach is clearly stated by Geyer and Baumeister:

> We do not presume to assess the validity of religious beliefs about supernatural processes here. We do not intend to imply anything about the possibility of religion providing supernatural help to self-control. Rather we are concerned with how beliefs and behaviours commonly associated with religion may be helpful to people trying to exercise control.[22]

This neutral stance treats Christian beliefs and practices as a meaning-making system which influences goals, life choices and behaviour. It seeks to discover the effects of religion on self-control and the processes that operate in exercising it. Clearly, for Christians, the place of prayer in a disciplined life, the impact of God as a source of strength and the role of the Holy Spirit, to name but a few, are realities in the Christian life which are integrated into their experience of self-control. That said, it is important that research in this area can provide helpful insights for ministry.

---

22 Geyer and Baumeister, 'Religion, morality and self control', pp. 415–16.

Religion provides standards. The Ten Commandments are a series of laws that indicate what we should and should not do. In the New Testament Jesus provides a model or pattern of behaviour and response for us to follow or imitate. The goal of Christian discipleship is to become Christlike expressed in the great commandment to 'love the Lord your God with all your heart, and with all your soul, and with all your strength, and with all your mind and your neighbour as yourself' (Luke 10.27). The New Testament provides a moral vision for the Christian life. There is an emphasis on holiness and self-denial. Sacrificing self-interest and self-denial is a sign of virtue although in contemporary society these are often viewed as countercultural.

Religion also serves as a motivator of self-control. The fact that God desires us to live and behave in a particular way is sufficient to motivate many believers to adopt what they perceive as essential in conforming to God's will. Self-control and virtuous living is also associated with the promise of salvation. The hope and promise of everlasting life is a strong motivating factor which enables people to transcend the immediate temptations of life and focus on more abstract goals. The opposite is also true. Many people associate immoral behaviour with the threat of hell and are motivated by the fear of severe judgement.

There are many other motivating factors for living the Christian life. The understanding that our lives are to be lived in a way which brings glory to God, blesses God and reflects God's love is a powerful motivator for many Christians; it affects their motivation for even the mundane tasks of life. As George Herbert suggests in his hymn, 'who cleans a room as for thy sake makes that and the action clean'.[23] The significance attached to the goals of the Christian faith and motivating power of God's love contribute to religion being both a potent and unique source of motivation for people's efforts at self-control.

One of the striking benefits associated with religion is the way it enables us to cope with feelings of distress and sadness. We have little control over feeling emotionally distressed or other negative

---

23 Herbert, G., 1633, 'The Elixir'.

emotions. When we experience these, the temptation of a little self-indulgence to change our emotional state is often acted upon.[24] Failure of our self-control is frequently associated with an attempt to relieve a negative mood. Geyer and Baumeister's[25] suggestion that 'behaviour pursues emotion' is an important insight. People do what they believe will produce positive feelings and avoid or alleviate negative feelings. The Christian tradition offers guidelines as to what we will find satisfying and what kind of lifestyle may lead to positive emotions such as joy, peace and thankfulness. It also offers teaching on the dangers of pursuing selfish desires in pursuit of satisfaction and happiness. Furthermore, faith in God's loving presence, omnipotence and benevolence provides a significant resource to draw upon when faced with challenging or distressing situations. The comfort derived from the knowledge that life has meaning and significance, even in times of trouble, enables many Christians to maintain their self-control and not be tempted by self-indulgence.

Baumeister, Heatherton and Tice[26] argue that there is a limit to our control which must be recognized. In fact, they suggest that it is counterproductive to believe that we can control those things we cannot, such as impulses. Sinful impulses cannot be eradicated but we can control the behaviour which the impulse urges. Not all Christians would agree with this, although most would acknowledge the work of the Holy Spirit in making the growth in holiness and grace possible. The belief in the work of the Holy Spirit in strengthening us in the struggle for holiness and holy living is important in sustaining many believers. The activity of God in and through our psychological resources enables our will to control the self to be strengthened in accordance with what we believe to be pleasing to God.

---

24 Geyer and Baumeister, 'Religion, morality and self control', pp. 424–5.
25 Geyer and Baumeister, 'Religion, morality and self control', p. 425.
26 Baumeister, Heatherton and Tice, *Losing Control*.

Guilt and Self-Control

Failures in self-control arouse the emotion of guilt. The main interest of psychology is the subjective feeling of guilt; what causes it, and how we respond to it. Guilt is a negative, moral emotion which causes emotional distress different from fear and anger. It is based on the actuality that we are in the wrong, the possibility that we may be wrong or that others may perceive that we are. The guilt we experience when we fail at self-control is caused by perceiving ourselves to be in the wrong. The desire to avoid feelings of guilt is also a very powerful motivator in moral behaviour and self-control.

Psychologists have understood guilt as a motivation for restoring or maintaining relationships.[27] When we feel guilty about upsetting or hurting someone, we might apologize, try to make amends and try not to repeat the action in the future. The standards of behaviour offered by religion and the central emphasis on relationships rooted in love serve to enhance the prosocial effects of guilt in those who hold a Christian faith. Furthermore, for the majority, being a Christian involves participating in the shared life of a Christian community with similar goals of self-control and a degree of moral accountability. An effect of this is to arouse feelings of guilt from monitoring the behaviour of other people in the community and then making comparisons between them and one's self. The belief that God knows all thoughts and deeds, even the very secrets of our hearts, also influences people's behaviour and self-regulation. In all of these examples, guilt functions psychologically as a motivator to avoid behaving in ways viewed as morally wrong. It acts as a warning and a deterrent.

Summary of Psychological Literature

The psychological literature provides a more detailed understanding of the behavioural and psychological processes which are involved in self-control, but fails to place self-control in a context of its broader meaning beyond a utilitarian framework which the

27 Baumeister, R. F., Stillwell, A. M. and Heatherton, T. F., 'Guilt: an interpersonal approach', *Psychological Bulletin*, 115 (2) (1994), pp. 243–67.

discipline so frequently operates in. Psychology's interest in the effects of religion on self-control focuses on how religious beliefs and behaviours help people to exercise self-control and do not extend beyond this. There is no real engagement with the goal of self-control and the motivations which drive it. As Bland states:

> from the psychological literature on self-control we no doubt have a greater understanding of the behavioural and psychological mechanisms operational in self-control, but we lack a compelling and inspirational reason to develop these mechanisms. If utilitarian subjective self-fulfilment and avoidance of pain is my operational motivation for developing self-control then I am left empty.[28]

The suggestion by Baumeister and Exline[29] that self-control is the 'master virtue' is indicative of its role in reducing the suffering of the individual, others and society. However, a Christian understanding of virtue places obedience to God or yielding to God's will as the ultimate virtue, and self-control as the fruit of the Holy Spirit's activity within a person. Furthermore, if as Baumeister states self-control restrains a person's sinful impulses and enables them to avoid temptation, how might this contribute to the Christian vocation to love God, others and self, since it is frequently more difficult to be loving than to restrain impulses which negatively impact on our personal standards or goals?

Theological Reflection

The adoption by psychology of the concepts of vices and virtues in some of its examination of self-regulation draws attention to the way in which the exercise of self-control is identified with goodness, and a failure of self-control with sin and a lack of self-discipline.

---

28 Bland, E. R., 'An appraisal of psychological and religious perspectives of self control', *Journal of Religion and Health*, 47 (2008), pp. 4–16.

29 Baumeister, R. F. and Exline, J. J., 'Virtue, personality and social relations: self control as the moral muscle', *Journal of Personality*, 67 (1999), pp. 1165–94.

Christian discipleship is a response to the call of Jesus to follow him and grow into his likeness. The model of virtue is Jesus. Central to his example is the embodiment of love: love God and others as one loves one's self. It is a life orientated away from self and obedient to God.

Augustine characterized fallen humanity by its neglect of its basic orientation towards God.[30] The abandonment of loving God above all else in favour of loving the self is the cause of human sin and sickness. Augustine believed that at the very core of the self is the will, and that it is the will that becomes faulty. The will foolishly chooses things which are inferior to God, and so sins, or it suffers from the more subtle affliction of causing the person to do what they do not will and not do what they will. For Augustine, the sinner, even though they may know what is good, cannot do it. In this way, he envisages a lack of freedom brought about by the distorted will as it becomes enslaved to sin and loses the freedom which is found through the grace of God. Sin becomes compulsive, and it is only by the reorientation of the will and desire through the grace of God providing a presentation of perfect goodness, and the desire for it identified as the spirit of love,[31] that sin's power is challenged. In this way, freedom is achieved through grace.

The division of the will undoubtedly causes anguish and distress for Augustine,[32] and he looks for an explanation of this inner turmoil in Paul's letter to the Romans (7.22–25). Cook[33] uses the theological understanding of the power of sin from both Augustine and Paul in his theological model of addiction, as he reflects on the experience of enslavement and captivity of self-indulgence. Drawing on McFadyen, who demonstrates in his analysis of the Holocaust and child sexual abuse that 'sin can so permeate the social environment that it engages as willing participants those who

---

30 Innes, R., 1999, *Discourse of the Self: Seeking Wholeness in Theology and Psychology, Religions and Discourse Vol. 4*, Bern: Peter Lang.

31 McFadyen, A., 2000, *Bound to Sin: Abuse, Holocaust and the Christian Doctrine of Sin*, Cambridge, Cambridge University Press, pp. 192–3.

32 Cook, C. C. H., 2006, *Alcohol, Addiction and Christian Ethics*, Cambridge: Cambridge University Press, p. 153.

33 Cook, *Alcohol, Addiction*, pp. 166–70.

are its victims',[34] Cook suggests that the combination of inherited predispositions, social pressures to conform in a drinking culture and the power of habit, leads to people being innocently drawn into drinking patterns which they continue, even though it is detrimental to themselves and their relationships. Addiction, an extreme form of self-regulation failure, can be described as having 'an apparent power'[35] which enslaves people and holds them captive. Hence, as part of our theological reflection on self-regulation, the notion of the divided will and the power of sin to hold people captive resonates with the psychological description of the experience of addiction and temptation more generally, and the difference that can exist between the self-regulatory will and self-regulatory competence. When we strive to live our lives according to our understanding of the gospel and fall prey to temptation and self-indulgence, we experience a division deep within the self, which is so eloquently described by Paul.

Paul goes on to ask 'Who will rescue me from this body of death? Thanks be to God through Jesus Christ our Lord' (Rom. 7.24b–25a). He recognizes that we cannot win this battle alone. It is by allowing the Holy Spirit to work within us that self-control, in line with God's loving purposes, is achieved.

This chapter has explored the psychological and behavioural understanding of self-control and the processes which enable it to be exercised. To understand the complex processes involved in self-regulation we need to know more than how the hot/cool system operates under stress or the major factors influencing the feedback loop which monitors behaviour. The way in which we evaluate ourselves and modify our behaviour cannot be extracted from an understanding of our personality or the moral framework we choose to adopt. Furthermore, our past experiences of self-control, the expectations of others, culture and faith shape this function and the way we assess any discrepancy between our behaviour and our standards or ideals. In this multifaceted understanding of self-control the significance of Christianity's perspective on the practice of self-discipline has an important contribution to make. There is a

34 Cook, *Alcohol, Addiction*, p. 166.
35 Cook, *Alcohol, Addiction*, p. 167.

great deal at stake here. Failure in self-control has been described as a major social pathology of our time.

The Christian faith provides the means of addressing this pathology. It provides a moral framework centred on love for God and others to shape human living. In a world of overwhelming choices and temptations, the tradition offers wisdom on ordering and managing our desires. It orientates us away from self towards God and calls us to strive to live holy lives. The challenge this presents is recognized from the early days of creation. In the story of Adam and Eve, the biblical narrative identifies this as the first sin. Adam and Eve failed to obey God's command not to eat the fruit of the tree of the knowledge of good and evil. They could not resist the temptation of the fruit and the beguiling serpent. The fall was the outcome of a lack of self-control. Our fallen nature can be reduced to a lack of self-control.

The story of the prodigal son provided valuable insight into the consequences of self-control failure, but it also offers the hope of grace. The return of the son to his father offers a rich metaphor for the search for meaning and redemption as they come together in a moment of extraordinary grace and forgiveness. Here the relationship between the father and son illustrates the extravagance of God's love for humanity and his desire to reach out to our fallen world and bring it back to himself through his works of grace. In the prodigal son the power of the father's love operated in and through the psychological processes of the son to bring him home. His spiritual union with his father was never completely broken, and God's redemptive purposes were ultimately fulfilled.

9

Self-Esteem

In his account of Peter's denial of Jesus, Luke notes that after Peter remembered Jesus' words, he wept bitterly (22.54–62). Peter, who had been told by Jesus he was to be 'the rock' on which he would build the Church and who was to be given the keys of heaven and hell, had here clearly failed to meet the standards expected of him. Peter, tired and stressed, had behaved not as he would want to. He had been tempted by the urge to protect himself, lying in response to a challenge by an unnamed woman, a stranger, and then finally by a third insistent man. After the cock crowed, he recalled the words of Jesus prophesying his denial. His tears are tears of grief and despair at himself. It is a poignant moment when Peter acknowledges he has betrayed the most important person in his life: his Lord. Prompted by the cock crowing, Peter's I-self evaluates itself, and the ensuing sense of failure has a profound effect on him. His tired and frightened state now also carries the additional burden of guilt and shame. As Peter reflected on himself as the dawn broke, we can only imagine his sense of self-loathing and unworthiness.

Later, as recorded in John's Gospel (21.15–19), the risen Jesus speaks to Peter on the beach after breakfast and questions him three times, 'do you love me?' Each challenge corresponds to the three denials, and serves as a reminder of the agony of guilt and failing not only his Lord, but also himself. Jesus goes to the heart of the pain and offers him forgiveness; but does more than this – he assures Peter that he trusts him. 'Feed my lambs', 'Tend my sheep' and 'Feed my sheep' are commands which express the confidence Jesus has in Peter to continue the work he has chosen for him. Not only does Jesus forgive Peter; Jesus restores his self-esteem.

A characteristic of Jesus' ministry is his concern for those who are counted as unworthy or marginalized by society: the poor, the disabled and women. The jubilee promise of lifting up the lowly and freeing the oppressed demonstrates the importance of self-worth in human flourishing. The miracle of love is wrought by affirming the other as a worthy recipient of such devotion. Throughout the Gospels the themes of love and acceptance for the lost and the outcast provide a model of the work of healing and redemption. These two characteristics shape the Christian response to the fundamental human need for relationship and belonging summarized in the Christian understanding of love. Although psychology rarely uses the word 'love', we find the affirmation of others, social acceptance and positive relationships are significant factors in the psychological understanding of self, self-esteem and psychological well-being.

Christian love proclaims the worthiness of each human being to receive the love of God and the love of others. Hence, to be loved is to be valued and deemed worthy of love. Love is accompanied by acceptance and positive self-regard. Reynolds defines love as 'life-giving generosity, a compassionate regard that draws near and attends to the beloved for its own sake with their good in mind'. He imagines love as summoning us into a 'relational space of giving'.[1] When Jesus commanded his followers to 'Love the Lord your God with all your heart, and with all your soul, and with all your strength, and with all your mind and your neighbour as yourself' (Luke 10.27), he was acknowledging the worthiness of all human beings to be loved and also to give love. We are all worthy to occupy that 'relational space of giving and receiving love'. When Jesus challenges Peter on the shore, it is Peter's love which he tests, not the degree of guilt he feels or his sense of self-abasement; and it is Jesus' love for Peter which both affirms him and facilitates the work of redemption. In his challenge to Peter, Jesus creates the relational space where the giving and receiving of love can take place.

Love is associated with affirmation in human experience. It affirms the other and, in the case of loving oneself, it is self-affirming. Psychologically affirmation is linked to self-esteem.

---

1 Reynolds, T. E., 'Love without bounds: theological reflections on parenting a child with disabilities', *Theology Today*, 62 (2005), pp. 193–209.

Receiving attention, praise and love from others raises self-esteem; just as being ignored, criticized and treated without respect lowers self-esteem. The concept of self-esteem is prevalent in popular and clinical psychology and has significant explanatory power especially in understanding emotions. However, it remains contentious in both theology and psychology.

The relationship between self-esteem, pride and humility continues to challenge any theological understanding of self which positively embraces self-esteem. How do we understand the virtue of humility and the sin of pride in the light of a growing awareness of the psychology of self-esteem? Moreover, the call to discipleship is a call to become Christlike and enter a way of life which involves daily self-denial and self-appraisal. Before making an initial step of commitment, there is an acknowledgement of not being the person we would like to be and recognition of the need for God's transforming grace. The words 'repent and believe the good news' emphasize the requirement to acknowledge our weakness and sinfulness, and then, through faith in the saving grace of God and the power of the Holy Spirit, a willingness to commit to striving to become more like the person of Christ. In prayers of confession, we declare before God our weakness and how we have sinned in thought, word and deed and admit to failing in our discipleship. We focus on the negative aspects of who we are and ask that we might be made 'new' again.

This newness of life is a life which requires a change of orientation away from self towards God and others. Jesus teaches that 'Those who try to keep their life secure will lose it, but those who lose their life will keep it' (Luke 17.33). If high self-esteem depends on positive self-regard, how are we to understand the Christian notion of losing oneself for Christ's sake? What view of the self is Jesus suggesting by losing their life?

Turning away from self and the danger of pride is a persistent theme in the Bible. Paul in his letter to the church at Philippi writes, 'Do nothing from selfish ambition or conceit, but in humility regard others as better than yourselves' (Phil. 2.3). Humility occupies the longest chapter in the Rule of St Benedict. There are twelve rungs on Benedict's ladder of humility in order that, through obedience, a monk must know his place in the monastery and, most import-antly, before God. How might the Christian virtue of humility be understood in the light of modern psychology's emphasis on the importance of self-esteem for human well-being? As always, care needs to be exercised in doing justice to the biblical texts as we bring modern psychology's understanding of self-esteem into conversation with the theological tradition. Humility is often mis-understood. In the letter to the Philippians, Jesus is described as the one who 'humbled himself and became obedient to the point of death' (2.8). Obedience is important. Humility in the Christian tradition is the virtue of obedience to God first and foremost. How might this demanding way of life be the way to finding one-self rather than self-diminishment? Furthermore, implicit in the Christian vision of human beings flourishing with all creation is the value which God ascribes to every human being. Can the psycho-logical understanding of 'optimal self-esteem' be helpful in putting the self in its rightful place?

A Contemporary Example of the Challenge of Self-Esteem

Anne is an attractive, lively, 18-year-old who has a place at an excellent university. She has lots of friends and is always perform-ing in school music concerts as well as representing her school at sport. At home her parents are worried by her constant anxiety and lack of self-confidence. She requires frequent reassurance about her abilities and often shares how bad she feels about herself and says that her friends don't understand because they just say that they wish they were half as good at their studies and music as she is. Her parents are perplexed by her low self-esteem.

What may be the cause of Anne's low self-esteem? It might be that even though she is high achieving academically, for her 90 per cent is not good enough. She may think she is not attractive, even though others think she is. In comparison with her friends, she experiences them as more socially competent, more confident, and she knows they get more invitations to parties. She might want a boyfriend, and although she has male friends the fact that no one has asked her out has a significant impact on her self-esteem. Objectively, from her achievements, social life and supportive home, Anne's low self-esteem seems puzzling. It is difficult to identify why Anne feels the way she does about herself.

Introducing Self-Esteem

Self-esteem is measured subjectively. Like other aspects of the self, it is dependent on the self's evaluation of itself. A distinguishing characteristic of human beings is their reflective consciousness. We know that we know something. We also have knowledge about ourselves and self-awareness which gives us the capacity for judgement, freedom and decision-making.

Most of us care about what kind of person we are. It matters what others think of us. It is important that we are seen to be a 'good person' who has concern for others, acceptable morals, is conscientious and competent in various roles, whether in a chosen occupation or social life. What's more, each of us has a model of an ideal who we aspire to be, and we evaluate ourselves against this. On the one hand, this aspiration self acts as a goal to motivate us to change our behaviour, attitudes and emotional responses and, on the other, it can be a source of failure and guilt which lowers self-esteem.

High self-esteem is universally considered to be important for well-being throughout life. Some would go so far as to claim that it is a basic human need.[2] The desire to be loved, to love and feel that we have value and are valued is a significant motive in determining how we respond to others and the situations we find ourselves in. The weight given to this human need is a notable feature in both European and American culture. Success and status are characterized by achievement, measured in intellectual performance, salary, material gains and positive relationships. The value which our culture places on individual success in these domains influences our personal sense

---

2 Greenberg, J., 'Understanding the vital quest for self esteem', *Perspectives on Psychological Science*, 3 (2008), pp. 48–55.

of individual worth and achievement and, ultimately, this has an impact on contentment and happiness. Poor achievement or failure in any of these domains lowers self-esteem and is associated with negative phenomena such as depression, alcohol abuse, teenage pregnancy, social anxiety and violence.[3] Furthermore, negative attitudes and beliefs about who we are and what we have achieved can easily set off a vicious circle of decreasing low self-esteem with the associated psychological and social disorders serving to lower self-esteem still further.

The Definition Maze – What is Self-Esteem?

How self-esteem is defined depends on the perspective which is adopted in relation to the concept at its centre: namely, the self. If the self is viewed as an object just like any other, then self-esteem is defined as the thoughts, feelings and attitudes we have towards our self. But what information do we draw upon to adopt this attitude at any particular time? First, we may compare our ideal self with our real self. As in self-regulation, the self we aspire to be and the actual self influence our behaviour by monitoring and controlling the self. In the case of self-esteem, the comparison between the self we aspire to be and the actual self causes self-esteem to rise or fall depending on how well we have matched up to our goal or ideal. We objectify the self, and our attitude towards it changes in relation to how well it performs. Hence, self-esteem is based upon the comparison between an aspect of our actual self with the same aspect of our aspirational self.

The second source of information in the evaluation process is a comparison with others. If others always seem to be more successful, attractive, popular or virtuous than us, this will also have an impact on our attitude towards ourselves. We will either feel good or bad about ourselves on the basis of these comparisons. It is important to note that this approach defines self-esteem as affective in nature. It is concerned with feelings towards the self and

---

3 Guindon, M. H., 2010, 'What is self esteem?', in Guindon, M. H. (ed.), *Self-Esteem across the Lifespan*, New York/Hove: Routledge, p. 3.

responsive to both these comparisons. Both of these comparisons suggest that self-esteem is a feature of personality and associated with self-regulation and motivation. When we fail to self-regulate our behaviour, we feel guilty and bad about ourselves which generally lowers self-esteem. When we resist temptation or generally feel pleased with ourselves our self-esteem is raised. Wells and Maxwell helpfully distil from these perspectives the two common features of self-esteem: evaluation and an emotional experience.[4]

The modern psychological concept of self-esteem was defined by William James as self-appreciation which he believed consisted of feelings and emotions towards the self.[5] He proposed that it was not based entirely on the opinion of others or on our achievements, but rather that we have an 'average tone of self-feeling' which is independent of any objective evaluation of why we might be satisfied or discontented. He called this trait self-esteem, and suggested that it rises and falls in relation to events which become for us our successes and failures. For James, self-esteem as a tone of self-feeling is innate and part of personality. However, self-esteem is not entirely at the mercy of all events, successes and failures or acceptances and rejections. James suggested that we are selective about the domains on which we stake our self-esteem, 'our self-feeling in this world depends entirely on what we back ourselves to be and do'.[6] In other words, the goals we set out to achieve constitute the domains on which our level of self-esteem depends.

Following James, Cooley in 1902 identified the importance of the opinion of significant others in the construction of self-esteem.[7] His notion of the 'looking-glass self' reminds us that our self-understanding and the attitudes we hold towards our self are shaped by the judgements of others. Cooley's insight that we imagine ourselves to be as others think of us, including our personalities, how we behave and even our looks, drew attention to the influence of

---

4 Wells, L. E. and Maxwell, G., 1976, *Self Esteem: Its Conceptualization and Measurement*, Beverly Hills, CA: Sage.

5 James, W., 1890, *The Principles of Psychology. Vol.1*, New York: Dover Publications, p. 310.

6 James, *The Principles*, p. 45.

7 Cooley, C. H., 1902, *Human Nature and the Social Order*, New York: Scribner's.

the social environment not only on our feelings concerning our-selves, but also what we believe about ourselves. In this way, we incorporate the responses of others into the self. He also concluded that we value some people's judgement more than others, such as parents, partners, close friends and family members, church leaders and others in positions of authority. Although the 'looking-glass self' has been influential in psychological understandings of the self, it has not been fully supported. A revised version suggested by Tice and Wallace proposes that we hold particular views of ourselves and these may bias our perceptions of how others see us.[8] It is this perception of how we think we are viewed by others, rather than how we are actually viewed by them, which has the most impact on our self-concept and consequentially influences self-esteem. How-ever, it seems to be the case that those with whom we have close and intimate relationships are most likely to be influential in the creation of the 'looking-glass self'.

Coopersmith studied self-esteem in pre-secondary school children, and proposed that self-esteem is a self-evaluation of personal-worthiness.[9] It is a judgement of the self against personal standards and values which develops during childhood. Thus, Coopersmith saw self-esteem as an acquired trait, not an innate one. In other words, we learn our sense of worth initially from our parents or caregivers, and as we proceed through life it is reinforced by others. He also drew attention to the distinction between true self-esteem and defensive self-esteem. True self-esteem is that which is seen in those who actually feel worthy and valuable, and defensive self-esteem is seen in those who feel unworthy but do not admit to this.

Even though variations in the definition of self-esteem persist and debates about the nature of it remain unresolved, the summary offered by Guindon helps to capture the main characteristics of the phenomenon supported by current research.[10] Self-esteem is an

---

8 Tice, D. M. and Wallace, H. M., 2003, 'The reflected self: creating your-self as (you think) others see you' in Leary, M. and Price Tangney, J. (eds), *Handbook of Self and Identity*, New York/London: Guilford Press, pp. 91–105.

9 Coopersmith, S., 1967, *The Antecedents of Self-esteem*, San Francisco: W. H. Freeman & Co.

10 Guindon, 'What is self-esteem?', p. 11.

attitude which is the individual's evaluation of the self. Both competence and achievement are integral elements of self-esteem and they form part of the judgement of self-worth. However, one of the complexities regarding self-esteem is its apparent dual nature since it appears to be both a general evaluation and a specific evaluation of parts of the self. We evaluate ourselves on a variety of qualities and aspects of the self to which we attach a varying amount of importance. We also add up these qualities to give us an overall evaluation of the self. Depending on our situation and what aspect of the self we are attending to, our self-esteem can vary and change from high to low from one moment to the next. Even though we might have a positive attitude about ourselves in general, we can have low self-esteem about a specific trait or quality. Hence global self-esteem is an overall estimate of general self-worth, which involves a level of self-acceptance or respect for oneself, and selective self-esteem is an evaluation of specific traits and qualities within the self which can vary with situations and over time. The salience or weight of different traits and qualities in selective self-esteem is indicative of what matters most to us and refers to different domains of the self which combine in the overall evaluation of the self or global self-esteem.

The Function of Self-Esteem

Early in the discipline of psychology self-esteem was recognized as important for psychological functioning. Since William James suggested that it is a fundamental aspect of our human nature, psychology has studied it within most, if not all, of its sub-disciplines. Even so, self-esteem's function and importance is still debated.[11] There are a number of different theories which make positive contributions to the debate, but as yet there is no general agreement regarding why this seemingly important characteristic of human experience has developed and occupies such a significant place in psychological well-being.

---

11 Leary, M. R., 'Making sense of self-esteem', *Current Directions in Psychological Science*, 8 (1) (1999), pp. 321–35.

Humanistic psychology proposes that self-esteem functions to communicate or feed back whether the person is functioning in an autonomous, self-determined way. Congruency between the real and ideal self generates high levels of self-esteem and, conversely, incongruence between the ideal and actual self is associated with low self-esteem. Humanistic psychologists, especially Carl Rogers, the founder of the movement, saw self-acceptance as important for healthy personality functioning. Those who struggle with low self-esteem generally recognize parts of themselves which they want to change, or view as unworthy or dislikeable. For humanistic psychology, unconditional positive regard is central. The process of self-acceptance involves discovering an underlying self which is worthwhile and lovable and being able to cast off the values of others in the experience of self to achieve autonomy.

Bednar, Wells and Peterson take a different approach, proposing that self-esteem functions as a form of subjective feedback regarding how adequate we are in coping with our circumstances.[12] It acts as a monitor of our achievement: how well we are doing at achieving our goals. When we are doing well, our self-esteem is high, and when we are struggling or structuring our lives to avoid threats, then self-esteem is negative. Self-esteem can then act as a warning system indicating that we need to seek help or readjust our goals. The role of self-esteem in facilitating goal achievement has also been recognized. It seems that high self-esteem increases people's willingness to strive towards goals and be tenacious in their pursuit of them, as shown by their motivation to persist in the face of obstacles and any setbacks.[13]

Solomon, Greenberg and Pyszczynski[14] controversially proposed a terror management theory of self-esteem. They suggest that self-esteem is the feeling associated with the conviction that you are

12 Bednar, R., Wells, G. and Peterson, S., 1989, *Self-Esteem: Paradoxes and Innovations in Clinical Theory and Practice*, Washington, DC: American Psychological Association.

13 Tedeschi, J. T. and Norman, N., 1985, 'Social power, self-presentation and the self', in Schlenker, B. R. (ed.), *The Self and Social Life*, New York: McGraw-Hill, pp. 293–322.

14 Solomon, S., Greenberg, J. and Pyszczynski, T., 'A terror management theory of social behavior: the psychological functions of self esteem and

of 'primary value in a meaningful universe'. In this understanding of how we function, self-esteem is needed as a central psychological process for protecting us from the anxiety that we experience from an awareness of our vulnerability and the prospect of death. The association between self-esteem and anxiety protection stems from the relationship that an infant has with parents or other caregivers. In these early stages of development the need for love, fulfilment and protection is provided by carers who are the primary source of security. As the infant develops, these essentials for well-being become more contingent on the child's meeting of the parents' standards of right behaviour and being good. In such a way, the child internalizes the parental standards and also the association between the knowledge of meeting these standards of value and feeling safe and secure. Self-esteem is understood to be the feeling associated with this relationship between standards and security. Furthermore, the relationship between being good or behaving in acceptable, respected ways is reinforced directly by the affirmation of others to certain behaviours and vicariously through cultural teachings that the good are rewarded and the wicked are punished. Self-esteem works to protect against anxiety as it is associated with being loved, good and safe and secure. So, the feeling of personal value reduces our susceptibility to anxiety, which is an important protective or defensive function that insulates us from fear. Although this theory has explanatory power, it can be argued that people who worry about their risks and insecurity might be more motivated to take the necessary precautions, hence the effect of self-esteem to lower anxiety might incur less rather than more protection.

Any understanding of the function of self-esteem must account for the well-documented relationship between self-esteem, emotion, adjustment or coping and well-being. Although some theorists suggest that some level of self-esteem is desirable for its own sake, emphasizing that self-esteem is primarily concerned with the self's need for integrity or a sense of adequacy, any explanation that suggests that self-esteem functions to maintain high levels of self-esteem fails to acknowledge the importance of realistic or accurate

cultural worldviews', *Advances in Experimental Social Psychology*, 24 (1991), pp. 3–159.

self-knowledge in human functioning. The risk that explanations of self-esteem are entirely inward or self-focused hardly needs drawing attention to. A more outward-facing approach, which recognizes the social nature of human experience and the role of self-esteem in relationships, is provided by the sociometer theory.[15] The sociometer theory suggests that the fundamental social aspect of human nature and the need to belong[16] is implicated in the main function of self-esteem; and as such affords this more explanatory power than those described earlier.

The basis of the sociometer theory lies in our need as human beings to belong to social groups. Chapter 6 has already explored the social nature of being human in considerable detail. Social living has an evolutionary benefit. In order to survive, we need to have lasting positive relationships. We become distressed when we are isolated or alone for long periods of time. Rejection is damaging, the devastating impact of exclusion by individuals or groups is without question. Social rejection and exclusion are used in all cultures to punish those who have broken the law. Incarceration diminishes the self through the deprivation of relationships with family and friends, while conveying upon the prisoners an unworthiness to be part of society.

We have an innate desire for frequent and pleasant interactions with others. The positive feelings which arise in relationships come from our perception that others value us and accept us as part of their social group or world. The quality of these relationships and the manner in which other people respond to us is an important source of information about ourselves and how others experience us. Much of our behaviour is directed by the goal of enhancing our interpersonal relationships and avoiding the experience of isolation or exclusion. To do this we need to be able to monitor the status of our relationships with significant others and groups especially, and then adjust our behaviour accordingly. This raises the question of what is the psychological mechanism that enables us to do

---

15 Leary, 'Making sense of self-esteem'.

16 Baumeister, R. F. and Leary, M. R., 'The need to belong: desire for interpersonal attachments as a fundamental human motivation', *Psychological Bulletin*, 117 (1995), pp. 497–529.

this and protect ourselves against rejection and exclusion? Leary suggests that this is the primary function of self-esteem. It acts as a sociometer whose primary function is to maintain our interpersonal relationships.[17]

The sociometer theory proposes that self-esteem acts as an indicator of the quality of our social relationships, especially the degree of inclusion and exclusion, and detects the extent to which we have a sense of social belonging. It challenges the main assumption in psychological literature that we have a need to maintain a certain level of self-esteem, and instead suggests that the level of self-esteem is concerned with minimizing the likelihood of being rejected by others rather than maintaining any level as such.[18] What this means is that we act in ways which we believe will increase our relational value and reduce our chances of being socially rejected or excluded. This explains why our self-esteem is affected more by events which are in the public domain than those which few, if anyone, has seen or has knowledge of. In general, the judgement of others has a greater impact on our self-esteem than our private self-judgements. It is this sensitivity to the opinions of others and what we believe they consider as important that influences the way we behave socially as we strive to be valued and accepted. Therefore criticism stings us and lowers our self-esteem. We fear rejection and failure because of the implications of these for our relationships with others or what is termed our relational value. It might not even be rejection itself, because even the fear of rejection can lower self-esteem. This suggests that self-esteem can also act as a warning system which enables us to change our current behaviour so as to prevent any rejection from happening in the future. It is important to note that the relationship between self-esteem and social acceptance is a direct challenge to the humanistic approach, which stresses that self-esteem based on the opinions of others is false or unhealthy. If, as the sociometer theory suggests, self-esteem works to avoid rejection, then it must be responsive to the reactions and opinions of others. This is not to say that the opinions of others are always

---

17 Leary, 'Making sense of self esteem'.
18 Leary, 'Making sense of self esteem'.

reliable sources of information about ourselves but, regardless, they are still a primary influence on our self-esteem. This is perhaps why on occasions some people will seemingly sacrifice personal integrity to maintain or protect a relationship which is important to them.

The sociometer theory also explains the relationship between low self-esteem and psychological difficulties in a different way from other theories. Instead of suggesting that low self-esteem is the cause of psychological problems, it proposes that a history of rejection or poor relationships causes low self-esteem and the combination of negative relationships results in emotional instability and distress. Furthermore, the theory suggests that the precursor to substance abuse, eating disorders, excessive dependency and membership of deviant groups is a difficulty in maintaining positive relationships and that these self-defeating behaviours are a maladaptive attempt to find acceptance or prevent rejection. Once this has become established, it is easy for a negative spiral to occur: one driven by relationship difficulties which then lower self-esteem, where the subsequent behaviour pattern fuels further rejection by others, thus lowering self-esteem even more. The theory's explanation of the link between self-esteem and relationships has important consequences for our understanding of community and belonging which was explored in Chapter 6.

Contingencies of Self-Worth

Being accepted or rejected by others, our successes and failures, doing the things which we consider to be good or bad, all contribute to our level of self-esteem. However, some things have a greater impact on our level of self-esteem than others. James argued that we are selective about the domains we stake our self-worth on. He concluded that 'our self-feeling in this world depends entirely on what we back ourselves to be and do'.[19] The idea that we differ in the contingencies we must satisfy in order to achieve high esteem has been developed into a model of self-esteem based on contingencies

---

19 James, *The Principles*, p. 310.

of self-worth (CSW).[20] Self-esteem is understood to depend on failure, success or meeting the standards in each of these domains or set of outcomes.

Each of us has our own contingencies of self-worth. For some people it might depend on being loved, academically successful, attractive and slim; for others it might be achieving a position of power in a company or institution, being virtuous or independent of others. Whatever they are, contingencies of self-worth are related to our emotions, goals and motivations: the way we interpret our experience and construct our personal narrative. Clearly our self-esteem is more vulnerable and likely to be more defended in the case of any event or happening which is relevant to a contingency of self-worth. However, it is not the event as such which has an impact on self-esteem, but rather our interpretation of the event or circumstances. For example, losing a tennis tournament in perfect conditions when I believed I was on top form will have a greater impact on my self-esteem than losing when the wind was gusting, the match was interrupted several times for rain, and I was nursing an ankle injury. I can attribute my failure to circumstances beyond my control in the latter, but not in the former, where it is likely that I was fairly beaten.

But where do our contingencies of self-worth originate? Why do we all have different contingencies of self-worth and how do we choose what to bet ourselves on? Although some have argued that we base our self-worth primarily on the things we know we are good at and can outperform others on, especially others who are close to us,[21] it seems that the development of contingencies of self-worth is influenced by a number of factors over time. Different social influences are especially prominent in determining our selection choices. The affirmation and acceptance of specific behaviours by parents and caregivers, peers, teachers and significant others, as well as cultural norms and values, all contribute to the establishment of our contingencies of self-worth. When a child is praised

20 Crocker, J. and Knight, K. M., 'Contingencies of self worth', *Current Directions in Psychological Science*, 14 (4) (2005), pp. 200–20.

21 Tesser, A., 2003, 'Self-evaluation', in Leary, M. R. and Price Tangney, J. (eds), *Handbook of Self and Identity*, New York/London: Guilford Press.

by her parents for high academic achievement, she may conclude that academic success is important for the approval and acceptance of her parents. Academic success then becomes a contingency of self-worth for the child, since she now associates it with warmth, acceptance and affirmation.

Crocker and Park suggest that we organize our lives around our contingencies of self-worth.[22] There are a number of psychological reasons for claiming that contingencies of self-worth play such an important role in our lives. First, they determine the goals and ambitions which we set for ourselves. These focus on which ones matter to us; if they did not, then there would be no point in setting them as goals. However, we do not select our contingencies of self-worth in isolation from the attitudes of others or the contingencies of self-worth of others as we perceive them. In fact, we select them partly to have our beliefs about what gives us self-worth validated by others through their sharing the same contingencies of self-worth as we do. Someone who sets high academic achievement as a goal and a contingency of self-worth knows that many others also strive for this and this validates their goal and influences the impact on their self-esteem when they succeed or fail in this domain.

Second, we are also influenced by the need to avoid losing self-esteem and select contingencies of self-worth which have the positive effect of increasing self-esteem. So, if we struggle with academic work, but are good at sport, we will select success in sport as a contingency of self-worth as opposed to academic achievement. Hence, our contingencies of self-worth are powerful influences on the situations and circumstances we choose to be in. We have a desire to be involved with and succeed in those experiences which are valued by others and also constitute the contingencies of self-worth of others. According to this theory, it is not surprising that many Christians spend most of their spare time in church-based activities and that most of their close friends are Christians or at least sympathetic to the Christian faith. Being in church and participating in the life of the church is a source of affirmation. It is valued among

---

22 Crocker, J. and Park, L. E., 2003, 'Seeking self-esteem: construction, maintenance and protection of self worth', in Leary and Price Tangney, *Handbook of Self and Identity*.

Christians who also share the same contingency, and contributes to a feeling of self-worth and raises self-esteem. Furthermore, by selecting situations, we allow these to shape our behaviour in order to maintain good relationships within the group and experience a positive sense of acceptance and belonging. We might volunteer to take on various roles in the church, offering our time for the benefit of the church community; an action others respond to with gratitude, which thus reinforces our self-worth with both affirmation and a sense of belonging.

Third, the goals we derive from our contingencies of self-worth also determine how we spend our time. People who have a contingency of self-worth based on achievement in their profession are likely to work longer hours than those who do not. Likewise, those whose self-esteem and contingency of self-worth is sensitive to their relationships in church are likely to spend more time in church-based activities than other social activities, such as going to the theatre or spending time with colleagues.

The effect of our contingencies of self-worth on our personal narrative and experience is such that Crocker and Park go so far as to claim that contingencies of self-worth create our reality.[23] In this self-focused appraisal, they suggest that we shape our lives around them and they provide a guide to the way we interpret events, make appraisals of events, and also how we respond to what happens to us both emotionally and in our behaviour. Because contingencies of self-worth are based on what matters to us, they provide an area of psychological understanding which offers useful insights into the life of faith and religious conversion in which we witness to contingencies of self-worth being changed or new ones adopted in the light of the knowledge of being loved by God, accompanied by new personal goals being set in the light of the gospel.

---

23 Crocker and Park, 'Seeking self-esteem', p. 298.

Failure and Threatened Self-Esteem

Contingencies of self-worth might well be the domains which we both back ourselves in and select in order to maximize the chances of enhancing or maintaining our self-esteem, but this also means that they are vulnerable to any threats. When we anticipate failure in any one of our contingencies of self-worth, we may respond in a number of different ways.[24]

First, we might avoid a threatening situation altogether, as someone whose self-esteem is contingent on being successful at work might very carefully select which jobs they apply for and not apply for any that they anticipate would be stretching for them, thus completely avoiding such a threatening situation. If the situation cannot be avoided, an alternative approach is to lower our expectations and avoid disappointment (defensive pessimism). For example, we might convince ourselves that being selected in the last three for interview would be good enough on this occasion. Sometimes we might even employ self-handicapping as a way to cope with an anticipated failure. By doing this we do not attribute the failure to our ability, but to the handicap. We may not make time to read all the background material on the company the night before the interview and blame the outcome on this rather than acknowledging we did not have the required skills profile for the job.

Psychological literature also suggests that threatened self-esteem can lead to a number of problematic responses which can cause damage to our relationships.[25] These include distancing oneself from the successful other, focusing on their shortcomings, generally acting with antagonism towards them, and maybe even responding with violence and aggression.[26] It is unsurprising, then, to discover

---

24 See 'Maintaining and Protecting Self-Esteem' for comprehensive list, in Crocker and Park, 'Seeking self-esteem', pp. 299–303.

25 Crocker and Park, 'Seeking self-esteem', p. 305.

26 Baumeister, R. F., Heatherton, T. F. and Tice, D., 'When ego threats lead to self regulation failure: negative consequences of high self-esteem', *Journal of Personality and Social Psychology*, 64 (1993), pp. 141–56; Baumeister, R. F., Smart, L. and Boden, J. M., 'Relation of threatened egotism to violence and aggression: the dark side of high self-esteem', *Psychological Review*, 103 (1996), pp. 5–33.

that prejudice and the derogation of others are often associated with threatened self-esteem and, as with other responses, this can cause antagonism in relationships.

Is Self-Esteem Worth It?

The negative effects of threatened self-esteem suggest that there is a dark side to self-esteem, but how do we reconcile this with its apparent significance for human flourishing? Indeed, how do we understand human nature if, as Crocker and Park claim, contingencies of self-worth create our reality? Is the construction of reality on the basis of how we feel about ourselves a worthy one? These are important questions, especially in a Christian context with its emphasis on self-denial. But before examining the implications of the psychological research for theology and ministry, it is necessary to review what psychology has to offer regarding the question of pursuing self-esteem at the expense of other possible goals and needs.

When we are successful, we usually feel happy, superior and secure for at least a while. We might also feel free from anxiety, with our raised level of self-esteem acting as an anxiety buffer.[27] But this feeling is usually transitory;[28] and as such we come to yearn for it again and again. In this way the pursuit of self-esteem can become a dominant force in our lives, and when this occurs there are a number of negative consequences.[29] The problems associated with self-esteem are not concerned with having it as such, but rather when one comes to pursue it above all else. Self-esteem itself is not negative. According to Crocker and Park, the pursuit of self-esteem

27 Greenberg, J., Solomon, S., Pyszczynski, T., Rosenblatt, A., Burling, J., Lyon, D., Simon, L. and Pinel, E., 1999, 'Why do people need self-esteem? Converging evidence that self-esteem serves an anxiety-buffering function', in Baumeister, R. F. (ed.) *The Self in Social Psychology*, New York/London: Psychology Press, pp. 105–18.

28 Crocker, J., Sommers, S. R. and Luhtanen, R. K., 'Hopes dashed and dreams fulfilled. Contingencies of self worth in the graduate school admissions process', *Personality and Social Psychology Bulletin*, 28 (2002), pp. 1275–86

29 Crocker, J. and Nuer, N., 'The insatiable quest for self worth', *Psychological Inquiry*, 14 (1) (2003), pp. 31–4.

can ultimately lead to people not attaining what they really need in life, such as competency and close caring relationships.[30]

From the discussion so far, it is evident that levels of self-esteem fluctuate according to our present experience and, as Crocker and Nuer note, this leads to a focus on 'what we are now, not what we need to become'.[31] A consequence of this can be that the pursuit of self-esteem leads to a resistance to learning and improvement, thus affecting competency. Attention remains on the present performance rather than learning from it for the future. This is due to the defence of self-esteem reducing the likelihood of a realistic appraisal of areas for improvement. Learning from our mistakes might become less and less likely as we look to blame any number of external factors rather than ourselves on those occasions when our performance is not what we had hoped for. Crocker and Nuer summarize the effects of the pursuit of self-esteem as preferring the illusion of competence and success to learning from failure, preferring being better than others to being non perfect; but also being mutually supportive of others and preferring feeling worthy to learning how we can better accomplish goals that emanate from our core self.

A second negative consequence of making self-esteem a primary goal is the effect on relationships. In constantly pursuing self-esteem, the self becomes the focus of almost all behaviour, and any awareness of others and their needs is diminished.[32] There is a predominance of the need to compete with and be better than others motivated by the desire for admiration and acceptance from others. However, the performance of others can also threaten self-esteem and this makes relationships vulnerable to the possibility of disintegration with the outcome of isolation and rejection by others.

Other identifiable costs from constantly striving for self-esteem are to mental health and physical health. If people assume that actively seeking and defending self-esteem will secure love, affirmation, respect and fulfilment, ironically the evidence suggests that

---

30 Crocker and Park, 'Seeking self esteem', p. 304.

31 Crocker and Nuer, 'The insatiable quest', p. 32.

32 Carver, C. S. and Scheier, M. F., 1998, *On Self-Regulation of Behavior*, New York: Cambridge University Press.

this is not the case. It appears that chasing after self-esteem limits the ability to learn and develop from experience, damages relationships and diverts attention away from goals which reflect core values and increases the risk of mental and physical health issues.

Given the findings that making the attainment of any self-esteem a goal in life can be self-defeating, psychology has sought to discover if there is an optimal self-esteem for human flourishing. Crocker and Nuer[33] insightfully suggest that, ironically, optimal self-esteem is achieved when self-esteem is not being pursued, but rather when our goals are rooted in inner values, which are larger than self and self-worth. Adopting such an approach, they believe, can lead to a state of authenticity and openness and honesty in close relationships. Furthermore, it appears that this is helped by identifying a higher goal in each situation which is concerned with what we can create or contribute, but one which is not self-focused and is consistent with our core values. They go on to say that structuring one's life in this way necessarily involves facing the fears we might have about being worthless, and persisting in reaching for the higher goal despite wanting to alleviate this fear by becoming self-focused. This resonates strongly with many of the challenges of Christian discipleship and the pursuit of holiness.

Theological Perspectives

The denial of Peter

After Peter denies Jesus three times he makes a sad exit from the Passion narrative. We are left to imagine the agony which remained with him after he wept. He has lied and denied Jesus, but he has also betrayed himself and his identity as a disciple. In the course of the events which followed in the final days of Holy Week, Peter's shame and self-degradation must have been unbearable. A consuming sense of unworthiness and deep despair must have infiltrated his very being. This is a dramatic example of how one event can have a devastating impact on self-esteem. The self's evaluation of itself

---

33 Crocker and Nuer, 'The insatiable quest', p. 34.

can reveal cruel truths about who we are, as well as who we long to be. When Peter denies Jesus a third time as the cock crows, Luke records that, 'The Lord turned and looked at Peter' (Luke 22.61). What might that look have revealed to Peter about his relationship with Jesus? Was it this which brought on the bitter tears? A look of rebuke, a look of disappointment, or a look of compassion and love? We are not told. But whatever we imagine the look of Jesus to convey, for Peter his identity and self-worth were contingent on his relationship with Jesus and because of this his shame and fear of the consequences of his denial cannot be underestimated.

It is the relational space on the lakeside which enables Peter's self-esteem to be restored. Here, after facing himself, Peter faces Jesus. When we face each other, we reveal our inner worlds. Meeting another's gaze influences both our sense of self and the other. From as early as three months of age, babies respond to the look and expression of their caregivers. At the heart of Peter's distress and low self-esteem might have been his fear of estrangement from Jesus. By turning to face Jesus, Peter receives an affirming presence, and thus the process of restoration of self-esteem begins to take place. The challenge of the three questions of Jesus to Peter of 'Do you love me?', as already noted, mirror the three denials, but also serve to stress the importance of love in the restoration of interpersonal relationships. The interrelationship between love of self and love of the other is necessary if self-esteem is to be restored.

From this reflection on Peter's denial and forgiveness, it is evident that Peter's self-esteem is contingent on his relationship with Jesus. In the moment when he realizes that his denial is a failure to honour their relationship and who Jesus is, he becomes deeply ashamed of himself. It is only after Jesus reasserts and reassures Peter of his love and acceptance of him that Peter can begin to face himself again; but Jesus does more than this: he demonstrates his unwavering confidence in Peter with the command to 'feed my sheep'. It is a recurring pattern in the Gospels. When Zacchaeus peers down at Jesus from the sycamore tree, Jesus affirms him by telling him that he will trust him to provide him with a meal. Matthew, a tax collector, trusted by no one, is selected by Jesus to be one of his disciples. The woman at the well in Sychar is trusted to provide him with a drink. It is as if Jesus is saying to each of them, 'you have something significant to offer to the son of God'.

Humility and Pride

Humility is a problematic word in contemporary understanding. For centuries humility has been associated with accepting an inferior status in society. Yet humility in ancient texts is primarily to do with relationships and the conviction that every human being is a beloved creature of God.[34] It also involves the recognition of our need for others and God. Hence, it acknowledges our dependence on others for our successes and almost everything we enjoy in life. Our lives and well-being depend on the love, care, expertise, knowledge and wisdom and much more from others. As Christians we also acknowledge our ultimate dependence on God. The notion of dependency stresses an awareness of relationship and connectedness in the world and the interdependencies of human life which draw us away from a self-centred orientation to one which is more outwardly focused. Rather than thinking about oneself in any grandiose way, or inflating one's self-esteem, a humble orientation is grounded and engages in realistic self-appraisal which is unpretentious and grasps the personal limits to any success that might have been achieved. This attitude of heart and mind presents a stark contrast to the pursuit of self-esteem, which seems to have become a preoccupation with Western society. The idea that our worth as people is contingent on what we achieve, our appearance or what we do is pervasive, but as we have seen, there is a cost to these kind of life goals. The notion of optimal self-esteem is helpful here, which, according to Crocker and Nuer, concerns 'a goal that is about what we can create and contribute, that is larger than the self and consistent with our core values'.[35]

The notion of a goal larger than the self is consistent with Hill's view that humility is an 'attitude which measures the importance

---

34 Bondi, R. C., 1987, *To Love as God Loves*, Philadelphia: Fortress Press, p. 42.
35 Crocker and Nuer, 'The insatiable quest', p. 34.

of things independently of their relation to oneself'.[36] There is a respect for others and their gifts and contribution to the world, and a deep appreciation of the wonder and grandeur of creation. The appreciation of that which extends beyond the self again suggests a recognition of personal limitations and seeing some worthwhile goal which is larger and more significant than that which might be only personally satisfying. Resonating with Crocker and Nuer's optimal self-esteem, adopting the virtue of humility draws us into desiring to make a contribution to larger goals which are married to our sense of purpose in life and ultimate concerns.

God as the author of our being is the creator and giver of all human gifts. We are called to look beyond ourselves to contribute to the larger goal of establishing the kingdom of God. As co-creators, we participate in the work of God, playing our part in the body of Christ in an interdependent community of love which is ultimately dependent on the love and grace of God for its flourishing. The link between the psychology of self-esteem and the psychology of humility has yet to be investigated in detail,[37] but this analysis has highlighted the close association between optimal self-esteem and the virtue of humility, and their role in promoting personal well-being and mutual human flourishing in community. Humility includes acceptance of oneself and affirmation of the contribution of others to one's achievements and well-being. The role of love and acceptance in the maintenance of self-esteem is another related topic where the dialogue between psychology and theology has the potential to positively inform both disciplines.

Love, Acceptance and Self-Esteem

Jean Vanier, founder of the L'Arche and Faith and Light Communities which provide a place of belonging to those with mental disabilities, reflects that 'insecurity is ... at the heart of one of the great human dichotomies: the need for belonging and the need to

36 Hill, T., 1991, *Autonomy and Self-Respect*, Cambridge: Cambridge University Press, p. 112.

37 Emmons, R. A. and Paloutzian, R. F., 'The psychology of religion', *Annual Review of Psychology*, 54 (2003), pp. 377–402.

be oneself, a real person, fully alive'.[38] In a similar vein, Peter van Breeman states that 'a life without acceptance is a life in which a most basic human need goes unfulfilled'.[39] To flourish is to experience acceptance. In the Benedictine tradition, on entering the community the novice says *'suspice me*, accept me O Lord as you have promised and I shall live; do not disappoint me in my hope'. This prayer is a plea to be cradled and treasured by God. From the Latin verb *sub-capere*, meaning to take underneath, it asks God for acceptance and support despite our failures, uncertainties, fears and limitations. There is a deep resonance with the psalmist's pleas when, surrounded by enemies and deserted by friends, he calls on God not to leave or forsake him. For the Benedictine novice as for all Christians, the love and acceptance of God becomes the bedrock of their self-esteem.

Psychology concurs with our need for a safe haven made up of close, mutually caring and supportive relationships. With acceptance comes belonging. The powerful image of Peter facing Jesus on the beach is one of Peter reconnecting with the constancy of Jesus' love as the good shepherd who knows all his sheep and will go out to retrieve the lost ones. The spiritual struggle so often is to believe and claim the acceptance and love of God. Self-rejection and contempt can be seemingly insurmountable barriers. A sense of unworthiness and shame frequently blights the flourishing which the grace of God freely offers; it ruptures relationships. To feel shame is often expressed as hiding one's face or losing face. Pattison notes that shame takes a person out of positive relationship with others.[40] It is a place of estrangement from love.

The Christian understanding of being created in love and for love is the supreme source of acceptance and belonging. We belong to God and are loved by God. It is this we accept and are called to reflect in loving not only ourselves but God and others. The act of loving in this way is a goal which focuses not exclusively on our-

---

38 Vanier, J., 1999, *Becoming Human*, London: Darton, Longman & Todd.

39 van Breemen, P., 1974, *As Bread that is Broken*, New Jersey: Dimensions, p. 10.

40 Pattison, S., 2013, *Saving Face: Enfacement, Shame, Theology*, Farnham: Ashgate.

selves, but on what we can create or contribute to in the life of God and the kingdom of God. It is larger than ourselves, but consistent with our core values. Embodying love and creating space for love is the vocation which God created us for. It is outward looking and selfless and free from the curse of the self. When this happens, then it is experienced as 'fundamental affirmation at work that exceeds estimation and escapes containment within any finite framework of value orientation'.[41] Reynolds senses this to be an experience of the divine, and it draws from us a deep sense of gratitude and hope.

Love leads to the acceptance of others and provides for them a sense of belonging. Love is humble. This is true for personal relationships and life in community. The Church as the body of Christ seeks to be the place where the love of God is found. As a community, the Church is called to be loving and inclusive. The place where those who feel worthless and struggle with relationships find acceptance, belonging and love. It is to be a place where they can discover that they have value and are lovable. But more than that, it is a place where people seek to live for God and God's glory. The loving purposes of God give it direction and set its goals. Those who are part of this community have contingencies of self-worth which centre on living faithfully in God's world. To minister to such a community is to model a self which knows the love of God for the world and for itself, and to live with integrity according to the values of the gospel. It is to adopt the orientation of the virtue of humility which draws attention, thinking and action away from self towards others and towards the world.

---

41 See Reynolds, 'Love without bounds', p. 203, referencing Ricoeur.

Memory, Narrative, Identity
and Ageing

As we progress through life, we become more able to answer the questions Erikson[1] suggested were directly concerned with personal identity: Who am I? How did I come to be the person I am? Where is my life going? The accumulation of life experiences and the ongoing development of our understanding of ourselves are part of the process of maturation. During our lives our interpretation of the past and our expectations for our future can change dramatically. For example, at the age of 20 the most significant life event might be going to university or starting an apprenticeship; by the age of 30, it may change to be working for a multinational company or getting married; at 60, a sudden family death or other tragedy may become the defining point in a life story. It is this progression that directs and shapes the story of who a person is and how they became that person. For example, Mary went to university at the age of 18 years and then decided to volunteer for an NGO working in Southern Sudan during which time the civil war restarted. She had never encountered such atrocity or witnessed death on such a scale. When she returned to England, she continued to work in overseas development, married and had three children. At the age of 56, her youngest son was tragically killed in a motor accident. Up to this point, her personal identity and narrative were still profoundly shaped by her experiences working in Southern Sudan. However, the experience of the death of her son transformed her interpretation of her many encounters with early deaths in Southern

---

1 Erikson, E. H., 1963, *Childhood and Society* (2nd edn), New York: Norton.

Sudan, while her understanding of herself as a parent also changed. New meanings emerged as she engaged in the demanding task of reflection and the integration of this unexpected tragedy into her person.

Who you have been, who you are, and who you will be are always under review because life is never static. Our personal narrative changes numerous times over the course of our lives, as do our goals and motivations. What we long for at the age of 20 and hope to have achieved by 50 are subject to many revisions in the light of new experiences and opportunities. It is fair to conclude that human beings are always subjected to change, whether of their own volition or by events and circumstances beyond their control. However, within the context of a constant flux of experience, we construct a sense of our personal identity from the narrative we tell about ourselves. It is a story of both continuity and change. New events replace older ones in significance, but the way we understand them bears some resemblance to our previous interpretation. Hence, our narrative serves to connect our experiences to each other, make sense of cause and effect, identify the major themes in our lives and, in later years particularly, to link them to large life themes and our overall worldview.

Over the past 20 years, there has been increased attention given to the role of constructing and sharing stories about ourselves and reflecting on particular episodes and phases of our lives as part of the process of developing our identity. I have already discussed the role of narrative in understanding our life experience in Chapter 2, and its significance for the interdisciplinary dialogue between psychology and theology in Chapter 3. In this chapter we re-engage with memory and narrative in order to understand human identity in adulthood – especially in old age – when our story nears completion and our life's ending comes sharply into focus.

All of us are biographically ageing. Each day our stories age and new stories are added to our personal narrative. The episodes of our story are stored in our autobiographical memory and from this we construct and internalize our changing and integrative personal story for life. Autobiographical memory enables us to reimagine our autobiographical past and look to the future from a place where our lives have a sense of coherence, purpose and meaning. As our ongoing narrative is added to with new events and experiences, we reappraise it to ascertain if we are nearer or farther away from the goals we hope to achieve in life, and we then adjust these accordingly. Throughout our lives we journey on a progression through the processes of story-making and meaning-making to wisdom accumulation which provides us with the experience and insight to meet the demands of life more ably and confidently. Our narrative has multiple functions. It is not only concerned with the construction of identity, but is also a source of learning, well-being and is necessary for social relationships. We learn from our narratives and find meaning in them which adds to our positive experience of life. As we draw wisdom from our experience, we can adjust to the demands of life and cope with stress. Furthermore, as we reflect on our story, we can adjust to the highs and lows of life by acknowledging and accepting what we have lost and what will perhaps never be.[2]

The storied nature of our experience is often emphasized in the later stages of life. During this stage of life, the pace of experience and events become slower and there is more time for reflection and processing our life story. But this stage is also associated with a decline in memory. When we can no longer recall our story, or it becomes fragmented, there are considerable implications for our personal identity and relationships. For this reason, this chapter will consider the place of memory in human experience, its role in narrative and identity, and how discovering life-meaning is an essential psychological process in late adulthood.

Simeon

There are more narratives which include older characters in the Old Testament than the New Testament. From Abraham to David, many of the great protagonists of that narrative live to a great age. In the New Testament, the number of examples is far more

---

2 Singer, J. A., 'Narrative identity and meaning-making across the adult life-span: an introduction', *Journal of Personality*, 72 (2004), pp. 437–59.

limited. In the Gospels, Luke opens his narrative with Zechariah and Elizabeth (Luke 1.7), and later we encounter Simeon and Anna (Luke 2.22–38). Meanwhile, John's Gospel leads us to believe that Nicodemus may be old, but this is not made explicit in the text (John 3.4). There are also a few references to older characters in the Epistles, but for our purposes I begin this exploration of memory, ageing, narrative and identity with Simeon, the elderly Jew who greets the child Jesus with his parents in the temple.

Simeon's narrative is a short one. We know very little about this elderly man, except that he is an old Jew and he longs for the 'consolation of Israel'. We are also told, in a phrase characteristic of Luke, that the 'Holy Spirit rested on him', and had revealed to him that before his death he would see the Messiah. Luke identifies Simeon as a holy man, he is 'righteous and devout' (Luke 2.25), who also has prophetic insight. He knew as he held the child Jesus in his arms that Jesus was the Messiah; but more than this, he also foresaw the destiny of Jesus and the pain which lay ahead for his mother Mary.

For Simeon this event in the temple when he at last sees the Messiah becomes the event which confirms his longings and his life purpose. Simeon's narrative identity was constructed from a life of devotional living shaped by his Jewish faith and centred round the temple, but his self-defining memory had become the revelation that at some point in his life he would see the Messiah. A self-defining memory is defined by Singer and Salovey[3] as an episode from the past that is 'vivid, affectively charged, repetitive, linked to similar memories and related to an unresolved theme or enduring concern in an individual's life'. It is also what has been called a personal event memory[4] which can include memorable or symbolic messages and events interpreted as holding implicit guidelines or the origin of a vocation or life goal. It is indeed likely that Simeon's experience of the Holy Spirit was both vivid and emotional. We can only imagine how many times he had longed for this truth deep within himself.

---

3 Singer, J. A. and Salovey, P., 1993, *The Remembered Self*, New York: Free Press, p. 13.

4 Pillemer, D. B., 1998, *Momentous Events, Vivid Memories*, Cambridge, MA: Harvard University Press.

For every Jew living in occupied Palestine under Roman rule at this time, it was a constant concern. Simeon's experience was a self-defining moment of revelation – the unresolved theme of salvation for the Jews was a constant focus of his devotional life. The moment of spiritual revelation had given him a new understanding of his life purpose. He was the one who saw the new Messiah, the one who brought salvation to all peoples, 'a light for revelation to the Gentiles' (Luke 2.32). Hence, it seems likely that this moment of prophecy was the transformational moment in his narrative. From that point, Simeon's past was reconstructed and he looked to his future with new purpose and meaning. As Simeon grew older, he knew he could face death when it came because he would have seen the Messiah. He had faith that he was to die comforted by the hope that Israel would be released at last from pain and torment.

Luke's narrative introduces old Simeon in the temple when his time has come. The years in which he had clung to the hope given to him by the Holy Spirit had reached fruition. No longer was his narrative identity determined by his foreknowledge of the arrival of the Messiah, but as he held the Messiah child in his arms this current experience heralds the next episode in his story – his hopeful release into death.

The intertwining of Simeon's narrative with that of the youthful Jesus and his parents is important in Luke's account. The old Simeon has a significant place in the story of what is to come. Simeon does not represent the past. He is not a nostalgic figure, but a figure whose hope for the future is embodied in Jesus, the one the Holy Spirit has identified as the Messiah. He does not know the full details of the future narrative, but it is enough for him to 'depart in peace' as a servant of the Lord. As an old man, Simeon goes to his death not thinking of what he is leaving behind, but of what is to come. He has lived a good life as one who was 'righteous and devout', but the fullness of his life and personal narrative no longer depend on him but on the narrative of the one who comes as the Messiah. The narrative identity of Jesus, as revealed by the Holy Spirit, has a profound impact on Simeon's personal narrative. The last chapters of his life are transformed by the new self-defining memory of cradling the child Jesus in the temple.

We have little detail of the rest of Simeon's life, but over his life-time he would have accumulated numerous episodes and stories stored in his autobiographical memory. By the end of our second year, we all have some memory of things which have happened to us as well as other stories from our lives.[5] During the course of our childhood, family and friends recall stories which we have been part of, reminding us of recent events, as well as other events which took place further into the past. The social context of our lives influences the shared interpretations of these stories, such as stories told round the table and at gatherings of family and friends. These stories are stored in our autobiographical memory. When these stories are recalled, they sometimes have new memories added to them, and so instead of facts and precise information about what happened when, with whom, by whom and who said what, the truth of events develops and becomes embedded in a story, which is interpreted, then reinterpreted. The memory is not static or fixed, but continues to be created and recreated. When we retrieve these memories in the process of telling and retelling them they become the means by which we achieve a sense of continuity in our lives. These are the stories which give our lives coherence and which we reflect on as we search for meaning.

Simeon's story is composed of memories of hopeful longing and promise. In old age, his story of faithful devotion is fulfilled when he sees and acknowledges the salvation embodied in the Christ child. His brief appearance at the beginning of Luke's Gospel opens the way for the greater story of the incarnation, but it is none the less important for its supporting role. Simeon signifies how his past narrative has directed his life, and now with the fulfilment of his longed-for future narrative, a new narrative emerges as he looks to depart in peace. Simeon's short appearance in the gospel story demonstrates the intricate interweaving of personal narratives, identity formation and memory not only in old age, but as a con-tinuous process throughout our lives. The boy Jesus will probably have been told the story of Simeon as an event in his life by Mary. Her memory of Simeon is added to Jesus' existing autobiographical

---

5 Howe, M. L. and Courage, M. L., 'The emergence and early development of autobiographical memory', *Psychological Review*, 104 (1997), pp. 499–523.

memory of the event and they merge to become integrated into his personal narrative which forms his identity. Luke records Simeon's part in God's narrative because of the self-defining memory it represents, foreshadowing Jesus' baptism when again the Holy Spirit reveals the identity of Jesus as the Messiah.

Self-defining moments held in memory become the scaffold for identity formation and direct the plot of the unfolding narrative. They are moments of divine revelation and presence, when a profound sense of identity and vocation becomes apparent. They are pivotal moments of meaning and purpose. Each of the Old Testament prophets is documented as having such a moment. Likewise, we can identify many incidents in the New Testament, when, in Jesus' ministry, moments of encounter, healing and teaching transformed an individual's perception of themselves and their future. The personal narrative of every disciple turns on the point of their response to the words 'follow me'.

From the example of Simeon, it is evident that the psychological relationship between experience, events, memory, narrative and personal identity has a profound effect on who we are, and become. But how does this take shape over the course of a life, and is there anything distinctive about our autobiographical memory, identity and narrative construction in old age?

Autobiographical Memory and Narrative Identity

For a long time, cognitive psychology has explored to what extent memories of personal events are accurate or subjective reconstructions of the past. What we store in memory is not usually a sequence of facts, but rather information about a sequence of events and the causal links between them in what are called schema.[6] While it is the case that some of our memories are vivid and detailed, others are misremembered events which become distorted by our schema as we make assumptions about events and fill in any gaps in our recollections. In short, we produce a seemingly plausible account

---

6 Schank, R. C. and Abelson, R. P., 1977, *Scripts, Plans, Goals and Understanding*, Hillsdale, NJ: Erlbaum.

of what happened which enables us to retain a sense of personal coherence and comprehension instead of an objective report of what happened in their lives. This explains why two people can give completely different stories of the same event. Hence Barclay,[7] taking a reconstructive position, described autobiographical memory as a form of improvisation, whereas others[8] suggest that the longer the time gap between the event and the recall, the more likely it is that the memory is reconstructed as opposed to reproductive. Whichever the case, our autobiographical memory contains an immense range of personal experience and knowledge, and is the main source of information for the construction of our self-narrative. However, our self-narrative is more than a selection from the store in autobiographical memory. It also contains our goals, our imagined future and the reconstructions and reinterpretations of the significant events in our lives. Specific memories from autobiographical memory are ascribed particular importance in our narrative and become self-defining events. They stand out as points of transformation or learning, or they may integrate themes in our lives. Some are notifiable as significant moments of insight or have symbolic significance and help to give our identity a sense of unity and purpose as we reflect on the past and anticipate our future.[9] In many respects the self-defining events are the building blocks of our self-narrative, giving it substance and shape as an embodied narrative. Often they are the clues to what we value and why, what we believe to be significant and our life themes.[10]

As we review our lives, we select certain events which define our identity and can help us tell the story of how we have changed over

7 Barclay, C. R., 1996, 'Autobiographical remembering: narrative constraints on objectified selves', in Rubin, D. (ed.), *Remembering Our Past: Studies in Autobiographical Memory*, Cambridge: Cambridge University Press, pp. 94–125.

8 Thompson, C. P., Skowronski, J. J., Laren, S. F. and Betz, A. L. (eds), 1996, *Autobiographical Memory: Remembering What and Remembering When*, Mahwah, NJ: Erlbaum.

9 McAdams, D. P., 'The psychology of life stories', *Review of General Psychology*, 5 (2001), pp. 100–22.

10 Csikszentimihalyi, M. and Beattie, O., 'Life themes: a theoretical and empirical exploration of their origins and efforts', *Journal of Humanistic Psychology*, 19 (1979), pp. 45–63.

time, as well as how our self has remained continuous. It seems that for most of us, many of the events we select cluster between the ages of 10 and 30, which is known as the memory bump, and is independent of whether we are recalling them at the age of 40 or 85 years. Hence, late childhood, adolescence and early adulthood appears to be the period of our lives which gives rise to the most autobiographical, the most vivid memories and the most important memories.[11] There is also some evidence to suggest that memories from this time are rich in emotional and motivational content. They are often disruptive life events and mark a change, such as memories of falling in love, significant illness, birth of a first child, getting married or first job, and as such they are more emotional, unusual, novel and surprising than subsequent similar experiences. These memories are frequently intimate memories that have been shared with others soon after the event as we try to make sense of them and their implications.[12] The memory bump also coincides with when we begin to form and develop our personal identity. It is the point at which narrative identity emerges as we begin to adopt a historical perspective on who we are and try to make sense of who we were in childhood, who we are now, and who we might become in the future. From late childhood, we begin to sort through our relatively short autobiographical memory and highlight the key events and transitional points so far, selecting the self-defining memories as we engage in the process of constructing our narrative identity.[13] It is the point at which our central task is to draw on memories of childhood and life to date and 'author a suitable narrative identity'.[14] Hence, autobiographical memory is not a repository of information and events, but a text that has meaning and significance for the

---

11 Conway, M. A., Wang, Q., Hanyu, K. and Haque, S., 'A cross-cultural investigation of autobiographical memory: on the universality and cultural variation of the reminiscence bump', *Journal of Cross-Cultural Psychology*, 36 (2005), pp. 1–11.

12 Thorne, A., 'Personal memory telling and personality development', *Personality and Social Psychology Review*, 4 (2000), pp. 45–56.

13 McAdams, D. P., 2002, *The Person: An Integrated Introduction to Personality Psychology* (3rd edn), New York: John Wiley & Sons, p. 652.

14 McAdams, D. P., 2015, *The Art and Science of Personality Development*, New York: Guilford Press, p. 316.

present and future. We select from it and use it in the formation of our current and future self-narrative and identity.

Further into the lifespan, during our middle adult years and following the memory bump, our goals and life trajectories have begun to crystallize. Erikson[15] described the task of these years as generativity, by which he meant caring for, and taking care of, the next generation and the valued things which will survive you. It is the phase of life which is directed towards our hopes for our children, making the world a better place, passing on values, improving things and contributing in ways which enhance the lives of those who follow on from us.[16] In other words, it is about the legacy we leave after death; what we want to be remembered for and the story which others will tell about us. These years already have a sense of our lives ending and how who we are and have been might be continued. The themes and emphases within our self-narrative begin to reflect this shift in goals and motivation.

The significance of the relationship between generativity and stories has been researched extensively by McAdams and his associates.[17] They have found that adults who score highly on self-reported measures of generativity, who have generative goals and participate in generative activities such as volunteering in the community, involvement in church, supporting education and charity work, were more likely to narrate their life story as a story of redemption. A redemptive story involves a transition from a negative situation to a notably positive one. Essentially, such a story includes a situation of suffering, loss, abuse, separation or other kinds of severe difficulty, which causes a strong negative emotional response. However, highly generative adults find and narrate a causal link between their

---

15 Erikson, E. H., 1963, *Childhood and Society* (2nd edn), New York: Norton.

16 McAdams, D. P., de St Aubin, E. and Logan, R. L., 'Generativity among young, midlife and older adults', *Psychology and Aging*, 8 (1993), pp. 221–30.

17 See McAdams, de St Aubin and Logan, 'Generativity among young, midlife and older adults'; McAdams, D. P., Diamond, A., de St Aubin, E. and Mansfield, E. D., 'Stories of commitment: the psychosocial construction of generative lives', *Journal of Personality and Social Psychology*, 72 (1997), pp. 678–94.

suffering and a subsequent positive and life-enhancing outcome or event. In other words, their suffering is understood to be redeemed, a failure ultimately resulted in victory, and apparent loss is seen as gain. In the process of autobiographical reasoning,[18] generative adults in particular are more likely to discover a positive meaning to a negative life event. Although this might well take place a considerable time after the event, as we ruminate and reflect on life events and identify new causal links, they come to suggest a story of hope, the promise of good things and ultimate redemption in life.

In these middle adult years our autobiographical memories may well contain unfortunate events such as divorce, unemployment, family illness and other difficulties. From these events our narrative might evolve to include either a redemption sequence as discussed above, which retains the hope that even experiences of sadness, loss, guilt and fear can lead eventually to good outcomes, or alternatively these events might lead to a contamination sequence, which holds the belief that even good things cannot be trusted to last and that bad outcomes inevitably follow the best times in our lives.[19]

At any stage of our life the major challenge for us is how we narrate negative life events and explain them or construct meaning from them. We deal with these in a number of ways. Sometimes we merely discount them, deny, repress or dissociate ourselves in some way from them. On other occasions, we exaggerate the positive events and skate over or diminish the significance of negative events. But these strategies are not always effective or desirable. Making narrative sense out of suffering can be, and often is, an important step on the way to healing and redemption. From a number of studies, it appears that exploring these experiences in depth is associated with psychological well-being.[20] However, there are some events that are too awful to be told. Freeman[21] suggests

---

18 McAdams, *The Art and Science*, p. 253.

19 McAdams, *The Person*, p. 660.

20 Lilgendahl, J. P. and McAdams, D. P., 'Constructing stories of self-growth: how individual differences in patterns of autobiographical reasoning relate to well-being in mid-life', *Journal of Personality*, 79 (2011), pp. 391–428.

21 Freeman, M., 'Charting the narrative unconscious: cultural memory and the challenge of autobiography', *Narrative Inquiry*, 12 (2002), pp. 193–211.

that these remain outside one's narrative identity and cannot be incorporated, as the narrator's world assumptions and cognitive apparatus are unable to make sense of them. They remain in the narrative unconscious or encapsulated and closed off in our minds. These horrendous events might never become meaningful to us, but when they re-emerge in our memory, triggered unexpectedly or revisited intentionally, we are often disposed to 'watch over [their] absent meaning'[22] rather than grasp at a cheap meaning that falsifies the experience and the whole integrity of our lives.[23] But this is not to say that hope of authentic and truth-bearing integration will not take place. There always remains the hope of an appropriate opportunity for re-engagement or a reopening of this episode in the story. However, it may never take place or not until many years have passed. Yet, the case remains, that if they are never assimilated into a personal narrative they can be a cause of hidden pain and distress continuing into the last stage of life.

The integration and healing of memories is part of the process of redeeming the past. For Christians, this is integral to our vision of salvation. To distort or repress these memories is unlikely to lead to healing; it requires remembering the event 'truthfully without being either tormented or in some way damaged by the memories'.[24] As Volf rightly suggests, the Christian convictions rooted in the biblical narrative, and the Christian story as a whole of 'creation, redemption and the final consummation ... frames what it means to remember rightly and the God of this story makes remembering rightly possible'.[25]

The integration of the Christian story within our personal narrative provides the hope that even the worst events and the memory traces they carve into our being cannot ultimately prevent God's work of redemption in us. Their meaning may be beyond us, but we have the hope that all will ultimately be revealed. The reality

---

22 Blanchot, M., 1986, *The Writing of the Disaster*, Lincoln: University of Nebraska Press, p. 42., cited in Volf, M., 2006, *The End of Memory: Remembering Rightly in a Violent World*, Grand Rapids, MI/Cambridge UK: Eerdmans, p. 77.

23 Volf, *The End of Memory*, p. 76.

24 Volf, *The End of Memory*, p. 76.

25 Volf, *The End of Memory*, p. 44.

of hope in the love and goodness of God and the remembrance of him and his promises may not guarantee complete healing of these memories and integration into our narrative, but it certainly helps. The healing agony may persist, but when the hope of God's redeeming love becomes integrated into our lives, the sting of pain is less sharp and the suffering we have endured no longer defines us.

Reading Memory – the Inner Text of Life in the Later Stages

So far I have considered how autobiographical memory is used in the construction of personal narrative and identity. In our later years we give special attention to reading this inner text or personal narrative and the meaning and wisdom we can draw from it. In this final stage of life, how might the psychological understanding of life as story contribute to human experience and meaning-making?

Freeman suggests that in the process of autobiographical reflection, 'a new relationship is being created between the past and present, a new poetic configuration, designed to give greater form to one's previous – and present – experience'.[26] The process of bringing our memories into our consciousness involves re-membering or re-creating the past experiences in the present moment. In doing so we recover what is left of the original experience along with how we and others have interpreted it over time. In a blending of fact and fiction, the experience is relived in our present context. Our memories have been edited; parts of them have been lost or corrupted, or changed by later experiences which have shed new light upon them. They are not static, sealed in our minds, but continue to evolve as they are subjected to the influence of our ongoing experiences and sense of self.

Our memories are a key source of our identity and meaning-making. Our self-perception is created from what we choose to remember about ourselves. Likewise, we reflect on our past experiences to understand who we are and make sense of the story of

26 Freeman, M., 1994, *Rewriting the Self: History, Memory, Narrative*, London: Routledge, p. 30.

our lives. I am the person I am because of what I have selected to remember about my childhood, university days, career and married life. But these memories are also the memories I ponder as I try to discern what the purpose of my life has been and is. What difference have I made, and what am I still striving to achieve? Where has God been present and what have I gleaned from these experiences about God's purpose in my life and the world?

The older we become the more meaning-making becomes a pressing need to cope with the losses and challenges that this life stage can bring. Late life crises are not uncommon. In retirement, questions such as 'Who am I? What is my purpose in life? Who needs me now that I am old?' may cause a crisis of meaning.[27] Furthermore, older people may adopt a 'narrative of foreclosure',[28] so that even though their life continues, they live as if their story has ended and there is no possibility of any new chapters or new interpretations of their personal narrative. Yet it remains the case that during our later years, evaluating and integrating our personal narrative to a point at which we can face the end of this earthly life with acceptance and thankfulness is drawn more into focus.

The reading and rereading of our text is a reflective process that most of us engage in at different times in our lives, and it is often precipitated by an unusual or significant life event. We also reminisce with others as we share our story and what we have learned from it. For our narrative to have continued meaning, it needs to be communicated to others. The topic of reminiscence has received a large amount of attention in the ageing literature, and it relates particularly to the challenging developmental task which Erikson[29] suggests as the final stage of human psychosocial development, when we deal with the issue of ego integrity versus despair. Ego integrity involves accepting graciously the life we have had; and

27 Missine, L., 2003, 'The search for meaning of life in older age', in Jewel, A. (ed.), *Ageing, Spirituality and Well-being*, London: Jessica Kingsley, pp. 113–23.

28 Freeman, M., 2011, 'Narrative foreclosure in later life: possibilities and limits', in Kenyon, G., Bohlmeijer, E. and Randall, W. L. (eds), *Storying Later Life: Issues, Investigations, and Interventions in Narrative Gerontology*, Oxford: Oxford University Press.

29 Erikson, *Childhood and Society*.

being able to critique it, but also ultimately accepting it, enjoying and savouring it. He believed that through this process new wisdom might be achieved. This phase is not so much about revising the personal narrative, but settling accounts and being grateful for the gift of life. Those who are unable to achieve this, according to Erikson, might experience bitter despair.

Reminiscence is closely associated with the concept of life review, introduced by Butler.[30] It reflects his concern with the need for repentance and release from guilt at this stage of life, but also implies the search for meaning from life's experiences as life draws to a close. However, research on reminiscence indicates that it can be both adaptive and maladaptive.[31] When we tell our story it facilitates conflict resolution and reconciliation, and integrates the past with the present in positive ways. But reminiscence can also become obsessive and characterized by rumination which does not achieve resolution. On the other hand, there is evidence suggesting that our stories might take on a more positive, warm tone in these years, which is suggestive of escapism as we avoid integrating the difficult events from the past or facing present realities.[32]

The reading and rereading of our narrative frequently involves a process of self-evaluation in older age. The questions we bring to our text are varied but may include: 'Have I lived my life well, and is my story a good story?' Guilt, regret and doubt may lead to despair as opposed to integration, resulting in low self-esteem and depression in the later chapters of life. Some individuals have never learned to value themselves and their achievements, and others are unable to integrate a hopeful future into their narrative envisioning only their ending. The questions of 'Who does my text tell me I am?' or 'What have I learned from life?' can be immensely painful.

A deepening awareness of the wisdom accumulated over the course of life is also part of the meaning-making process in later

---

30 Butler, R. N., 'The life review: an interpretation of reminiscence in old age', *Psychiatry*, 26 (1963), pp. 65–76.

31 Wong, P. T. and Watt, L. M., 'What types of reminiscence are associated with successful aging?', *Psychology and Aging*, 6 (1991), pp. 272–9.

32 Coleman, P. G., 'Creating a life story: the task of reconciliation', *The Gerontologist*, 39 (1999), pp. 133–9.

life. Psychologists have generally taken a pragmatic approach to wisdom, relating it to acquired knowledge and judgements for coping and managing the pragmatics of life.[33] But wisdom can also be understood to include self-understanding and self-knowledge. Over the years, we learn from our experience and our story: the mistakes we have made as well as the decisions which were wise and led to self-fulfilment or success. We also spend time reflecting on our feelings and the consequences of our behaviour. Being able to reflect on our experiences from different perspectives is seen as especially important for the growth of wisdom. Self-awareness in the process of reflexivity enables us to acknowledge that our personal hermeneutic might have created distortions in our interpretation of different episodes in our lives. Wisdom comes from developing some critical distance, and increases the likelihood that we can see the reality and truth of different episodes in our story. Psychologists also assert that reflection on emotions is important for wisdom. With a better understanding of people and how they feel, we are more likely to be compassionate, which many researchers believe as essential for wisdom.[34] Knowledge is related to intelligence and has cognitive significance, but it is not the same as wisdom. Wisdom is being able to tell the story well, whatever its content might be, in order to discern the truth of who you are and how to flourish in life.

The Content of the Narrative in Later Life

Encouragingly, psychological research into old age reveals a different picture from the frequently imagined one of loss, decline, dependency and hopelessness. Instead, there is evidence of a determination to set goals which focus on close rewarding relationships and are adapted to fall in line with shorter time scales. The most significant content in the narrative of these years are relationships which seem to improve in old age. In the face of declining physical

33 Baltes, P. and Smith, J., 1990, 'Toward a psychology of wisdom and its ontogenesis', in Sternberg, R. (ed.), *Wisdom: Its Nature, Origins and Development*, New York: Cambridge University Press, pp. 87–100.

34 Coleman, P. G. and O'Hanlon, A., 2004, *Ageing and Development*, London: Hodder Education, p. 60.

well-being and some cognitive decline, Fingerman et al. found that older adults reported better marital relationships, more supportive friendships, less conflict with children and siblings, and closer ties with their social network than younger adults.[35] This investment in relationships has been explained by Carstensen[36] and her colleagues as a consequence of older people being aware that time might be 'running out' and making the right choices so as not to waste the time left. Hence, rather than investing time in trivial or superficial relationships, older people are more likely to focus on deepening the close relationships which are most emotionally meaningful and positive in their lives. It appears that knowing that time is limited influences the goals older people set and increases their focus in pursuing that which is most likely to provide them with comfort, satisfaction and meaning in life.

It is unsurprising that we change our behaviour in the light of this steady reduction in the remaining time we believe we have left. As our narrative draws to a close, we are less likely to prolong conflicts or start them, and also more predisposed to be forgiving. We would prefer to end our story well and invest in making our relationships rewarding. Although we can never ensure that our story will end well, we are likely to contemplate what a good ending might be for us.

Coleman[37] associates our story's end with the search for truth. Quoting Freeman's reflection on Tolstoy's *Death of Ivan Ilyich*, he comments that:

Ivan Ilyich had been living his life without an ending in mind and without a sense of an ending there could be no story, but only a series of events, experiences, moments, valued only for their

---

35 Fingerman, K. L., Hay, E. L. and Birditt, K. S., 'The best of ties, the worst of ties: close, problematic, and ambivalent relationships across the lifespan', *Journal of Marriage and Family*, 66 (2004), pp. 792–808.

36 Carstensen, L. L., Isaacowitz, D. M. and Charles, S. T., 'Taking time seriously: a theory of socioemotional selectivity', *American Psychologist*, 54 (1999), pp. 165–81.

37 Coleman, P. G., 'Creating a life story: the task of reconciliation', *The Gerontologist*, 39 (1999), pp. 133–9.

pleasure or avoidance of pain. It was devoid of narrative integrity.[38]

As we strive for meaning and the truth of who we are, the sense of what our end might be becomes increasingly important. We tell the truth of our lives as we know it. It is authenticity rather than truth per se that is important. The truth we tell is composed of our memories which, as already discussed, are a conglomerate of facts, interpretations, other people's memories, and memories of memories all steeped in meaning and feelings. These memories are the truth for us, they are our story and provide the evidence of our goals and motivations, our convictions and commitments which we have lived by and the meaning we have searched for. They reflect our beliefs about what might be at the end as much as how to live life well in the present. Heidegger[39] suggested that, although we are always at some point in the middle of our story, our identity is always configured from the prospect of its end. In later years, as our sense of an ending becomes stronger, the way we have authored our identity might be reappraised in the light of any changes in our understanding of death and what comes after it. The need for reconciliation, forgiveness and healing can typically be a response to a search for meaning, coherence and personal identity in the last stage of life, reflecting the desire for a hopeful end.

The Loss of the Text and Personal Identity: Alzheimer's Disease and Dementia

The essential role of memory in personal identity dominates the psychological literature and raises the profound question of what happens to a person's identity when they have no episodic or autobiographical memory. The question of, 'Who am I when I no longer can recall my narrative alongside the events and experiences which

---

38 Freeman, M., 'Death, narrative, integrity and the radical challenge of self understanding: a reading of Tolstoy's *Death of Ivan Ilyich*', *Ageing and Society*, 17 (1997), pp. 373–98.

39 Heidegger, M., 1962, *Being and Time* (J. Macquarrie and E. Robinson, trans.), New York: Harper & Row. (Original work published 1927).

have formed my identity?' presents a challenge both to psychology and theology. Without our memory, how do we know who we are? No one can carry our true identity on our behalf, however well they know us and our story. Although others play an important part in our identity construction, they do not know us like we know ourselves. Our memories are ours and no one else's. They are stored in our minds to be recalled by us alone. It is from *my* memory that I construct *my* identity and from which I derive the essence of who *I* am.

Augustine, writing in Book 10 of his *Confessions*, echoes this understanding. Memory is a 'great storehouse',[40] an 'inner place'[41] which 'without it I could not speak of myself',[42] 'it is my mind: it is myself'.[43]

Keck[44] also shares this sentiment in his reflection on dementia, suggesting: 'The loss of memory entails a loss of self, and we can no longer be secure in our notions of "self-fulfilment." Indeed our entire sense of personhood and human purpose is challenged.'

Without memory, there is no content to the narrative of the past and no basis for hope in the future. In our self-perception, we are our memories. Likewise, we are to others what they remember about us. Memory and identity are intricately bound up with each other. Our identity is constructed from the memories we select as self-defining in an ongoing process throughout our lives which ceases with dementia.

For the sufferer of dementia, episodic memory which provides the raw material of the narrative self slowly diminishes or fragments, the self-defining memories are no longer available to them, and the story they live by eventually disappears. The personal backwards story and the forward facing story no longer exist. But this is not the full picture. Our personal identity is not formed in isolation from others. We are social beings and our identity is shaped by

---

40 Augustine, *Confessions*, trans. R. S. Pine-Coffin (London: Penguin Classics, 2002), X.8.

41 Augustine, *Confessions*, X.9.

42 Augustine, *Confessions*, X.16.

43 Augustine, *Confessions*, X.17.

44 Keck, D., 1996, *Forgetting Who We Are: Alzheimer's Disease and the Love of God*, Nashville: Abingdon Press, p. 15.

an intricate web of relationships. Indeed, we only acquire a full sense of our personal identity through our relationship with others. The personal narrative is a story of relating, responding, giving and receiving to and from others. It is from our patterns of relating that a sense of our personal identity emerges in childhood. We come to know much of who we are through what people remember and tell us about ourselves, and how they respond to us. So within the complexity of each human person, there is a need to account for the influence of others in the process of personal integration and identity. To conclude that loss of memory means a loss of identity and personhood, and hence to forget oneself is to lose oneself, rests on an individualistic and cognitive view of personhood which is rightly to be challenged.

Swinton[45] suggests that the fact that we are remembered both by others and by God is a powerful theological response which preserves the 'vanishing self' in dementia. A conception of personal identity which shifts the emphasis onto the relational aspects of identity and personhood with God and others suggests that identity should not be conceived as entirely subjective and entirely individualistic, but to be a remembered person or to be a present person in the company of others is sufficient for one's identity.

Swinton makes this point as he suggests that those with dementia become:

> More and more ... dependent on other people to hold them in their identities through the stories that are told about them and the names that these others give them ... People who are losing their ability to tell their own stories need others to tell their stories well. They need people who will hold and remember them properly.[46]

In this way, we can conceive of how others maintain the personal identity of another, both in life and afterwards in death, through faithfully telling their narratives. But this still makes identity dependent on being known and remembered. In other words, it

---

45 Swinton, J., 2012, *Dementia: Living in the Memories of God*, London: SCM Press, p. 205.
46 Swinton, *Dementia*, p. 241.

is relational. However, Swinton[47] also asserts that persons exist independently of their relationships. Drawing on Spaemann,[48] who defines a person as one with 'biological membership of the human race', he claims that 'to be a person is to be born into and to participate in the human family'.[49] The difficult point here is participation, which implies purposeful action or relations, when to be is to have a personal identity.

Each of us has a created biological identity which in itself makes us worthy of love and care. From before we are born, God's prevenient grace establishes our relationship with him and our part in his story. Before we have any knowledge of God, by his own initiative he has participated in our story and loves us. As Christians, our identity is bestowed upon us as children of God, not constructed by us or others. Whether we remember our past or not, our identity is found in God, who loved us before we were born. Therefore, our narrative identity is always present, because as a human being we have a relationship with God our creator and we play a part in his narrative. Our life and identity are gifts from God, and even though our personal identity might develop and change over the course of our lives, it remains unique and contingent on God.

Time and Hope

Psychological understandings of identity are based on a model which stresses the role of past experience and future goals in the identity formation process. But as noted already, at different life stages our narrative changes with changing experience and life goals. Our story is never static and neither is our related identity. We engage in a process of ongoing reflection as we seek coherence and direction in the drama of life. Our identity draws on the modalities of past and future, yet only exists in the modality of the present.

47 Swinton, *Dementia*, p. 159.

48 Spaemann, R., 2006, *Persons: The Difference between 'Someone' and 'Something'*, trans. O. O'Donovan, Oxford: Oxford University Press, pp. 255–6, quoted in Swinton, *Dementia*, p. 156.

49 Swinton, *Dementia*, p. 156.

We can only be in the present moment when the memory of our previous experience and anticipated future influence our current identity. To anticipate a good future is to hope. Simeon's personal narrative is one of hope which he embodied in the present. Throughout his life he kept the hopeful story of salvation going and this marked his identity. Giddens[50] argues that in the contemporary world 'a person's identity is not to be found in behaviour – nor important though it is – in the reactions of others, but in the capacity to keep a particular narrative going'. Any good story explains the goals and intentions of the characters as they embody their narrative in time. The hoped-for future of a meaningful end sustains and drives the personal narrative; it keeps it going.

For Christians, death is not the end of their story. Simeon could embrace death at the end of a good life because of his glimpse of the continuing story of salvation. McAdams[51] observes that those who tell a personal narrative containing redemptive sequences – when bad episodes are redeemed by the subsequent good or emotionally positive experiences which follow – sustain hope and commitment in their narrative. But sustaining a narrative of hope does not deny the truthful reality of painful episodes, rather it continues to seek their positive meaning and trusts in the ultimate redemption of all creation in the fullness of time. There is a not-yet dimension to this way of thinking which constructs a narrative in which death is not the end, and becomes instead a source of meaning. It is only God's narrative, when it reaches completion, which will provide a meaningful end. As Christians, wherever we are in the course of life, our narrative is woven into the story of God, which tells of both our beginning and ultimate ending. Until then we live in the hope of seeing God's salvation.

50 Giddens, A., 1991, *Modernity and Self-identity: Self and Society in the Late Modern Age*, Stanford, CA: Stanford University Press, p. 54, cited in McAdams, D. P., 2015, *The Art and Science of Personality Development*, New York: Guilford Press, p. 240.
51 McAdams, *The Person*, p. 659.

Bibliography

Ainsworth, M. D. S. (1973), 'The development of infant-mother attachment', in Caldwell, B. M. and Ricciuti, H. N. (eds), *Review of Child Development Research*, Vol. 3, Chicago: University of Chicago Press.

Ainsworth, M. D. S., Blehar, M., Waters, E. and Wall, S., 1978, *Patterns of Attachment*, Hillsdale, NJ: Erlbaum.

Apter, M. J., 1985, 'Religious states of mind: a reversal theory of interpretation', in Brown, L. B. (ed.), *Advances in the Psychology of Religion*, Oxford: Pergamon.

Arnold, M., 1960, *Emotion and Personality: Vol. 1 Psychological Aspects*, New York: Columbia University Press.

Augustine, *Confessions*, trans. R. S. Pine-Coffin (London: Penguin Classics, 2002), X.8.

Baltes, P. and Smith, J., 1990, 'Toward a psychology of wisdom and its ontogenesis', in Sternberg, R. (ed.), *Wisdom: Its Nature, Origins and Development*, New York: Cambridge University Press.

Bandura, A., 1986, *Social Foundations of Thought and Action: A Social Cognitive Theory*, Englewood Cliffs, NJ: Prentice-Hall.

Bandura, A., 1999, 'Social cognitive theory', in Pervin, L. A. and John, O. P. (eds), *Handbook of Personality: Theory and Research* (2nd edn), New York/London: Guilford Press.

Barclay, C. R., 1996, 'Autobiographical remembering: narrative constraints on objectified selves', in Rubin, D. (ed.), *Remembering Our Past: Studies in Autobiographical Memory*, Cambridge: Cambridge University Press.

Barton, S., 1994, *People of the Passion*, London: Triangle, SPCK, pp. 15–17.

Baumeister, R. F., 1991, *Meanings of Life*, New York: Guilford Press.

Baumeister, R. F. (ed.), 1999, *The Self in Social Psychology*, New York/London: Psychology Press.

Baumeister, R. F., 2005, *The Cultural Animal: Human Nature, Meaning and Social Life*, Oxford: Oxford University Press.

Baumeister, R. F., Leith, K. P., Muraven, M. and Bratslavsky, E., 1998, 'Self-regulation as a key to success in life', in Pushkar, D., Bukowski,

W. M., Schwartzman, A. E., Strack, D. M. and White, D. R. (eds), *Improving Competence across the Lifespan*, New York, Boston, Dordrecht, Moscow: Kluwer Academic/Plenum Publishers.

Baumeister, R. F. and Tice, D. M., 'Anxiety and social exclusion', *Journal of Social and Clinical Psychology*, 9 (1990), pp. 165–95.

Baumeister, R. F. and Exline, J. J., 'Virtue, personality and social relations: self control as the moral muscle', *Journal of Personality*, 67 (1999), pp. 1165–94.

Baumeister, R. F. and Leary, M. R., 'The need to belong: desire for interpersonal attachment as a fundamental human motivation', *Psychological Bulletin*, 117 (1995), pp. 497–529.

Baumeister, R. F. and Tierney, J., 2012, *Will Power: Rediscovering Our Greatest Strength*, London: Allen Lane.

Baumeister, R. F. and Vohls, K. D. (eds), 2004, *The Handbook of Self-Regulation*, New York/London: Guilford Press.

Baumeister, R. F. and Wilson, B., 'Life stories and the four needs for meaning', *Psychological Enquiry*, 7 (1996), pp. 322–5.

Baumeister, R. F., Bratslavsky, E., Muraven, M. and Tice, D. M., 'Ego depletion: is the active self a limited resource?', *Journal of Personality and Social Psychology*, 74 (1998), pp. 1252–65.

Baumeister, R. F., Heatherton, T. F. and Tice, D., 'When ego threats lead to self regulation failure: negative consequences of high self-esteem', *Journal of Personality and Social Psychology*, 64 (1993), pp. 141–56.

Baumeister, R. F., Smart, L. and Boden, J. M., 'Relation of threatened egotism to violence and aggression: the dark side of high self-esteem', *Psychological Review*, 103 (1996), pp. 5–33.

Baumeister, R. F., Heatherton, T. F. and Tice, D., 1994, *Losing Control: How and Why People Fail at Self-Regulation*, San Diego, CA: Academic Press.

Baumeister, R. F., Stillwell, A. M. and Heatherton, T. F., 'Guilt: an interpersonal approach', *Psychological Bulletin*, 115 (2) (1994), pp. 243–67.

Baumeister, R. F. and Heatherton, T. F., 'Self-regulation failure: an overview', *Psychological Inquiry*, 7 (1) (1996), pp. 1–15.

Baumeister, R. F. and Heatherton, T. F., 'Self-regulation failure: past, present and future', *Psychological Inquiry*, 7(1) (1996), pp. 90–8.

Baumrind, D., 'Current patterns of parental authority', *Developmental Psychology*, 4 (1971), pp. 1–103.

Baumrind, D., 'The influence of parenting style on adolescent competence and substance use', *Journal of Early Adolescence*, 11 (1991), pp. 56–95.

Bednar, R., Wells, G. and Peterson, S., 1989, *Self-Esteem: Paradoxes and Innovations in Clinical Theory and Practice*, Washington, DC: American Psychological Association.

Blanchot, M., 1986, *The Writing of the Disaster*, Lincoln: University of Nebraska Press.

Bland, E. R., 'An appraisal of psychological and religious perspectives of self control', *Journal of Religion and Health*, 47 (2008), pp. 4–16.

Boisen, A. T., 1936, *The Explorations of the Inner World: A Study of Mental Disorder and Religious Experience*, Chicago/New York: Willet, Clark & Company.

Bondi, R. C., 1987, *To Love as God Loves*, Philadelphia: Fortress Press.

Bourdieu, P., 1998, *Practical Reason: On the Theory of Action*, Stanford: Stanford University Press.

Bowen, E., 1999, *The Collected Stories of Elizabeth Bowen*, London: Vintage Books.

Bowlby, J., 'Separation anxiety', *International Journal of Psychoanalysts*, 61 (1959).

Bowlby, J., 1965, *Child Care and the Growth of Love* (2nd edn), London: Penguin.

Bowlby, J., 1969, *Attachment and Loss. Vol. 1: Attachment*, New York: Basic Books.

Bowlby, J., 1973, *Attachment and Loss. Vol. 2: Separation*, London: Pimlico.

Bowlby, J., 1988, *A Secure Base*, New York: Basic Books.

Brueggemann, W., 1982, *Genesis: Interpretation: A Bible Commentary for Teaching and Preaching*, Louisville, Kentucky: Westminster John Knox Press.

Brueggemann, W., 2003, *An Introduction to the Old Testament: The Canon and Christian Imagination*, Louisville, Kentucky: Westminster John Knox Press.

Bruner, J., 1986, *Actual Minds, Possible Worlds*, Cambridge, MA: Harvard University Press.

Bruner, J., 'Life as narrative', *Social Research*, 54 (1) (1987), pp. 11–32.

Bucci, W., 1997, *Psychoanalysis and Cognitive Science*, New York: Guilford Press.

Buss, D. M., 'Toward a biologically informed psychology of personality', *Journal of Personality*, 58 (1990), pp. 1–16.

Butler, R. N., 'The life review: an interpretation of reminiscence in old age', *Psychiatry*, 26 (1963), pp. 65–76.

Cantor, N., 'From thought to behavior: "having" and "doing" in the study of personality and cognition', *American Psychologist*, 45 (1990), pp. 735–50.

Carlson, R., 'Studies in script theory: I. Adult analogs of a childhood nuclear scene', *Journal of Personality and Social Psychology*, 40 (1981), pp. 501–10.

Carr, D., 1986, *Time, Narrative and History*, Bloomington: Indiana University Press.

Carstensen, L. L., Isaacowitz, D. M. and Charles, S. T., 'Taking time seriously: a theory of socioemotional selectivity', *American Psychologist*, 54 (1999), pp. 165–81.

Carver, C. S. and Scheier, M. F., 1998, *On Self-Regulation of Behavior*, New York: Cambridge University Press.

Cassidy, J. and Shaver, P. R. (eds), 2008, *Handbook of Attachment: Theory, Research and Clinical Applications*, New York/London: Guilford Press.

Coleman, P. G., 'Creating a life story: the task of reconciliation', *The Gerontologist*, 39 (1999), pp. 133–9.

Coleman, P. G. and O'Hanlon, A., 2004, *Ageing and Development*, London: Hodder Education.

Conway, M. A., Wang, Q., Hanyu, K. and Haque, S., 'A cross-cultural investigation of autobiographical memory: on the universality and cultural variation of the reminiscence bump', *Journal of Cross-Cultural Psychology*, 36 (2005), pp. 1–11.

Cook, C. C. H., 2006, *Alcohol, Addiction and Christian Ethics*, Cambridge: Cambridge University Press.

Cooley, C. H., 1902, *Human Nature and the Social Order*, New York: Scribner's.

Coopersmith, S., 1967, *The Antecedents of Self-esteem*, San Francisco: W. H. Freeman & Co.

Cox, M. J. and Paley, B., 'Families as systems', *Annual Review of Psychology*, 48 (1997), pp. 243–67.

Craighead, W. E., Kimball, W. H. and Rehak, P. J., 'Mood changes, physiological responses and self-statements during self-rejection imagery', *Journal of Consulting and Clinical Psychology*, 47 (1979), pp. 385–96.

Crites, S., 'The narrative quality of experience', *The Journal of the American Academy of Religion*, 39 (1971), pp. 291–7.

Crocker, J., Sommers, S. R. and Luhtanen, R. K., 'Hopes dashed and dreams fulfilled. Contingencies of self worth in the graduate school admissions process', *Personality and Social Psychology Bulletin*, 28 (2002), pp. 1275–86.

Crocker, J. and Nuer, N., 'The insatiable quest for self worth', *Psychological Inquiry*, 14 (1) (2003), pp. 31–4.

Crocker, J. and Knight, K. M., 'Contingencies of Self Worth', *Current Directions in Psychological Science* 14 (4) (2005), pp. 200–20.

Crossley, M. L., 'Narrative psychology, trauma and the study of self/identity', *Theory & Psychology*, 10 (4) (2000), pp. 527–46.

Csikszentimihalyi, M. and Beattie, O., 'Life themes: a theoretical and empirical exploration of their origins and efforts', *Journal of Humanistic Psychology*, 19 (1979), pp. 45–63.

Deci, E. L. and Ryan, R. M., 1985, *Intrinsic Motivation and Self-determination in Human Behavior*, New York: Plenum.

Diener, E. and Wallbom, M., 'Effects of self-awareness on autonormative behaviour', *Journal of Research in Personality*, 10 (1976), pp. 107–11.

Diener, E. and Seligman, M. E. P., 'Very happy people', *Psychological Science*, 13 (1) (2002), pp. 81–4.

Dienstbier, R. and Ryan. R. M. (eds), *Nebraska Symposium on motivation: 1990*, Lincoln, NE: University of Nebraska Press.

Donaldson, M., 1992, *Human Minds*, London: Penguin.

Dostoevsky, F., *The Idiot*, 1868, Penguin Classics, new edn (2004), London: Penguin Classics.

Ekman, P., 1980, *Face of Man: Universal Expression in a New Guinea Village*, New York: Garland.

Emmons, R. A., 1999, *The Psychology of Ultimate Concerns*, New York: Guilford Press.

Emmons, R. A. and Paloutzian, R. F., 'The psychology of religion', *Annual Review of Psychology*, 54 (2003), pp. 377–402.

Erikson, E. H., 1963, *Childhood and Society* (2nd edn), New York: Norton.

Fingerman, K. L., Hay, E. L. and Birditt, K. S., 'The best of ties, the worst of ties: close, problematic, and ambivalent relationships across the lifespan', *Journal of Marriage and Family*, 66 (2004), pp. 792–808.

Fleeson, W., 'Toward a structure and process-integrated view of personality: traits as density distributions of states', *Journal of Personality and Social Psychology*, 80 (2001), pp. 1011–27.

Folkman, S., 'Positive psychological states and coping with severe stress', *Social Science and Medicine*, 45 (1997), pp. 1207–21.

Frank, A., 1995, *The Wounded Storyteller: Body, Illness and Ethics*, Chicago, IL: University of Chicago Press.

Frankl, V. E., 1969, *The Will to Meaning*, New York: New American Library.

Franklin, C. and Nurius, P. A. (eds), *Constructivism in Practice*, Milwaukee, WI: Families International Press.

Freeman, M., 1994, *Rewriting the Self: History, Memory, Narrative*, London: Routledge.

Freeman, M., 'Death, narrative, integrity and the radical challenge of self understanding: a reading of Tolstoy's *Death of Ivan Ilyich*', *Ageing and Society*, 17 (1997), pp. 373–98.

Freeman, M., 'Charting the narrative unconscious: cultural memory and the challenge of autobiography', *Narrative Inquiry*, 12 (2002), pp. 193–211.

Frijda, N., 1986, *The Emotions*, Cambridge: Cambridge University Press.

Gerhardt, S., 2004, *Why Love Matters: How Affection Shapes a Baby's Brain*, Hove, Sussex: Routledge.

Gerkin, C. V., 1984, *The Living Human Document: Revisioning Pastoral Counselling in a Hermeneutical Mode*, Nashville: Abingdon Press.

Giddens, A., 1991, *Modernity and Self-identity: Self and Society in the Late Modern Age*, Stanford, CA: Stanford University Press.

Graham, E., Walton, H. and Ward, F., 2007, *Theological Reflection: Sources*, London: SCM Press.

Greenberg, J., 'Understanding the vital quest for self esteem', *Perspectives on Psychological Science*, 3 (2008), pp. 48–55.

Guindon, M. H. (ed.), 2010, *Self-Esteem Across the Lifespan*, New York/ Hove, Sussex: Routledge.

Haidt, J., 2012, *The Righteous Mind: Why Good People are Divided by Politics and Religion*, New York: Vintage.

Hamlin, J. K., Wynn, K. and Bloom, P., 'Social evaluation by pre-verbal infants', *Nature*, 450 (2007), pp. 557–60.

Harlow, H. F. and Zimmermann, R. R., 'Affectional responses in the infant monkey', *Science*, 130 (1959), pp. 421–32.

Harrison, P. (ed.), *The Cambridge Companion to Science and Religion*, Cambridge: Cambridge University Press.

Hauerwas, S. and Gregory Jones, L. (eds), 1989, *Why Narrative? Readings in Narrative Theology*, Grand Rapids, MI: Eerdmans.

Hazan, C. and Shaver, P., 'Romantic love conceptualized as an attachment process', *Journal of Personality and Social Psychology*, 52 (1987), pp. 511–24.

Heidegger, M., 1962, *Being and Time* (J. Macquarrie and E. Robinson, trans.), New York: Harper & Row. (Original work published 1927).

Hesse, E. and Main, M., 'Disorganised infant, child and adult attachment: collapse in behavioral and attentional strategies', *Journal of the American Psychoanalytical Association*, 48 (2000), pp. 1097–127.

Hill, T., 1991, *Autonomy and Self-Respect*, Cambridge: Cambridge University Press.

Hofmann, W., Baumeister, R. F., Förster, G. and Vohs, K. D., 'Everyday temptations: an experience sampling study of desire, conflict, and self-control', *Journal of Personality and Social Psychology*, 102(6) (2012), pp. 1318–35.

Howe Jr, H. E. and Dienstbier, R. A. (eds), 1979, *Nebraska Symposium on Motivation* (Vol. 26), Lincoln, NE: University of Nebraska Press.

Howe, M. L. and Courage, M. L., 'The emergence and early development of autobiographical memory', *Psychological Review*, 104 (1997), pp. 499–523.

Innes, R., 1999, *Discourse of the Self: Seeking Wholeness in Theology and Psychology*, Religions and Discourse Vol. 4, Bern: Peter Lang.

James, W., 1890, *The Principles of Psychology. Vol. 1*, New York: Dover Publications.

James, W., 1902, *The Varieties of Religious Experience*, new edn (1985), London: Penguin Classics.

Jewel, A. (ed.), 2003, *Ageing, Spirituality and Well-being*, London: Jessica Kingsley, pp. 113–23.

Jones, S. L., 2009, *Trauma and Grace: Theology in a Ruptured World*, Louisville, Kentucky: Westminster John Knox Press.

Kasser, M. and Ryan, R. M., 'Further examining the American Dream: differential correlates of intrinsic and extrinsic goals', *Personality and Social Psychology Bulletin*, 22 (1996), pp. 280–7.

Keck, D., 1996, *Forgetting Who We Are: Alzheimer's Disease and the Love of God*, Nashville: Abingdon Press.

Kenyon, G., Bohlmeijer, E. and Randall, W. L. (eds), 2011, *Storying Later Life: Issues, Investigations, and Interventions in Narrative Gerontology*, Oxford: Oxford University Press.

Kirkpatrick, L. A., 'An attachment-theory approach to the psychology of religion', *Journal for the Psychology of Religion*, 2 (1992), pp. 3–28.

Kirkpatrick, L. A., 'God as a substitute attachment figure: a longitudinal study of adult attachment style and religious change in college students', *Personality and Social Psychology Bulletin*, 24 (1998), pp. 961–73.

Klinger, E., 1977, *Meaning and Void: Inner Experience and the Incentives in People's Lives*, Minneapolis, MN: University of Minnesota Press.

Lazarus, R. S., 1991, *Emotion and Adaptation*, New York/Oxford: Oxford University Press.

Leary, M. R., 'Making sense of self-esteem', *Current Directions in Psychological Science*, 8 (1) (1999), pp. 321–35.

Leary, M. R. and Price Tangney, J. (eds), 2003, *Handbook of Self and Identity*, New York/London: Guilford Press.

Lilgendahl, J. P. and McAdams, D. P., 'Constructing stories of self-growth: how individual differences in patterns of autobiographical reasoning relate to well-being in mid-life', *Journal of Personality*, 79 (2011), pp. 391–428.

Little, B. R., 'Free traits, personal projects and idio-tapes: three tiers for personality psychology', *Psychological Inquiry*, 7 (1996), pp. 340–4.

Lynch, J. J., 1979, *The Broken Heart: The Medical Consequences of Loneliness*, New York: Basic Books.

Mandler, J. M., 1984, *Stories, Scripts and Scenes: Aspects of Schema Theory*, New York: Lawrence Earlbaum Associates.

Martin, L. L. and Tesser A. (eds), 1995, *Striving and Feeling: Interactions Among Goals, Affect and Self-regulation*, Mahwah, NJ: Erlbaum.

Maslow, A. H., 1954, *Motivation and Personality*, New York: Harper Row.

Maslow, A. H., 1968, *Toward a Psychology of Being* (2nd edn), New York: D. Van Nostrand.

McAdams, D. P., 1985, *Power, Intimacy, and the Life Story: Personological Inquiries into Identity*, New York: Guilford Press.

McAdams, D. P., 1993, *The Stories We Live By: Personal Myths and the Making of the Self*, New York: Guilford Press.

McAdams, D. P., 'What do we know when we know a person?', *Journal of Personality*, 63 (1995), pp. 365–96.

McAdams, D. P., 'The psychology of life stories', *Review of General Psychology*, 5(2) (2001), pp. 100–22.

McAdams, D. P., 2002, *The Person: An Integrated Introduction to Personality Psychology*, New York: John Wiley & Sons.

McAdams, D. P., 2015, *The Art and Science of Personality Development*, New York: Guilford Press.

McAdams, D. P., Diamond, A., de St Aubin, E. and Mansfield, E. D., 'Stories of commitment: the psychosocial construction of generative lives', *Journal of Personality and Social Psychology*, 72 (1997), pp. 678–94.

McAdams, D. P. and Pals, J. L., 'A new Big Five: fundamental principles for an integrative science of personality', *American Psychologist*, 61 (3) (2006), pp. 204–17.

McAdams, D. P., Anyidoho, N. A., Brown, C., Huang, Y. T., Kaplan, B. and Machado, M. A., 'Traits and stories: links between dispositional and narrative features of personality', *Journal of Personality*, 72 (4) (2004), pp. 761–84.

McAdams, D. P., de St Aubin E. and Logan, R. L., 'Generativity among young, midlife and older adults', *Psychology and Aging*, 8 (1993), pp. 221–30.

McAdams, D. P., Josselson, R. and Lieblich, A. (eds), 2001, *Turns in the Road: Narrative Studies of Lives in Transition*, Washington, DC: American Psychological Association.

McClelland, D. C., Koestner, R. and Weinberger, J., 'How do self-attributed and implicit motives differ?', *Psychological Review*, 96 (1989), pp. 690–702.

McCrae, R. R. and John, O. P., 'An introduction to the five factor model and its applications', *Journal of Personality*, 60 (1992), pp. 175–215.

McFadyen, A., 2000, *Bound to Sin: Abuse, Holocaust and the Christian Doctrine of Sin*, Cambridge: Cambridge University Press.

McLean, K. C., Pasupathi, M. and Pals, J. L., 'Selves creating stories, stories creating selves: a process model of self development', *Personality and Social Psychology Review*, 11 (2007), pp. 262–78.

Metz, J. B., 'A short apology of narrative', *Concilium*, 85 (1973), pp. 84–96.

Miller-McLemore, B., 2012, *Christian Theology in Practice: Discovering a Discipline*, Grand Rapids, MI: Eerdmans.

Milton, J., 1667, *Paradise Lost Book III*, Penguin Classics (2003), London: Penguin.

Mischel, W., 'Toward an integrative science of the person', *Annual Review of Psychology*, 55 (2004), pp. 1–22.

Mischel, W., Schoda, Y. and Peake, P. K., 'Delay of gratification in children', *Science*, 224 (1988), pp. 933–8.

Moffitt, T. E., Arseneault, L., Belsky, D., Dickson, N., Hancox, R. J., Harrington, H., Houts, R., Poulton, R., Roberts, B. W., Ross, S., Sears, M. R., Thomson, W. M. and Caspi, A., 'A gradient of childhood self-control predicts health, wealth, and public safety', *Proceedings of the National Academy of Sciences* (2011), www.pnas.org/content/early/2011/01/20/1010076108.

Murray, H. A., 1938, *Explorations in Personality*, New York: Oxford University Press.

Myers, D. G., 1992, *The Pursuit of Happiness*, New York: Morrow.

Myers, D. G., 2012, *Psychology* (10th edn), New York: Worth Publishers.

Neimeyer, R. A., 'Fostering posttraumatic growth: a narrative elaboration', *Psychological Enquiry*, 15 (1) (2004), pp. 53–9.

Novak, M., 1971, *Ascent of the Mountain, Flight of the Dove*, San Francisco: Harper & Row.

Nussbaum, M. C., 2001, *Upheavals of Thought: The Intelligence of Emotions*, Cambridge: Cambridge University Press.

Oatley, K., Keltner, D. and Jenkins, J. M., 2006, *Understanding Emotions* (2nd edn), Oxford: Blackwell.

Paloutzian, R. F. and Park, C. L. (eds), *Handbook of the Psychology of Religion and Spirituality*, New York/London: Guilford Press.

Pargament, K. I., Magyar-Russell, G. M. and Murray-Swank, N. A., 'The sacred and the search for meaning', *Journal of Social Issues*, 61(4) (2005), pp. 665–87.

Parkes, C. M. and Stevenson-Hinde J. (eds), 1982, *The Place of Attachment in Human Behavior*, New York: Basic Books.

Pattison, S., 2007, *The Challenge of Practical Theology: Selected Essays*, London/Philadelphia: Jessica Kingsley.

Pattison, S., 2013, *Saving Face: Enfacement, Shame, Theology*, Farnham: Ashgate.

Pervin, L. A., 1996, *The Science of Personality*, New York: John Wiley & Sons.

Pervin, L. A. and John, O. P., 2001, *Personality Theory and Research* (8th edn), New York: John Wiley & Sons.

Pervin, L. A. and John, O. P. (eds), 1991, *Handbook of Personality: Theory and Research* (2nd edn), New York/London: Guilford Press.

Pillemer, D. B., 1998, *Momentous Events, Vivid Memories*, Cambridge, MA: Harvard University Press.

Polkinghorne, D. E., 1988, *Narrative Knowing and the Human Sciences*, New York: State University of New York Press.

Reynolds, T. E., 'Love without bounds: theological reflections on parenting a child with disabilities', *Theology Today*, 62 (2005), pp. 193–209.

Ricoeur, P., 1992, *Oneself as Another*, Chicago: University of Chicago Press.

Roberts, R. C., 2007, *Spiritual Emotions: a Psychology of Christian Virtues*, Grand Rapids, MI/Cambridge, UK: Eerdmans.

Rochat, P., 'Five levels of self-awareness as they unfold in early life', *Consciousness and Cognition*, 12 (2003), pp. 717–31.

Root, M., 'The narrative structure of soteriology', *Modern Theology*, 2 (2) (1986), pp. 145–57.

Ruffing, J. K., 2011, *To Tell the Sacred Story: Spiritual Direction and Narrative*, Mahwah, NJ: Paulist Press.

Russell, J. A., 'Core affect and the psychological construction of emotion', *Psychological Review* 110 (1) (2003), pp. 145–72.

Rutter, M., 'Nature, nurture and development: from evangelism through science to policy and practice', *Child Development*, 73 (2002), pp. 1–21.

Ryan, R. M. (ed.), 2012, *The Oxford Handbook of Human Motivation*, Oxford: Oxford University Press.

Santrock, J. W., 1999, *Life Span Development* (7th edn), McGraw-Hill.

Sapiro, T. and Emde, R. (eds), *Affect, Psychoanalysis Perspectives*, New York: International Universities Press.

Sarbin, T. R., 1986 (ed.) *Narrative Psychology: The Storied Nature of Human Conduct*, New York: Praeger.

Sarbin, T. R., 'The narrative quality of action', *Theoretical & Philosophical Psychology*, 10 (2) (1990), pp. 49–65.

Sbarra, B. A, 'Taking stock of loneliness: special section', *Perspectives on Psychological Science*, 10 (2) (2015), pp. 200–1.

Schaffer, H. R., 1996, *Social Development*, Oxford: Blackwell.

Schank, R. C. and Abelson, R. P., 1977, *Scripts, Plans, Goals and Understanding*, Hillsdale, NJ: Erlbaum.

Schlenker, B. R. (ed.), 1985, *The Self and Social Life*, New York: McGraw-Hill.

Seligman, M. E. P., Railton, P., Baumeister, R. F. and Chandra, S., 'Navigating into the future or driven by the past', *Perspectives on Psychological Science*, 8 (2) (2013), pp. 119–41.

Shaver, P. R. and Rubenstein, C., 'Childhood attachment experience and adult loneliness', *Review of Personality and Social Psychology*, Beverly Hills, CA: Sage, 1 (1980), pp. 42–73.

Siegel, D. J., 2001, *The Developing Mind: How Relationships and the Brain Interact to Shape Who We Are*, New York: Guilford Press.

Siegel, D. J. and Hartzell, M., 2004, *Parenting from the Inside Out*, New York: Jeremy P. Tarcher.

Silberman, I., 'Spiritual role modelling: the teaching of meaning systems', *The International Journal for the Psychology of Religion*, 13 (3) (2003), pp. 175–95.

Silberman, I., 'Religion as a meaning system: implications for the new millennium', *Journal of Social Issues*, 61 (4) (2005), pp. 641–63.

Singer, J. A., Narrative identity and meaning-making across the adult life-span: an introduction, *Journal of Personality*, 72 (2004), pp. 437–59.

Singer, J. A. and Salovey, P., 1993, *The Remembered Self*, New York: Free Press.

Solomon, S., Greenberg, J. and Pyszczynski, T., 'A terror management theory of social behavior: the psychological functions of self esteem and cultural worldviews', *Advances in Experimental Social Psychology*, 24 (1991), pp. 93–159.

Sorrentino R. M. and Higgins E. T. (eds), *Handbook of Motivation and Cognition*, Vol. 1, New York: Guilford Press.

Spaemann, R., 2006, *Persons: The Difference between 'Someone' and 'Something'*, trans. O. O'Donovan, Oxford: Oxford University Press.

Spilka, B., Hood, R. W. Jr, Hunsberger, B. and Gorsuch, R., 2003, *The Psychology of Religion: An Empirical Approach* (3rd edn), New York: Guilford Press.

Swinton, J., 2007, *Raging with Compassion*, Grand Rapids, MI/Cambridge, UK: Eerdmans.

Swinton, J., 2012, *Dementia: Living in the Memories of God*, London: SCM Press.

Tedeschi, R. G. and Calhoun, L. G., 'Posttraumatic growth: conceptual foundations and empirical evidence', *Psychological Enquiry*, 15 (1) (2004), pp. 1–18.

Tellegan, A., Lykken, D. T., Bouchard, T. J. Jr, Wilcox, K. J., Segal, N. L. and Rich, S., 'Personality similarity in twins reared apart and together', *Journal of Personality and Social Psychology*, 54 (6) (1988), pp. 1031–9.

Thompson, C. P., Skowronski, J. J., Laren, S. F. and Betz, A. L. (eds), 1996, *Autobiographical Memory: Remembering What and Remembering When*, Mahwah, NJ: Erlbaum.

Thorne, A., 'Personal memory telling and personality development', *Personality and Social Psychology Review*, 4 (2000), pp. 45–56.

van Breemen, P., 1974, *As Bread that is Broken*, New Jersey: Dimensions.

Vanier, J., 1999, *Becoming Human*, London: Darton, Longman & Todd.

Volf, M., 2006, *The End of Memory: Remembering Rightly in a Violent World*, Grand Rapids, MI/Cambridge, UK: Eerdmans.

Voorwinde, S., 2011, *Jesus' Emotions in the Gospels*, London: T & T Clark.

Vormbrock, J. K., 'Attachment theory as applied to war-time and job related marital separation', *Psychological Bulletin*, 114 (1993), pp. 122–44.

Wallace, W., 1993, *Personality Theories*, Boston: Allyn and Bacon.

Walton, H., 'Speaking in signs: narrative and trauma', *Pastoral Theology, Scottish Journal of Healthcare Chaplaincy*, 5 (2) (2002), pp. 2–5.

Watts, F., 'Psychological and religious perspectives on emotion', *Zygon*, 32 (1997), pp. 243–60.

Watts, F., 2002, *Theology and Psychology*, Aldershot: Ashgate.

Weiner, B., 1992, *Human Motivation: Metaphors, Theory and Research*, Thousand Oaks, CA: Sage.

Wells, L. E. and Maxwel, G., 1976, *Self Esteem: Its Conceptualization and Measurement*, Beverly Hills, CA: Sage.

Wentzel van Huyssteen, J. and Weibe, E. P. (eds), 2011, *In Search of the Self: Interdisciplinary Perspectives on Personhood*, Grand Rapids, MI/ Cambridge, UK: Eerdmans.

Winter, D. G., John, O. P., Stewart, A. J., Klohnen, E. C. and Duncan, L. E., 'Traits and motives: towards an integration of two traditions in personality research', *Psychological Review*, 105 (1998), pp. 230–50.

Wong, P. T. P. and Watt, L. M., 'What types of reminiscence are associated with successful aging?', *Psychology and Aging*, 6 (1991), pp. 272–9.

Wong, P. T. P. and Fry, P. S., 2012 (eds), *The Human Quest for Meaning*, Mahwah, NJ: Erlbaum.

Woodward, J. and Pattison, S. J. (eds), 2000, *The Blackwell Reader in Pastoral and Practical Theology*, Oxford: Blackwell.

Zajonic, R., 'Feeling and thinking: preferences need no inferences', *American Psychologist*, 35 (1980), pp. 151–75.

Biblical index

Index of Names and Subjects